Message about zagat.com

We are inviting you to become a Charter Member of our recently launched zagat.com subscription service for a special introductory price of only $9.95 (a 33% discount off the normal membership charge).

The benefits of membership include:

- **Ratings and Reviews:** Our trademark restaurant ratings and reviews for 70 cities worldwide.
- **New Restaurants:** A look at restaurants as they open throughout the year.
- **ZagatWire:** Our monthly e-mail newsletter covering the latest restaurant openings, closings, chef changes, special offers, events, promotions and more.
- **Advanced Search:** With 50+ criteria, you'll find the perfect place for any occasion.
- **Discounts:** Up to 25% off at our online Shop.
- **Dining Diary:** An online record of your restaurant experiences, both positive and negative.

Given all these benefits, we believe that your zagat.com membership is sure to pay for itself many times over — each time you have a good meal or avoid a bad one.

To redeem this special offer, go to zagat.com and enter promotional code PHIL2003 when you subscribe.

Please join us.

Nina and Tim Zagat

P.S. Voting at zagat.com will continue to be free of charge.

Y0-CUW-278

Offer expires 2/28/04. Cannot be combined with any other offer.

Message about zapal.com

We are inviting you to become a Charter Member of our recently launched rapa.com subscription service for a special introductory price of just $24.95 to 5% discount off the normal membership prices.

The benefits of membership:

- Ratings and Reviews by consumers, restaurants, hotels, and more to help in your search.

- New Restaurants, Attractions, Shopping and more added periodically.

- Zapal free or modified prices newsletters; dining tips, reservations, concierge service, price changes, special offers, events, promotions, and more.

- Advanced Search with advanced search filters the options of menu.

- Exclusive invitations on that codes, etc.

- Bundle many of top restaurants in your area to our own member, high quality business receptions.

Spread the word regardless to believe about your about your members, just one to join them for join me so you an loved them by a landscape of book-loved and of...

To accept this special offer, go to rapa.com and enter promotional code Feb 2016 when you subscribe.

Thank you in advance,

[signature]

Reserve a reservation of us continues the free of charge.

ZAGATSURVEY®

2003/04

PHILADELPHIA RESTAURANTS

Local Editor: Michael Klein

Local Coordinator: Marilyn Kleinberg

Editor: Sinting Lai with Betsy Andrews

Published and distributed by
ZAGAT SURVEY, LLC
4 Columbus Circle
New York, New York 10019
Tel: 212 977 6000
E-mail: philadelphia@zagat.com
Web site: www.zagat.com

Acknowledgments

We thank Fran and Joe Alberstadt, Charlotte Ann and Dick Albertson, Cindy and Richard Blum, Norman and Suzanne Cohn, Gerald Etter, Ellen and Steve Goldman, Margaret Grace, Eric Hegedus, Tom and Loretta Jordan, René, Rachel and Lindsay Klein, Sybil and Dave Rothstein and the *Inquirer*'s food crew and news desk: Sandy Clark, Anne Gordon, Craig LaBan, Marilynn Marter, Rick Nichols, Lance Parry and Barb Sadek for their help and support. We'd also like to thank the Philadelphia Chapter of Women in Communications, the Philadelphia Convention and Visitors Bureau and the Philadelphia Public Relations Association for their invaluable assistance with survey distribution.

This guide would not have been possible without the hard work of our staff, especially Reni Chin, Anna Chlumsky, Schuyler Frazier, Jeff Freier, Shelley Gallagher, Randi Gollin, Katherine Harris, Natalie Lebert, Mike Liao, Dave Makulec, Laura Mitchell, Jennifer Napuli, Rob Poole, Robert Seixas, Yoji Yamaguchi and Sharon Yates.

The reviews published in this guide are based on public opinion surveys, with numerical ratings reflecting the average scores given by all survey participants who voted on each establishment and text based on direct quotes from, or fair paraphrasings of, participants' comments. Phone numbers, addresses and other factual information were correct to the best of our knowledge when published in this guide; any subsequent changes may not be reflected.

© 2003 Zagat Survey, LLC
ISBN 1-57006-516-0
Printed in the United States of America

Contents

About This Survey	5
What's New	6
Key to Ratings & Symbols	7
TOP RATINGS	
• Most Popular Places	9
• Food; Cuisines, Features, Locations	10
• Decor; Outdoors, Romance, Rooms, Views	14
• Service	15
• Best Buys	16
RESTAURANT DIRECTORY	
Names, Addresses, Phone Numbers, Ratings and Reviews	
• Philadelphia	18
• Lancaster/Berks Counties	130
• New Jersey Suburbs	136
• Wilmington/Nearby Delaware	145
INDEXES	
Cuisines	154
Locations	164
Special Features	
Additions	172
Breakfast	172
Brunch	172
Buffet Served	173
Business Dining	174
BYO	174
Catering	175
Child-Friendly	177
Cigars Welcome	178
Critic-Proof	179
Dancing	179
Delivery/Takeout	180
Dining Alone	182
Entertainment	182
Fireplaces	184
Game in Season	185
Historic Places	186
Hotel Dining	186
"In" Places	187
Jacket Required	188
Late Dining	188
Meet for a Drink	188
Microbreweries	189
Offbeat	189
Outdoor Dining	189
Parking	191
People-Watching	192
Power Scenes	193

Pre-Theater Menus	193
Private Rooms	194
Prix Fixe Menus	196
Quiet Conversation	197
Raw Bars	197
Reserve Ahead	198
Romantic Places	199
Senior Appeal	199
Singles Scenes	200
Sleepers	200
Tasting Menus	201
Views	201
Visitors on Expense Account	201
Waterside	201
Winning Wine Lists	202
Worth a Trip	202
Wine Chart	204

About This Survey

For 24 years, Zagat Survey has reported on the shared experiences of diners like you. This *Philadelphia Restaurant Survey* is an update reflecting developments since our last *Philadelphia Survey* was published. For example, we have added 60 places not in the previous edition, as well as indicated new addresses, phone numbers, chef turnovers and other major developments. All told, this guide covers some 800 restaurants.

By regularly surveying large numbers of avid local restaurant-goers, we hope to have achieved a uniquely current and reliable guide. For this book, more than 2,700 people participated. Since they dined out an average of 2.6 times per week, this *Survey* is based on roughly 372,000 meals annually. We sincerely thank each of these surveyors; this book is really "theirs."

Of course, we are especially grateful to our editor, Michael Klein, a columnist at the *Philadelphia Inquirer*, and to our coordinator, Marilyn Kleinberg, Director of Special Events for the Chamber of Commerce of Southern New Jersey.

To help guide our readers to Philadelphia's best meals and best buys, we have prepared a number of lists. See Top Ratings, including Most Popular (pages 9-15), and Best Buys (page 16). In addition, we have provided 46 handy indexes and have tried to be concise. Finally, it should be noted that our editors have synopsized our surveyors' opinions, with their comments shown in quotation marks.

As companions to this guide, we also publish guides to restaurants, hotels, resorts, spas and golf courses worldwide, as well as maps. Most of these guides are also available on mobile devices and at **zagat.com**, where you can vote and shop as well.

To join any of our upcoming *Surveys,* just register at **zagat.com**. Each participant will receive a free copy of the resulting guide when it is published.

Your comments and even criticisms of this guide are also solicited. There is always room for improvement with your help. You can contact us at philadelphia@zagat.com or by mail at Zagat Survey, 4 Columbus Circle, New York, NY 10019. We look forward to hearing from you.

New York, NY
June 24, 2003

Nina and Tim Zagat

What's New

Despite the cool local economy, the dining scene here is far from cooling off. Though some high-end places have had a decline in business, most neighborhood eateries are as busy as ever, and there's been no slowdown in the spate of openings.

Shining Starr: Golden boy Stephen Starr (Buddakan, The Continental, Pod, et al) continues to expand his empire with the debut of Jones, an American comfort-food haven down the block from his Japanese hit Morimoto. He's already working on another project, an Italian trattoria.

The Square Look: Wallet-watching may be common these days, but chic still means something in swanky Rittenhouse Square. Just take a look at the luxuriously appointed Lacroix at the Rittenhouse, with a classic French kitchen helmed by Fountain alum Jean-Marie Lacroix. Or Salt, David Fields' no-expense-spared Eclectic standout. Not quite as showy but still sumptuous is Loie, a French brasserie that's become an instant magnet .

The Suburban Boom: High style has made it to the Main Line thanks to the addition of Roux 3, a smart-looking Asian-tinged New American bistro in Newtown Square. Credit too Margaret Kuo, who converted an old diner in Wayne into a handsome bi-level shrine to Chinese-Japanese cooking. Just around the corner, the trendy Italian wine bar Vivo Enoteca exudes a definite urban attitude.

Double the Pleasure: Why own one restaurant when you can own two? Mustapha Rouissiya of Figs is making a splash with his Adriatica seafood house in Old City. Hibachi is stepping up the teppanyaki craze by cloning itself at the spectacular Penn's Landing site last occupied by Meiji-En, while Dahlak, an Ethiopian-Eritrean favorite in West Philly, is poised to open an offshoot in Germantown. And David Mantelmacher, of circa, has rolled out Plate, providing a new American comfort-food option for the Ardmore crowd.

Retooling Time: Georges Perrier turned his taste of Provence, Le Mas Perrier, into the lower-priced Le Mas. After losing the lease on its Avenue of the Arts site, Pompeii Cucina D'Italia is about to set up shop a few blocks away in City Center. In Old City, the loungey, exotic Marmont went into the beef business, reinventing itself as the Marmont Steakhouse.

Easy Eating: Despite all the diversity offered by the City of Brotherly Love's thriving dining scene, the average cost of a meal out is a reasonable $29.75, while Philadelphians lead the nation in tipping at a generous average of 18.7%.

Philadelphia, PA
June 24, 2003

Michael Klein

Key to Ratings/Symbols

Name, Address & Phone Number

Zagat Ratings

Hours & Credit Cards

	F	D	S	C
Tim & Nina's ◐ S ⊄	▽ 23	9	13	$15

3408 S. Hoagie Pl. (bet. Mayo & Roll Drs.), 215-555-1234

◪ "Yo!" – join all the Iggles and Phils fans who flock to this "run-down" 24-hour joint for its "belly-busting" cheese steaks and "five-pound" hoagies served up proudly with a side of "sass" by "Port Richmond girls" dripping with "attitude"; though your cardiologist surely thinks of this "classic" Philly grub as a "heart attack on a plate", you'll probably run into him "in line" too.

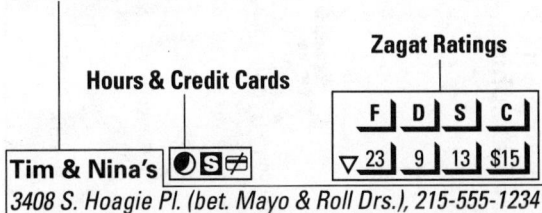

Review, with surveyors' comments in quotes

Restaurants with the highest overall ratings and greatest popularity and importance are printed in CAPITAL LETTERS.

Before reviews a symbol indicates whether responses were uniform ■ or mixed ◪.

Hours: ◐ serves after 11 PM
S open on Sunday

Credit Cards: ⊄ no credit cards accepted

Ratings: Food, Decor and Service are rated on a scale of **0** to **30.** The Cost (C) column reflects our surveyors' estimate of the price of dinner including one drink and tip.

F Food	D Decor	S Service	C Cost
23	9	13	$15

0–9	poor to fair	**20–25**	very good to excellent
10–15	fair to good	**26–30**	extraordinary to perfection
16–19	good to very good	▽	low response/less reliable

For places listed without ratings or a numerical cost estimate, such as an important newcomer or a popular write-in, the price range is indicated by the following symbols.

I	$15 and below	**E**	$31 to $50
M	$16 to $30	**VE**	$51 or more

Most Popular

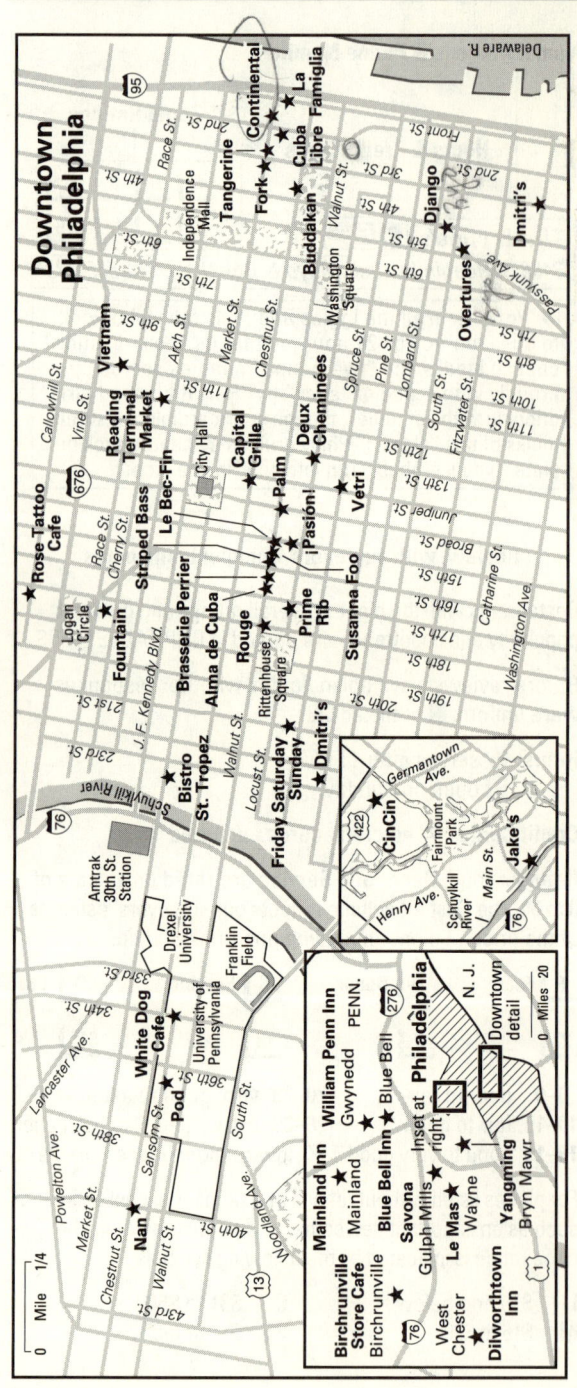

Top Ratings

Excluding places in Lancaster/Berks Counties, New Jersey Suburbs and Wilmington/Nearby Delaware, and those with low voting. An asterisked restaurant is tied with the one directly above it.

40 Most Popular

1. Fountain
2. Le Bec-Fin
3. Buddakan
4. Striped Bass
5. Brasserie Perrier
6. Susanna Foo
7. Vetri
8. Fork
9. Dilworthtown Inn
10. Tangerine
11. Yangming
12. ¡Pasión!
13. Jake's
14. Dmitri's
15. Deux Cheminées
16. White Dog Cafe
17. Prime Rib
18. Capital Grille
19. Savona
20. Palm
21. CinCin
22. Continental
23. Le Mas
24. La Famiglia
25. Mainland Inn
26. Nan
27. Rose Tattoo
28. William Penn Inn
29. Django
30. Alma de Cuba
31. Bistro St. Tropez
32. Pod
33. Friday Sat. Sun.
34. Cuba Libre
35. Overtures
36. Vietnam
37. Rouge
38. Blue Bell Inn
39. Birchrunville Store
40. Reading Term. Mkt.*

It's obvious that many of the restaurants on the above list are among Philadelphia's most expensive, but if popularity were calibrated to price, we suspect that a number of other restaurants would join the above ranks. Given the fact that both our surveyors and readers love to discover dining bargains, we have added a list of 80 Best Buys on page 16. These are restaurants that give real quality at extremely reasonable prices.

vote at zagat.com

Top Food

Top 40 Food

- **29** Fountain
  Le Bar Lyonnais
  Le Bec-Fin
- **28** Vetri
- **27** Django
  Deux Cheminées
  Buddakan
  Swann Lounge
- **26** Striped Bass
  Koch's Deli
  La Famiglia
  Susanna Foo*
  Mainland Inn
  Jake's
  Prime Rib
  Dilworthtown Inn
  Birchrunville Store
  Savona
  Inn at Phillips Mill
  ¡Pasión!

  Nan
  Founders
  Brasserie Perrier
- **25** Dmitri's
  Overtures
  Tacconelli's
  Tre Scalini
  Monte Carlo Liv. Rm.
  Pif
  La Bonne Auberge
  Kristian's
- **24** Saloon
  Le Petit Café
  Yangming
  Alisa Cafe
  Tangerine
  Morton's of Chicago
  Rib Crib
  Umbria
  EverMay/Delaware

By Cuisine

American (New)
- **29** Fountain
- **27** Swann Lounge
- **26** Mainland Inn
  Jake's
  Dilworthtown Inn

American (Regional)
- **23** Carversville Inn
- **22** Kimberton Inn
- **19** bluezette
  Azalea
  Jack's Firehouse

American (Traditional)
- **23** Old Guard House
  Rose Tree Inn
- **22** Duling-Kurtz Hse.
  Friday Sat. Sun.
  Judy's Cafe

Chinese
- **26** Susanna Foo
- **24** Yangming
  CinCin
  Peking
- **23** Lee How Fook

Continental
- **23** Rouge
  Barrymore Room
- **22** Vickers Tavern
  Kennedy-Supplee
- **21** Seven Stars Inn

Eclectic
- **27** Django
- **24** Umbria
- **21** Mirna's Cafe
  Latest Dish
- **20** Bridgid's

French (Bistro)
- **29** Le Bar Lyonnais
- **26** Inn at Phillips Mill
- **25** Pif
- **24** Cafe Arielle
- **23** Bistro St. Tropez

French (Classic)
- **29** Le Bec-Fin
- **27** Deux Cheminées
- **26** Birchrunville Store
- **25** La Bonne Auberge
- **24** Le Petit Café

10   subscribe to zagat.com

Top Food

French (New)
- **26** Brasserie Perrier
- **24** Rest. Taquet
  Passerelle
- **23** Gourmet
- **22** Grasshopper

Indian
- **23** Khajuraho
- **21** Cafe Spice
  Tandoor India
  Minar Palace
- **20** Palace of Asia

Italian
- **28** Vetri
- **26** La Famiglia
- **25** Tre Scalini
  Monte Carlo Liv. Rm.
  Kristian's

Italian (Northern)
- **26** Savona
- **24** La Locanda
- **23** Moonstruck
- **22** DiPalma
  La Vigna

Italian (Southern)
- **22** Trinacria
  Ralph's
- **21** Il Sol D'Italia
  Gnocchi
- **20** Marra's

Japanese
- **23** Kisso Sushi
  Genji
  August Moon
- **22** Shiroi Hana
- **20** Hikaru

Latin
- **26** ¡Pasión!
- **22** Tierra Colombiana
  Valanni
- **21** Alma de Cuba
- **19** Cibucán

Malaysian/Vietnamese
- **24** Vietnam
- **23** Vietnam Palace
- **22** Penang
  Pho 75
- **21** Pho Xe Lua▽

Mediterranean
- **25** Dmitri's
  Overtures
- **24** Tangerine
  Figs
- **22** Bitar's

Mexican
- **23** Las Cazuelas
- **21** Zocalo
  Tamarindo's
- **20** Coyote Crossing
- **18** El Azteca

Pizza
- **25** Tacconelli's
- **23** Celebre's Pizzeria
- **21** Mama Palma's
- **20** Marra's
  Lombardi's

Seafood
- **26** Striped Bass
- **22** Little Fish
- **21** Devon Seafood
  Philadelphia Fish
- **20** Sansom St. Oyster

Steakhouses
- **26** Prime Rib
- **24** Saloon
  Morton's of Chicago
  Capital Grille
  Palm

Thai
- **26** Nan
- **24** Alisa Cafe
- **23** Thai Orchid
  Jasmine Thai
- **22** Lemon Grass

vote at zagat.com

Top Food

By Special Feature

Breakfast†
- 24 Carman's
- 23 Reading Term. Mkt.
  - Tony Luke Jr.'s
  - Morning Glory
- 20 Blue in Green

Brunch
- 29 Fountain
- 27 Swann Lounge
- 26 Striped Bass
  - Mainland Inn
  - Jake's

BYO
- 27 Django
- 26 Birchrunville Store
  - Inn at Phillips Mill
  - Nan
- 25 Overtures

Cigar Scenes
- 29 Le Bar Lyonnais
- 26 Prime Rib
- 25 Monte Carlo Liv. Rm.
- 24 Morton's of Chicago
- 21 Happy Rooster

Hotel Dining
- 29 Fountain
  - Four Seasons
- 27 Swann Lounge
  - Four Seasons
- 26 Prime Rib
  - Radisson Warwick
- 24 Rest. Taquet
  - Wayne Hotel
- 23 Rist. Panorama
  - Penn's View

"In" Places
- 28 Vetri
- 27 Django
  - Buddakan
- 26 ¡Pasión!
- 25 Dmitri's

Newcomers/Unrated
- Chops
- Jones
- Lacroix/Rittenhouse
- Ravenna
- Salt

Offbeat
- 25 Tacconelli's
- 24 Carman's
- 23 Shank's & Evelyn's
  - Morning Glory
- 22 Penang

People-Watching
- 27 Buddakan
- 26 Koch's Deli
  - Prime Rib
  - ¡Pasión!
  - Brasserie Perrier

Power Lunch
- 29 Fountain
- 26 Striped Bass
- 24 Capital Grille
  - Palm
- 19 Smith & Wollensky

---

† Other than hotels

Top Food

By Location
Pennsylvania

Bucks County
- 26 Inn at Phillips Mill
- 25 La Bonne Auberge
- 24 EverMay/Delaware
- 23 Carversville Inn
  - Blue Sage

Center City
- 29 Fountain
  - Le Bar Lyonnais
  - Le Bec-Fin
- 28 Vetri
- 27 Deux Cheminées

Chester County
- 26 Dilworthtown Inn
  - Birchrunville Store
- 22 Duling-Kurtz Hse.
  - Vickers Tavern
  - Kimberton Inn

Chinatown
- 24 Vietnam
- 23 Lee How Fook
  - Vietnam Palace
  - Ray's Cafe
  - Charles Plaza

Delaware County
- 24 Le Petit Café
  - Alisa Cafe
  - Carmine's Cafe
  - Peking
- 23 Nais Cuisine

Lancaster/Berks Counties
- 26 Green Hills Inn
- 25 Gracie's
- 24 Log Cabin
- 23 Rest. at Doneckers
- 22 Lemon Grass Thai

New Jersey
- 29 Siri's
- 26 Sagami
  - Fuji
  - La Campagne
- 25 Little Café

Main Line
- 26 Savona
- 24 Yangming
  - Rest. Taquet
  - Tratt. San Nicola
  - Passerelle

Montgomery County
- 26 Mainland Inn
- 24 Carambola
  - Totaro's
- 23 Sullivan's
  - Thai Orchid

Old City/Northern Liberties
- 27 Buddakan
- 26 La Famiglia
- 25 Tacconelli's
- 24 Tangerine
  - Fork

South Philly
- 25 Tre Scalini
  - Pif
  - Kristian's
- 24 Saloon
  - Carman's

South St./Queen Village
- 27 Django
- 25 Dmitri's
  - Overtures
  - Monte Carlo Liv. Rm.
- 24 New Wave Café

West Philly/University City
- 26 Koch's Deli
  - Nan
- 23 Dahlak
  - White Dog Cafe
- 22 Bitar's

Delaware
- 26 Green Room
  - Restaurant 821
  - Eclipse
  - Brandywine Rm.
  - Deep Blue

Top 40 Decor

- **29** Fountain
- **28** Le Bec-Fin
     Striped Bass
- **27** Swann Lounge
     Barrymore Room
     Founders
     Buddakan
     Deux Cheminées
- **26** Dilworthtown Inn
     Tangerine
     Savona
     Grill
     Prime Rib
     La Bonne Auberge
     Cuba Libre
     Inn at Phillips Mill
- **25** Passerelle
     Kennedy-Supplee
     Susanna Foo
     Le Mas

     EverMay/Delaware
     Brasserie Perrier
     Duling-Kurtz Hse.
- **24** Le Bar Lyonnais
     Roselena's Coffee
     ¡Pasión!
     Pod
     La Famiglia
     Opus 251
     Capital Grille
     Inn Philadelphia
     William Penn Inn
- **23** Toto
     Kimberton Inn
     Mainland Inn
     Rest. Taquet
     Azalea
     circa
     Alma de Cuba
     City Tavern

Outdoors

Carmella's
Cresheim Cottage
Devon Seafood
Dilworthtown Inn

Inn Philadelphia
Opus 251
Rouge
Sonoma

Romance

Carversville Inn
Deux Cheminées
Duling-Kurtz Hse.
EverMay/Delaware

Golden Pheasant
Le Bec-Fin
Roselena's Coffee
Vetri

Rooms

Alma de Cuba
Brasserie Perrier
Buddakan
Le Mas

Morimoto
Pod
Striped Bass
Tangerine

Views

Barrymore Room
Bistro St. Tropez
Black Bass Hotel
EverMay/Delaware

La Veranda
Moshulu
Simon Pearce
Upstares/Varalli

Top 40 Service

- **29** Fountain
- **28** Le Bec-Fin
- **27** Swann Lounge
- **26** Deux Cheminées
  - Vetri
  - Le Bar Lyonnais
  - EverMay/Delaware
- **25** Dilworthtown Inn
  - Founders
  - Mainland Inn
  - Striped Bass
  - Susanna Foo
  - La Famiglia
  - Barrymore Room
  - La Bonne Auberge
- **24** Prime Rib
  - Savona
  - ¡Pasión!
  - Brasserie Perrier
  - Buddakan
  - Inn at Phillips Mill
  - Jake's
- **23** Django
  - Overtures
  - Capital Grille
  - Grill
  - Monte Carlo Liv. Rm.
  - Duling-Kurtz Hse.
  - Kimberton Inn
  - Morton's of Chicago
  - Passerelle
  - Abacus
  - Tangerine
  - Gourmet
  - Charles Plaza
  - Rist. La Buca
  - Carman's
- **22** Yangming
  - William Penn Inn
  - Le Mas

Best Buys

Top 40 Bangs for the Buck

1. La Colombe Panini
2. Koch's Deli
3. Pink Rose Pastry
4. Dalessandro's
5. Jim's Steaks
6. Geno's Steaks
7. Pat's King of Steaks
8. Reading Term. Mkt.
9. Bitar's
10. Nifty Fifty's
11. Izzy & Zoe's
12. Pho 75
13. Tony Luke Jr.'s
14. Carman's
15. Taco House
16. Dahlak
17. Minar Palace
18. Morning Glory
19. Celebre's Pizzeria
20. Hank's Place
21. Shank's & Evelyn's
22. Alyan's
23. Melrose Diner
24. New Delhi
25. Pepper's Cafe
26. Mayfair Diner
27. Blue in Green
28. More Than/Ice Cream
29. Day by Day
30. Cosi
31. Vietnam
32. Ruby's
33. Silk City
34. Trolley Car Diner
35. Rib Crib
36. Tandoor India
37. Mama Palma's
38. Tacconelli's
39. Beijing
40. Vietnam Palace

Other Good Values

Abacus
Ben & Irv Deli
Blue Sage
Cafette
Campo's Deli
Charles Plaza
Chun Hing
Country Club
Dark Horse Pub
Down Home Diner
El Azteca
El Sombrero
Famous 4th St.
Garnian Wa
Harmony
H.K. Golden Phoenix
House of Jin
Jamaican Jerk Hut
Kim's
La Boheme
Las Cazuelas
Le Bus
Little Pete's
Lombardi's
Maccabeam
Main-ly Café
Marathon Grill
Marigold Din. Rm.
McGillin's Olde Ale
North Sea
N. 3rd
Pietro's Coal Oven
Ray's Café
Roselena's
Sang Kee
Singapore Kosher
Standard Tap
Tamarindo's
Taqueria Moroleon
Time Out Falafel

subscribe to zagat.com

Restaurant Directory

Philadelphia

| F | D | S | C |

Abacus ⑤   23 | 19 | 23 | $23
North Penn Mktpl., 1551 S. Valley Forge Rd. (Sumneytown Pike), Lansdale, 215-362-2010

■ You can count on "amusing, albeit corny jokes" from "funny guy"/host Joe Chen at this "top-notch" Montco Chinese BYO, but even "without his descriptions" the dishes are "innovative and very good", so "abandon your preconceived notions" and enjoy a "gourmet" meal with a "family feel", whether you can stomach the "wit" or not.

Abbaye ◐⑤   – | – | – | M
637 N. Third St. (Fairmount Ave.), 215-627-6711

Pub crawlers are flocking to this bright and airy Northern Liberties newcomer for its ever-changing selection of beers served at a copper-topped bar, as well as its Belgian-French bistro fare (the oyster po' boys are the house specialty); the laid-back vibe is conducive to conversation, but even if you come stag you'll likely encounter a gabby local, possibly accompanied by his pooch.

Abilene ◐⑤   14 | 11 | 15 | $21
429 South St. (bet. 4th & 5th Sts.), 215-922-2583

■ "If you're hungry from a day on South Street" and need something "cheap" and "quick", take a seat at a "beat-up table" and dig into some "must-have garlic mashed potatoes" at this "gritty" Eclectic "joint" where "pierced student types" get "noisy" at "happy hour" and "blues" fans whoop it up to "great live bands."

Abyssinia ◐⑤   ∇ 22 | 12 | 13 | $15
229 S. 45th St. (Locust St.), 215-387-2424

☒ "Eating with your hands is sexy" at this West Philly Ethiopian – just "go with people as adventurous as you", and you're sure to have a "wonderful", if "novel, dining experience"; the "service is slow as molasses", but the "cheap eats" (including "many veggie options") are "worth the wait", even amid the "grim" surrounds.

Aden ⑤   18 | 15 | 20 | $25
614 N. Second St. (bet. Fairmount Ave. & Spring Garden St.), 215-627-9844

■ Dining at this "cute" Northern Liberties Mediterranean is "like finding out you really do have relatives" in the old country: the "family atmosphere" is "warm and homey", the brother-sister owners "greet everyone as a long-lost friend" and the booze is strictly BYO; as for the "upscale"

Philadelphia   F | D | S | C

eats, they're "worth the extra bucks", especially when sampled in the garden "in summer."

Adobe Cafe S   16 | 13 | 16 | $23
4550 Mitchell St. (Leverington Ave.), 215-483-3947
☑ On the Roxborough side of Manayunk, this "inexpensive" "neighborhood" Southwestern is "great for kids", especially if the tykes are herbivorous, as the menu boasts some "incredibly tasty vegetarian" dishes; meat-eating adults complain "the only good thing served here is the margarita", though a recent ownership change may improve "mediocre" meals, a "seedy" setting and "spotty service."

Adriatica S   – | – | – | M
217 Chestnut St. (Strawberry St.), 215-592-8001
Mustapha Rouissiya, owner of Figs, has returned to Old City with this spacious, boldly decorated Mediterranean seafood venture complete with a gourmet fish market; insiders, noting the menu's French, North African and Turkish influences, are partial to the baked brie with honey and lavender appetizer, followed by one of the day's five whole fish offerings and washed down with a selection from the 150-bottle wine list, all reasonably priced.

Alberto's S   19 | 19 | 18 | $36
191 S. Newtown Street Rd. (½ mi. south of West Chester Pike), Newtown Square, 610-356-9700
☑ The "many rooms" at this "well-run" Delco Italian work "for corporate luncheons and parties", but some say the meals and decor "lack the glamour for the price" you pay; if you want to "take your parents" "for a birthday celebration" amid the "mostly older clientele", regulars suggest the "super Sunday brunch."

Al Dar Bistro S   15 | 14 | 15 | $24
281 Montgomery Ave. (Levering Mill Rd.), Bala Cynwyd, 610-667-1245
☑ Bala babies warn "if you can't say anything nice, don't say anything" about this "casual" "neighborhood place"; nevertheless, plenty of disappointed diners do dismiss the "tired menu" of "typical" Med–Middle Eastern eats, the "noisy" room and the "slow" servers who act "like they're doing you a favor by letting you dine" here.

ALISA CAFE   24 | 13 | 22 | $33
109 Fairfield Ave. (bet. Garrett Rd. & Terminal Sq.), Upper Darby, 610-352-4402
■ Chef-owner "Tony Kanjanakorn is as consistent as the sunrise" in turning out "superb" "bargain" French-Thai fare that makes this "unprepossessing" Upper Darby "storefront BYO" shine; servers who are "anxious to please" add to the "warmth", but "bring earplugs", as the "noise" in the "tight space" can be intense.

vote at zagat.com

Philadelphia

| F | D | S | C |

Alison at Blue Bell ⌀ | - | - | - | M |
721 Skippack Pike (Penllyn-Blue Bell Pike), Blue Bell, 215-641-2660
The crowds that overflowed Central Montco's Alison Cafe have followed chef Alison Barshak (of Striped Bass fame) down the pike to her new, larger New American BYO in Blue Bell, where she works the mesquite grill in the open kitchen; the airy atmospherics and cheery service enhance the meal, but keep in mind that it's cash-only.

ALMA DE CUBA S | 21 | 23 | 22 | $46 |
1623 Walnut St. (bet. 16th & 17th Sts.), 215-988-1799
☒ Celeb chef Douglas Rodriguez and über-restaurateur Stephen Starr help the "beautiful" people "forget where they are" at this "hip" Restaurant Row Cuban collaboration; where the "mojitos have mojo", the fare is "fabulous fusion" and the decor features "flashing scenes" of the island, it is indeed "hard to believe you're in Philly", though diners who find it "too dark", "too loud" and "too trendy" pout that "a trip to Havana should be more fun."

Alyan's S | 19 | 9 | 15 | $13 |
603 S. Fourth St. (South St.), 215-922-3553
■ "Shove your way" into this "tiny", "bare-bones" Middle Eastern off South Street for a "tasty", "quick bite" at a "definite value"; though adherents particularly "go for the falafel, hummus and fries", they swear "you can't go wrong with anything on the menu."

Amara Cafe S | 20 | 12 | 19 | $22 |
105 S. 22nd St. (bet. Chestnut & Sansom Sts.), 215-564-6976
☒ "Imagination is used in the food preparation, not the decor" at this "no-frills" Center City Thai where "BYO makes it perfectly reasonable" for "young couples" on a budget to enjoy a "solid" meal; when you dine at East of Amara's "tiny" Siamese twin, just "don't share your secrets, or the whole place will hear them."

America Bar & Grill S | 18 | 17 | 17 | $31 |
Shops at Lionville Station, 499 E. Uwchlan Ave. (Lionville Station Rd.), Chester Springs, 610-280-0800
☒ "It's slim pickings in this part of the suburbs", so Lionvillers call this "upscale-casual" New American "convenient", particularly for a "nice martini" or the "delicious Sunday brunch"; even so, most admit they "wouldn't go out of their way" for "overpriced", "ordinary" eats.

Aoi S | 18 | 12 | 17 | $26 |
1210 Walnut St. (bet. 12th & 13th Sts.), 215-985-1838
☒ "All-you-can-tolerate sushi is the main attraction" at this "decent" Center City Japanese – just "don't get caught with leftovers" because "they charge you per piece" you can't stomach; design divas diss decor

Philadelphia   F | D | S | C

that "looks like they took over a cheesy nightclub and didn't change anything."

Ardmore Station Cafe S ⊄   ▽ 20 | 15 | 20 | $22
6 Station Rd. (bet. Anderson & Lancaster Aves.), Ardmore, 610-642-3889
■ "It's about time the Main Line had a decent breakfast joint" say Ardmore commuters about this "cute" New American near the train depot; the "caring" team of "alums" from Center City top spots "tries very hard" and turns out "consistent" lunches too.

Ariana S   ▽ 25 | 16 | 23 | $21
134 Chestnut St. (bet. Front & 2nd Sts.), 215-922-1535
■ Considered by a cadre of critics to be "even better" than its sib, this "friendly" "Kabul spin-off" down the block in Old City offers "inventive", "bold" Afghan fare, "exquisitely seasoned" and "delightfully served" as you sit on pillows on the floor (conventional table seating is also available); it's a "very good value for your money."

Arpeggio S   23 | 11 | 19 | $20
542 Spring House Village Ctr. (Bethlehem Pike & Norristown Rd.), Spring House, 215-646-5055
■ "Not just your average pizza joint", this Montco Med BYO serves up "fantastic" brick-oven pies and other "hearty", "fair-priced" fare; though diners have reservations about "no reservations", the business' "cheerful busyness" seduces "crammed-in" regulars to "sit on top of each other" (good news: an expansion will soon double the seating), and "complimentary appetizers" "help calm hunger pangs nagging at the bellies" of "waiting patrons."

Astral Plane S   19 | 20 | 19 | $31
1708 Lombard St. (bet. 17th & 18th Sts.), 215-546-6230
◨ Take a "nostalgic trip down groovy memory lane" at Center City's "flower child" of a New American; "after all these years", this "classic" remains as "upscale rummage-sale" "romantic" as it wants to be, and the fare is "reliably creative"; some may find it "*très passé*", but "campy" groupies still gush over a dining experience that's "like eating in a faded starlet's dressing room."

Athena S ⊄   17 | 14 | 17 | $21
264 N. Keswick Ave. (Easton Rd.), Glenside, 215-884-1777
◨ A "good-value" "best bet for those on their way to the Keswick Theater" is a meal at a "terrace table" at this "informal" Greek BYO in a Montco "strip center"; though fans say the "ok joint" puts out "authentic" eats, including a "spinach pie too good for Popeye", opposing Olive Oyl aficionados find no muscle in the "boring" chow and say service can be as "rude" as Bluto.

vote at zagat.com

Philadelphia   F | D | S | C

Audrey Claire ⓈⒻ   22 | 16 | 19 | $29
276 S. 20th St. (Spruce St.), 215-731-1222
▨ There's still a "buzz" surrounding Audrey Taichman's "reliable" Rittenhouse Square Med BYO, though it could just be the "cell phones" of all the "friends" who "jam" the "minimalist" room "to be seen" or to "listen in on someone else's date"; "even the pickiest eater" can ask for something "inventive" and "tasty", though when "bedlam" ensues among the "trendies", "the staff can't hear the orders."

August Moon Ⓢ   23 | 16 | 20 | $28
300 E. Main St. (Arch St.), Norristown, 610-277-4008
▪ "Main Liners don't know what they're missing" if the "lousy location" keeps them away from this "hidden gem" in Norristown; until word is out, it's "easy to get into" the "elegant" Japanese-Korean, so "grab friends" or "a date" and try out the "great" Asian BBQ, or sample the "amazing sushi" served by a "polite", "attentive" staff.

Avalon Ⓢ   – | – | – | E
312 S. High St. (Union St.), West Chester, 610-436-4100
Chef Michael Merlo of Brasserie Perrier fame has added to West Chester's dining scene with this romantic American-Continental BYO set up in a California-style room complete with a rock-bordered fountain and pool; those in-the-know suggest that the best time to visit is on weeknights, when a reasonably priced bistro menu is offered.

Azafran Ⓢ   22 | 17 | 20 | $26
617 S. Third St. (bet. Bainbridge & South Sts.), 215-928-4019
▨ "*Siempre fantastico*" cry amigos of this "intimate" South American BYO off South Street, where the fare is "melt-in-your-mouth" good; the whole joint "hums with energy", but if you want to really impress "a date", tell 'em to go powder their nose, as the "funky" bathrooms are nearly as "beautiful" as the courtyard.

Azalea Ⓢ   19 | 23 | 20 | $43
Omni Hotel at Independence Park, 401 Chestnut St. (bet. 4th & 5th Sts.), 215-931-4260
▨ "One of Philadelphia's best-kept secrets" is tucked into the Omni, where the American dining room is so "classy, it's flirting with opulence"; though the "great view" of Independence National Historical Park dazzles noshers at the "excellent" Sunday brunch, detractors say with "so much potential", it's a "shame" that the fare is "uneven" and the "service so slow even a snail would be impatient."

Bamboo Club Ⓢ   – | – | – | M
Pavilion at King of Prussia Mall, 640 W. DeKalb Pike (bet. Allendale & Long Rds.), King of Prussia, 610-265-0660
Shoppers at the Pavilion at King of Prussia Mall feel transported amid acres of bamboo and rattan at this way-

Philadelphia F | D | S | C

cool outpost of the lively Pacific Rim chain; while the 'happiness-hour' crowd enjoys nibbling potstickers and crispy crab won tons, chased by a few 'sake bombers', families feel right at home with the kid-friendly menu that includes such Anglo-familiar treats as egg rolls.

Bards, The S 16 | 16 | 16 | $21
2013 Walnut St. (bet. 20th & 21st Sts.), 215-569-9585

☑ "There's no better place on a cold winter night" wax beery bards than this "neat little Irish bar" in Center City, where the Gaelic fare is "authentic" and the Guinness oils the "conversation" "with your mates"; "health-conscious individuals", however, complain it gets "smoky" and "you need earplugs" when "rowdy footballers" "pack" the pub.

BARRYMORE ROOM S 23 | 27 | 25 | $42
Park Hyatt at the Bellevue, 200 S. Broad St. (Walnut St.), 215-790-2814

■ "A lovely, old hotel with a fresh, young staff" makes an "exquisite" combination for an "elegant" afternoon tea at this Continental; while the Park Hyatt servers treat you right, sip your cup, yes, but drink in the "magnificent views" of Center City and the "gorgeous ambiance" of what some stylists call Philly's "most beautiful room."

Basil Bistro & Bar S 18 | 16 | 17 | $28
522 King Rd. (Lancaster Ave.), Paoli, 610-647-1500

☑ This "boisterous" "barn of a place" in Paoli offers "zesty" New American eats in "large portions" to a "smartly casual" crowd; "happy hour" revelers say "we're not talking serious dining, we are talking entertainment and convivial surroundings", and to that end, management has added carpeting to lower "unnerving" "noise levels."

Bay Pony Inn S 18 | 20 | 19 | $33
Bay Pony Inn, 508 Old Skippack Rd. (Salfordville Rd.), Lederach, 215-256-6565

☑ "Romantic traditionalists" say the "picturesque country setting" makes this "out-of-the-way" American-Continental in Montco "the place to propose" over "flavorful" "comfort food"; though the banquet room and attached "old railway car" have been redone, modernists mumble that it's "time for renovations" in the "rather musty" main room, while the "tired food and service" "need a change" to match.

Beau Monde S 20 | 23 | 19 | $25
624 S. Sixth St. (Bainbridge St.), 215-592-0656

☑ "Very romantic on a cold night when they have the fire going", this "beautiful music box" of an off–South Street crêperie is "the perfect date restaurant"; dine with your darling on an "unbelievable selection" of "*délicieux*" "savory and sweet" French creations; the "portions are small", but the prices won't "break the bank", and the

Philadelphia   F | D | S | C

"arrogant, aloof servers" might actually help you "pretend you're in Paris"; N.B. L'Etage, its new second-floor lounge, is already quite the scene, especially on theme nights.

Beijing S   17 | 8 | 18 | $15
3714 Spruce St. (bet. 37th & 38th Sts.), 215-222-5242
■ "Hectic" with "Penn students" and other budget-wise University City-zens scarfing down "acceptable" Chinese, this "bright", "inexpensive" BYO has "blink-of-an-eye" service that gets you "in and out" "fast" so you won't miss your next class; even the cheapest chowhounds chirp that it's "worth a splurge" "if the food carts are closed."

Bella, an American Bistro S   – | – | – | E
2000 Lombard St. (20th St.), 215-985-3222
Run by an eager-to-please transplanted New Yorker, this homey New American bistro in Rittenhouse Square hews to the 'Slow Food' movement; the kitchen bases its creative, seasonal Mid-Atlantic–focused menu (think pretzel-coated fish) on the freshest ingredients from local purveyors who practice sustainable agriculture and aquaculture, while the dining room gives off an appropriately funky vibe.

Bella Luna ⊄   ∇ 21 | 16 | 19 | $27
816 W. Lancaster Ave. (Bryn Mawr Ave.), Bryn Mawr, 610-527-4666
■ The "mussels are great", the "chicken is excellent" and there are "interesting pastas" to boot, all at "reasonable prices", so naturally the crowds "stand in line" in the beautiful moonlight for a table at this "dreamy" Italian BYO in Bryn Mawr, but forget about reservations on weekends.

Bella Trattoria S   17 | 15 | 16 | $25
4258 Main St. (bet. Cotton & Rector Sts.), 215-482-5556
◪ "When the lines are too long at the other Manayunk places", this "come-as-you-are" Italian is "reliable" for "inexpensive", "straightforward" pizzas and red-gravy grub ferried by "friendly" folks; snobs say it's "not worth searching for parking" unless, "weather permitting", you can pull your bumper up to a table in the "*bella*" outdoor cafe and get in some "great people-watching" "alfresco."

Ben & Irv Deli Restaurant S   17 | 9 | 16 | $15
1962 County Line Rd. (Davisville Rd.), Huntingdon Valley, 215-355-2000
◪ Huntingdon Valley "Jewish boys" say "even my grandma has no complaints" about this "no-frills" strip-mall deli where "tasty" Ashkenazi "comfort-food" faves are served in "big portions" by "lovable waitresses" with a knack for "making you feel you're on the *Seinfeld* set"; nevertheless, "long lines" of "Jackie Mason" ringers have outsiders to the tribe kvetching if you're "not stuffed into a warm-up suit with stones, stay home" – "oy vey!"

24   subscribe to zagat.com

Philadelphia

F | **D** | **S** | **C**

Bertolini's S
16 | 16 | 16 | $24

Plaza at King of Prussia Mall, 160 N. Gulph Rd. (bet. DeKalb Pike & Mall Blvd.), King of Prussia, 610-265-2965

King of Prussia Plazaholics "rest mall-weary feet" at this "casual", "convenient" Italian franchise where the "decent" pasta "beats the food court" offerings; however, gourmands "won't rush back" for fare as "unimaginative" as that at "a thousand other chains."

Big George's Stop-N-Dine S⊄
▽ 18 | 8 | 17 | $12

285 S. 52nd St. (Spruce St.), 215-748-8200

"Whoo-whee – that's some good eatin'!" holler the gaggle of Southern food fanciers who feast at this "down-home" West Philly joint known as much for its "nice portions" of "genuine" vittles as for Bill Clinton's 1998 stop-n-dine; it's a meal fit for a presidential "finger licking", "frantic" pace regardless.

Billy Wong's ●S
– | – | – | M

50 S. Second St. (bet. Chestnut & Market Sts.), 215-829-1128

A former partner at Mustard Greens has struck out on his own with this eponymous eatery offering "fresh Chinese without attitude" amid a "beautiful" white-on-white room in Old City; diners "go for the dumplings", while the black-on-gray bar gets lots of high-decibel, late-night action from young vodka and schnapps fans.

BIRCHRUNVILLE STORE CAFE ⊄
26 | 20 | 22 | $40

1407 Hollow Rd. (Flowing Springs Rd.), Birchrunville, 610-827-9002

"Half the joy is finding" Francis Trzeciak's Italian-French BYO "retreat" "in the woods" of "nowheresville", aka the Chester County "hills"; as they "make reservations waaay in advance", aficionados' "mouths water" for the "exquisite" "country" fare presented in a "cute" "village store" setting; the only exception to "impeccable everything" is the "cash-only" policy.

Bistro La Baia S⊄
21 | 14 | 20 | $27

1700 Lombard St. (17th St.), 215-546-0496

"Fantastic grilled squid", "divine lobster ravioli" and other signatures are "so good you forget there's no room to breathe" says a "fiercely loyal clientele" "crammed like sardines" into this charming, cash-only trattoria near Graduate Hospital; the BYO policy helps keep this "eager-to-please" "neighborhood charmer" "a true bargain."

Bistro La Viola S⊄
▽ 23 | 15 | 23 | $36

253 S. 16th St. (bet. Locust & Spruce Sts.), 215-735-8630

Among Center City sorts, this "wonderful" Italian BYO "gets high marks" for the kitchen's "careful attention" to "excellent" dishes served at "moderate prices" by a

Philadelphia F | D | S | C

"suave" staff; it's "tiny", so when it's "crowded" it's "way too noisy", but the food? – "wow."

Bistro Romano S 17 | 17 | 18 | $30
120 Lombard St. (bet. Front & 2nd Sts.), 215-925-8880

◪ "For a change of pace, try the Murder Mystery Dinner with friends" on weekends at this "rustic" Italian off Head House Square; it's no mystery, however, that the joint "needs to work on even the famous Caesar salad" made tableside, "endearing" as it is, and surface-dwellers say "basement" dining is only "romantic" "if you like caves."

BISTRO ST. TROPEZ 23 | 20 | 20 | $35
2400 Market St., 4th fl. (23rd St.), 215-569-9269

◪ Patrice Rames "has French bistro style down pat" at his "imaginative" fourth-floor "hideaway" in the Marketplace Design Center; "arty" urbanites "send suburbanites" here for "imaginative" prix fixes, "kitschy" decor and a "groovy bar", "spectacular" "views of the Schuylkill" and an après-meal "browse through the displays" in the building; a few *non*-sayers sniff that the "rude", "indifferent" staff displays a bit too much Gaul.

Bitar's 22 | 9 | 16 | $11
Bourse Bldg., 111 Independence Mall E. (bet. 5th & Market Sts.), 215-625-4877
947 Federal St. (10th St.), 215-755-1121
Moravian Cafe Food Ct., 3401 Walnut St. (34th St.), 215-222-4513 S ⌿

■ "There are better decorations in a Bedouin tent" than at this "no-frills", "friendly" Mediterranean clan, but with falafel and hummus (and pita sandwiches and combo platters) "this cheap and good, you can't go wrong" when you're seeking a "fast-food alternative."

Black Bass Hotel S 21 | 22 | 20 | $43
Black Bass Hotel, 3774 River Rd. (north of Greenhill Rd.), Lumberville, 215-297-5770

◪ "King George–oriented" "romantics" have been "beating a path" to this New American Bucks County inn since the 1740s; the "dreamy" riverbank location affords a "lovely view", and an "outstanding collection" of antiques makes the "old building" feel as if "nothing has changed since it opened except electricity and indoor plumbing"; to wit, despite the "amazing champagne brunch", modernists say the "unimaginative" cuisine could use an update.

Black Sheep Pub ●S 16 | 17 | 16 | $22
247 S. 17th St. (Latimer St.), 215-545-9473

◪ This "Dublin-like" Rittenhouse pub set in a former gay strip club is "alive with young people" of all persuasions guzzling glasses from the "super beer selection" and gobbling "decent" Eclectic grub; it "fills a void in the

Philadelphia   F | D | S | C

pretentious Square scene", though the "high-decibel" "after-work" crunch downstairs has yucksters bleating that the joint should be named the "Black Sardine."

Bleu S   20 | 20 | 18 | $35
Sheraton Rittenhouse Square Hotel, 227 S. 18th St. (Locust St.), 215-545-0342

◪ Even Rittenhouse Squares enjoy the "nice energy" of Neil Stein's "overly trendy" French bistro where "the food is great, but hey, you go for the face time"; the "outside tables" are "perfect for people-watching", but "slow service" and "big prices" have "see-and-be-seensters" seeing Rouge – those who prefer its ruddy sib up the block say "if it wasn't on the park, this would be just another average restaurant" with an "overinflated sense of worth."

BLUE BELL INN   20 | 18 | 19 | $37
601 Skippack Pike (Penllyn-Blue Bell Pike), Blue Bell, 215-646-2010

◪ Montco mealsters say it "seems like eons" since this "oldie but real goodie" first served béarnaise-smothered Traditional American "classics", and with a pre-1776 pedigree, that's not such an exaggeration; whippersnappers "make fun of its clientele", grunting it's a "great place for an afternoon snooze", but senior scenesters harrumph "so we have gray hair – it's reliable, and we love it."

Blue in Green S⌀   20 | 14 | 15 | $15
7 N. Third St. (Market St.), 215-928-5880
719 Sansom St. (bet. 7th & 8th Sts.), 215-923-6883

◪ Their "super pancakes" and "excellent omelets" are "why brunch was invented", so if you can stomach the "none-too-cheery" "slacker Gen X" servers at this "retro-beatnik" daytime duo in Old City and on Jewelers Row, belly up to a booth and dig in; penny-pinchers pout that the "glorified diners'" "touch of NYC" extends to the tab, griping that the "green in the name is an allusion to the cost."

Blüe Ox Brauhaus S   19 | 19 | 19 | $28
7980 Oxford Ave. (Rhawn St.), 215-728-9440

■ There's "real butter" and lots of it in the "old-world, authentic" cooking at this Fox Chase Bavarian, but if it's "not the place for dieters", you can don your "lederhosen" and burn a few calories when the "live accordion" music gets you "waving your hands and stomping your feet in pure bliss"; your tongue will get a workout too, since "speaking German helps you fit in at the bar."

Blue Pacific S   – | – | – | M
Plaza at King of Prussia Mall, 160 N. Gulph Rd. (bet. DeKalb Pike & Mall Blvd.), King of Prussia, 610-337-3078

Sushiphiles and Chinese traditionalists both get what they want at this neon-glitzy Asian newcomer (a $1 million

Philadelphia F | D | S | C

modernization of the long-running Jade Garden) at the Plaza at King of Prussia Mall; regulars who talk up the small-plate selections (best washed down with sake) also get a kick out of the wisecracking chefs who put on a lively floor show at the sushi bar.

Blue Sage Vegetarian Grille 23 | 13 | 20 | $22
772 Second Street Pike (Street Rd.), Southampton, 215-942-8888

■ "These are vegetables! – the chef has them jumping through hoops" say Southampton surveyors; seasonal specialties "gorgeously presented" in "generous" portions at this "creative Vegetarian" BYO have even "meat lovers" oohing and aahing, not to mention "feeling healthy" and promising to "return many times."

bluezette ●S 19 | 22 | 18 | $34
246 Market St. (bet. 2nd & 3rd Sts.), 215-627-3866

At Delilah Winder's "snazzy, jazzy" Old City Southern-Caribbean, it's "hip to hang" and "people-watch" the "great-looking crowd" while "late-night snacking" in the "fabulous upstairs bar" or sidewalk cafe; in the "sultry" back room on the first floor, serious diners "satisfy their cravings" for "citified soul food", even though a few fret that the "menu is more ambitious than accomplished."

Bomb Bomb Bar-be-que Grill ⊄ 18 | 9 | 18 | $21
1026 Wolf St. (Warnock St.), 215-463-1311

"Da ribs are da bomb", so "check your attitude at the door", but not your appetite, at this Italian BBQ "joint"/"neighborhood bar" whose "time-warp" "atmosphere defines South Philly", where "smoky, noisy and local" are "virtues" and "folksy" servers "never fail to call you 'hon.'"

Bookbinders 15th St. 16 | 14 | 16 | $38
Seafood House S
215 S. 15th St. (bet. Locust & Walnut Sts.), 215-545-1137

"Time forgot" this "well-established" seafooder in Center City, and while that's a plus for those who expect "no surprises" from the shucker at the oyster bar and "generous portions" from the "good-buy early-bird special", most scoff "tradition shmadition", claiming it's "riding on its reputation" and in "need of a makeover."

Bourbon Blue S – | – | – | M
2 Rector St. (Main St.), 215-508-3360

The good times roll nightly at this handsome stone-and-brick addition on the Manayunk Canal, whose French Quarter theme attracts Cajun-Creole seekers with its better-than-average oyster sampler, andouille meatloaf and bananas Foster served by a competent staff; the real calling card, though, is the live entertainment (blues, funk) featured in the downstairs lounge Thursday–Saturday.

Philadelphia   F | D | S | C

Brasil's 🆂   20 | 17 | 19 | $32
112 Chestnut St. (Front St.), 215-413-1700

■ If your crowd is carnivorous, then "a great place for the group to laugh, eat, dance and have fun" is this Old City Brazilian favorite where Tuesday and Thursday's "perfectly grilled" rodizio is definitely a "beef-eater's delight"; the fish-tank-and-waterfall decor may be "tacky", but the staff is "gorgeous", and the upstairs "disco", complete with "lessons", adds to the joint's "spice" – "just watch the house drink, the caipirinha", or you might samba over your own toes.

BRASSERIE PERRIER 🆂   26 | 25 | 24 | $52
1619 Walnut St. (bet. 16th & 17th Sts.), 215-568-3000

■ "Bring your best client" to Georges Perrier's other Center City outpost because, though the New French belle is known as the "poor man's Le Bec-Fin", the "almost perfect dining experience" here will make you seem "rich and trendy"; "Armani-clad clientele" slouch about the "power bar" jabbering on "cell phones" while an "arty" staff glides through the "sleek", "Manhattanesque" room delivering Chris Scarduzio's "scrumptious" Asian–Italian-inflected fare to diners who only wish the portions weren't so "tiny."

Bravo Bistro 🆂   20 | 18 | 20 | $33
175 King of Prussia Rd. (Lancaster Ave.), Radnor, 610-293-9521

■ There's "strong local interest" on the Main Line for a "casual alternative to fancy" "date places", and supporters say that Passerelle's "informal" sibling delivers with consistently "pretty, satisfying" New American plates, accompanied by "good wines by the glass" and served overlooking a pond populated by swans, all at "half the price" of the upscale joints.

Brew HaHa! 🆂⌀   16 | 14 | 15 | $11
Giant Shopping Ctr., 2749 Street Rd. (Mechanicsville Rd.), Bensalem, 215-633-7780
Whitpain Shopping Ctr., 1510 DeKalb Pike (Yost Rd.), Blue Bell, 610-239-2422
1967 Norristown Rd. (Welsh Rd.), Maple Glen, 215-619-9950
163 E. Lancaster Ave. (bet. Louella & Wayne Aves.), Wayne, 610-995-2757
9 W. Gay St. (High St.), West Chester, 610-429-9335
See review in the Wilmington/Nearby Delaware Directory.

Brick Hotel, The 🆂   – | – | – | E
The Brick Hotel, 1 E. Washington Ave. (State St.), Newtown, 215-860-8313

Newtown is a "pleasant" neighborhood "for wandering", but when you get hungry, lots of "locals" advise stop for a "beautifully presented" bite at this "charming" American-

vote at zagat.com

Philadelphia   F | D | S | C |

Continental quarter in a "lovely old hotel" dating from 1764; with "imaginative", "delicious" seasonal dishes like Black Angus fillet Asagio with purple mashed potatoes, the kitchen in this brick house sure is mighty, mighty – it's letting it all hang out.

Bridget Foy's ●S   17 | 16 | 17 | $28 |
200 South St. (2nd St.), 215-922-1813

◪ Even "grandma likes to sit and watch the crowds on South Street" from the "nice" porch at this New American "tourist" "magnet", but tasters tsk tsk that the old gal ain't no gastronome, considering that the "tavern-food" menu is quite "lackluster"; "cheesy" surroundings and green "servers who have a lot to learn" further inspire the nickname "Bridget Phooey."

Bridgid's S   20 | 14 | 19 | $23 |
726 N. 24th St. (Meredith St.), 215-232-3232

■ "Eye-poppingly low" prices on "interesting, hearty" Eclectic eats and "fascinating beers" dazzle Fairmount feeders at this "smoke-free bar" ("what a great idea!") with a "neighborhood" vibe somewhere "between trendy chic and working class"; dining has expanded to the second floor, though the downstairs is still "cramped."

Buca di Beppo S   15 | 17 | 17 | $24 |
258 S. 15th St. (bet. Latimer & Manning Sts.), 215-545-2818
1 W. Germantown Pike (DeKalb Pike), East Norriton, 610-272-2822
300 Main St. (Bartlett Ave.), Exton, 610-524-9939
309 Old York Rd. (bet. Greenwood & West Aves.), Jenkintown, 215-885-6342

◪ "Fun"-loving "large groups" "gorge themselves" at "the Pope's table" at these "lively" links in a "gaudy" Italian chain where the "obscene portions" of "just average" chow would have the pontiff doling out Hail Marys to the kitchen; "screaming" "kids love to tour" the "kitsch"-filled, "Disney"-like joints, but "woe unto the table of two" looking for quiet fine dining – gourmands suggest couples are better off "staying home and eating canned pasta."

BUDDAKAN S   27 | 27 | 24 | $47 |
325 Chestnut St. (bet. 3rd & 4th Sts.), 215-574-9440

■ Stephen Starr serves up the "wow factor" at his "edgy" Asian Fusion "production" in the Historic District, where the "'in' crowd" achieves "gastronomic nirvana" on chef Scott Swiderski's "beautiful", "family-style" dishes "in the shadow of the big, gold Buddha"; though there's nothing "zen-like" about "deafening" noise and "people-watching", you may "enjoy a more relaxed dinner" upstairs where "you get no stares", except from "servers who are as stone-faced" as the statue of the Enlightened One himself.

Philadelphia F | D | S | C

Bunha Faun S 23 | 12 | 20 | $31
152 Lancaster Pike (¼ mi. east of Morehall Rd.), Malvern, 610-651-2836
■ This "unpretentious" French-Asian BYO in Malvern just might win the prize for "best use of an old Dairy Queen"; thinly "disguised with pretty linens and candles", it looks "like a remodeled office", but what it "lacks in atmosphere", it more than makes up for in "delicious", "subtly sauced" dishes and "wonderful service."

Butcher's Cafe S⊘ 20 | 15 | 18 | $28
Italian Mkt., 901 Christian St. (9th St.), 215-925-6200
◪ "Not much has changed decor-wise" at this "former butcher shop" in the Italian Market, where "meat hooks" and a cold case add a certain "charm" to this "casual", "cash-only" BYO joint that serves "basic", satisfying "home cooking" from all over The Boot; fussy foodies, however, say the fare can "vary wildly" from feasts "fit for Tony Soprano" to "mediocre" meals, and snobs roast the "unrefined" service.

Cadence S – | – | – | VE
Kimmel Center for the Performing Arts, 300 S. Broad St. (Spruce St.), 215-670-2388
The Kimmel Center's handsome, high-ticket French is picking up the beat as it steps up hours (it's open for dinner Tuesday–Saturday, plus show nights and for Sunday brunch); the signature iced seafood platter strikes the right note for a lavish nosh before a concert, and the staff has been brushing up on its performance, but the biggest bravo goes to the view of the Avenue of the Arts; there's also a lounge for lighter brasserie fare.

Cafe Arielle S 24 | 22 | 21 | $42
100 S. Main St. (Ashland St.), Doylestown, 215-345-5930
◪ The "beautiful place settings" pique expectations, and chef-owner Jacques Colmaire "does not disappoint" fans with "fabulous" "south-of-France cuisine" at his "high-class", "European-style" bistro in Doylestown; coinwise critics crave "more spark for the price"; N.B. noted that lunch is served Wednesday–Friday and dinner is offered Wednesday–Sunday.

Café Habana S 16 | 20 | 18 | $30
102 S. 21st St. (bet. Chestnut & Sansom Sts.), 215-561-2822
◪ It "feels like Havana" at this "upscale" but "low-key" Center City Cuban where "cute", "friendly" servers from the island nation pour some of "the city's best mojitos" to fuel fancy footwork during Saturday's *Buena Vista*-esque "fun late-night parties"; still, spice queens "don't get" how a *casa* with such a "cool", "authentic" vibe can put out fare that's "so bland."

vote at zagat.com

Philadelphia | F | D | S | C |

Cafe Preeya ⑤   21 | 15 | 19 | $32
Village Ctr., 2651 Huntingdon Pike (Red Lion Rd.), Huntingdon Valley, 215-947-6195

■ Huntingdon Valley denizens rally behind this "long-running neighborhood hit" that hyperbolic diners call "the Buddakan of the suburbs without the noise" or, for that matter, the "aspiration to greatness"; the bare-bones but "pleasant" surroundings "serve their purpose", providing a comfortable backdrop for an Eclectic, "inventive mix of French and Thai" flavor to "tantalize" tastebuds and help "locals" "recover from shopping the mall."

Cafe San Pietro ⑤   – | – | – | M
41 W. Lancaster Ave. (Ardmore Ave.), Ardmore, 610-896-4740

It "feels like Italia" at Ristorante Positano's "low-key" "satellite" in Ardmore, where thrifty locals are pleased by the fine, if limited, Mediterranean menu, "friendly" service and weekend entertainment, all at "half the price"; if you're looking for cozy, this is it.

Cafe Spice ⑤   21 | 22 | 20 | $30
35 S. Second St. (bet. Chestnut & Market Sts.), 215-627-6273

■ You "feel like a movie star" sipping "wickedly poured cocktails" with the "beautiful people" at the "extra-trendy bar" before you tuck into a "private booth" at this "chic" Old City link in the New York–based "nuevo" Indian mini-chain; the "sensually stimulating" experience "fills a need after a hundred buffets" in bare-bones joints, and the "exquisite" fare keeps pace with the "hot" design, even if skinflints don't like feeling as if they're helping to "pay the interior decorator."

Cafette ⑤∌   19 | 12 | 17 | $17
8136 Ardleigh St. (Hartwell Ln.), 215-242-4220

■ "One of the few places" in Chestnut Hill, where "tree huggers" and "carnivores" alike "can be happy", this "tiny", "quirky" Eclectic BYO offers a menu of "solid home cooking" featuring "something for everyone"; there are "healthful selections", sure, but Friday's "fried chicken is the definition of comfort food" at a place that feels "like you're eating in your own kitchen."

Caffè Bellissimo ⑤   18 | 15 | 19 | $23
1001 Baltimore Pike (Sproul Rd.), Springfield, 610-328-2300

See review in the Wilmington/Nearby Delaware Directory.

Caffe Casta Diva ∌   – | – | – | E
227 S. 20th St. (Locust St.), 215-496-9677

The demanding Rittenhouse Square crowd has fallen for this chef-owned Italian cafe nestled in a shoebox-size

---

32   subscribe to zagat.com

Philadelphia F | D | S | C

storefront; the atmosphere may be unassuming, but the traditional cooking is serious and generously portioned and the service warm; keep in mind, though, that it's BYO and cash-only.

California Cafe S — 20 | 19 | 19 | $29
Plaza at King of Prussia Mall, 160 N. Gulph Rd. (bet. DeKalb Pike & Mall Blvd.), King of Prussia, 610-354-8686

■ Where else would a gaggle of "17-year-old girls using their fathers' credit cards" "after a day at Neiman's" "gladly sit down" but this "cool" "California wanna-be" serving "great salads" and such in King of Prussia Plaza?; in fact, with "appealing" fare, a "West Coast–chic" vibe and a "well-trained staff", the chain link is an "unexpected oasis" for anyone who has "shopped till they dropped" at the mall.

California Pizza Kitchen S — 18 | 14 | 17 | $19
Court at King of Prussia Mall, 470 Mall Blvd. (DeKalb Pike), King of Prussia, 610-337-1500

☒ The "potpourri of toppings" at this chainster in the Court is "sure to get you out of the pizza doldrums" proclaim King of Prussians; beyond the "fun, fast and flavorful" "designer" pies, it "doesn't try to be fancy", so it's "a favorite destination for kids", but be forewarned of a "prohibitive wait."

Campo's Deli — ▽ 22 | 15 | 17 | $11
214 Market St. (Strawberry St.), 215-923-1000

☒ The hoagies, grinders and cheese steaks sure are "fresh" and "yummy" at this sandwich joint in Old City; nevertheless, big bellies blubber over "small portions for the price", and "too much attitude" Philly-style has Misses Manners mumbling that the staff is "very rude."

CAPITAL GRILLE S — 24 | 24 | 23 | $49
1338 Chestnut St. (Broad St.), 215-545-9588

☒ Take "a welcome trip back to the '50s, when food was guiltless fun", at this "clubby", "old-school" Avenue of the Arts beef palace; the "expense-account" legions "feel like senators" chomping on "melt-in-your-mouth" meat and swilling "great martinis" amid a "dark wood" interior brightened by a "sunny staff"; jaded jurists jibe "seen one chophouse, you've seen them all", but how many have servers "who send out thank-you notes?"

Capriccio's Cafe S — 15 | 14 | 12 | $15
Radisson Plaza Warwick Hotel, 1701 Locust St. (17th St.), 215-735-9797

☒ The Radisson Plaza Warwick Hotel's coffee shop is a veritable home away from home for all the "bohemian" denizens of the local "art and music" schools, so brace yourself for a lot of "smoke" to accompany your "late" "cup of joe" or "pre-packaged" lunch "on the run", and

vote at zagat.com   33

Philadelphia   F | D | S | C

don't expect refined service from a lackluster staff that seems to "change daily."

Carambola S   24 | 15 | 19 | $31
Dreshertown Plaza, 1650 Limekiln Pike (Dreshertown Rd.), Dresher, 215-542-0900

■ At this "gem of the suburbs", a "friendly" father-son team puts out "delicious" New American–Italian dishes with "magnificent presentation", and Dresher diners enjoy every bite, even if "earsplitting noise" means they "can't hear themselves chew"; urbanites say "if it were in the city, you couldn't get near this place", and given its popularity and "no-reservations" policy, you'll "wait for a table on weekends" as it is.

Caribou Cafe S   20 | 19 | 17 | $29
1126 Walnut St. (bet. 11th & 12th Sts.), 215-625-9535

◪ With "great open front windows", "nice outdoor seating", a "beautiful bar" and an air so "civilized" you can "bring an ex for dinner", this "offbeat", "sun-filled" French bistro strikes up an "authentic rendition of Paris" in Center City; "you either like it or you don't – there's no in-between" – but "new chef" Oliver de Saint Martin's dishes might garner a consensus in the future.

Carman's Country Kitchen S⊘   24 | 15 | 23 | $16
1301 S. 11th St. (Wharton St.), 215-339-9613

■ Housed in an old bookmaker's shop in South Philly, it "ain't quite a country kitchen, but it sure is tasty" for a "hearty" breakfast with an "exotic" Eclectic flair; the staff is "so friendly it's scary", but "everyone should experience Carman" and her "crazies" "at least once", especially alfresco in the "pickup-truck seating" out front.

Carmella's S   - | - | - | M
1 Leverington Ave. (Main St.), 215-487-1400

Manayunk über-restaurateur Derek Davis (Kansas City Prime, Sonoma) has retooled the Southwestern Arroyo Grille into this bustling new red-gravy Italian trattoria that serves everything in big, family-style portions at moderate prices; meanwhile, the late-night bar action, especially on the pleasant deck, promises to remain among the neighborhood's top draws.

Carmine's Cafe S⊘   24 | 13 | 20 | $29
5 Brookline Blvd. (Darby Rd.), Havertown, 610-789-7255

■ Havertowners let "*les bon temps*" roll at this "festive" Cajun-Creole BYO "favorite" to which "crowds" "drive over an hour" for chef-owner John Mims' "decadent" duck and other "spicy", "imaginative" N'Awlins creations in an "unpretentious", "tiny" space filled with "noise and crowds" served by a "rushed" staff; if you're in a mellow mood, "take out and have a marvelous meal at home."

34   subscribe to zagat.com

Philadelphia   **F | D | S | C**

Carversville Inn ⑤   23 | 23 | 22 | $42
6205 Fleecydale Rd. (Aquetong Rd.), Carversville, 215-297-0900
◪ Gastronomes gladly "take the journey" to Bucks County "to have a splendid adventure" dining on "delicious" Southern-style dishes at this "romantic", "rustic" "old building" where a table "by the fire" and a "friendly" staff that treats guests like "part of the family" leave loyalists with a "warm feeling"; however, budget travelers say "ho-hum" fare "does not warrant the price."

Casablanca ⑤   ▽ 18 | 21 | 20 | $31
7557 Haverford Ave. (City Ave.), 215-878-1900
Warrington Mews Plaza, 1111 Easton Rd. (Bristol Rd.), Warrington, 215-343-7715
■ You must remember this pair of "traditional" Moroccan eateries in Overbrook and (BYO) Warrington when you crave "a delicious evening" of "theatrical fun"; "good belly dancing", "fabulous decor" and "enjoyable" seven-course feasts will "take you back to the casbah", and it may well be the beginning of a beautiful friendship.

Cassatt Lounge & Tea Room ⑤   ▽ 24 | 26 | 24 | $29
Rittenhouse Hotel, 210 W. Rittenhouse Sq. (bet. Locust & Walnut Sts.), 215-546-9000
■ Far from the madding crowds of Center City "shoppers", the Earl Grey group has "an elegant escape in this sunny tea-filled haven" at the Rittenhouse Hotel; when the weather is warm, the "lovely tradition" seeps out onto the terrace garden so that afternoon sippers can swoon over the "orgasmic sandwiches", scones and tarts in broad daylight.

Cedars ⑤   20 | 14 | 18 | $20
616 S. Second St. (bet. Bainbridge & South Sts.), 215-925-4950
■ A "refuge from bustling South Street" is this "reliable" spot serving "enjoyable", "simple Mediterranean" dishes that go well with "funky Lebanese wines"; regulars "like the pickle platter" for a "reasonably priced" nibble while perched amid all the pillows.

Celebre's Pizzeria ●⑤   23 | 10 | 16 | $14
Packer Park Shopping Ctr., 1536 Packer Ave. (Broad St.), 215-467-3255
■ The owner "fills you up and sends you on your way before games and concerts" "at the stadium and arenas" near this South Philly pizzeria; stars of the team of "great" "down-home" pies include the "to-die-for" "Pizzazz pizza with American cheese" and the "great white veggie" version.

Centre Bridge Inn ⑤   18 | 21 | 20 | $41
Centre Bridge Inn, 2998 River Rd. (Upper York Rd.), New Hope, 215-862-9139
■ It's "worth a trip out of Philly" with "the person you love" to dine at this "high-class" New Hoper, either "outside on

vote at zagat.com   35

Philadelphia　　　　　　　　　　　F | D | S | C

the veranda with a view of the canal, river and bridge"
"in the warmer months" or inside by the "fire in winter";
"especially if you stay over" at the inn "after a wonderful
meal" of Continental dishes, it's ohhh "sooo romantic."

Century House S　　　　　　　　20 | – | 20 | $34
*Bethlehem Pike (north of Unionville Pike), Hatfield,
215-822-0139*
◪ "Does decor really matter?" – it does to the Montco crowd
that's been cheering the recent redo at this "reliable"
"landmark" in Hatfield that had been sporting the "same
look for over 25 years"; the Traditional American menu has
likewise been perked up with more interesting, updated
specials, though the real appeal remains the "bargain"
four-course early-bird deal that "can't be surpassed" for
"tasty cooking at a great price."

Chadds Ford Inn S　　　　　　18 | 20 | 19 | $35
*Chadds Ford Inn, Baltimore Pike & Creek Rd., Chadds Ford,
610-388-7361*
◪ When you're "taking out-of-town visitors sightseeing in
the area", this "classic" American with an "Andrew Wyeth"-
esque Brandywine bent delivers "lots of tradition"; that
"revolutionary feel" is "delightful" if you "like olde" things,
but for those who don't, note that a post-*Survey* change of
chef has brought the menu into at least the 20th century.

Charles Plaza S　　　　　　　23 | 15 | 23 | $21
234-236 N. 10th St. (Vine St.), 215-829-4383
■ "Charles is a love" say surveyors smitten with the "smiley,
solicitous" eponymous owner of this "upbeat" Chinatown
Chinese where "the man's" "recommendations" are so
"reliable" that "patrons return week after week, year after
year" for more "healthy" "standards" and "exceptional
vegetarian dishes"; the "gracious" host has also recently
remodeled, so decor ratings may rise in the future.

Chart House S　　　　　　　　17 | 20 | 17 | $38
*Penn's Landing, 555 S. Columbus Blvd. (Lombard St.),
215-625-8383*
◪ "Bring your Hawaiian shirt and Nikon to blend in with the
other tourists" snapping shutters at the "spectacular" river
views from this "Disneyland" of a seafood chainster on
Penn's Landing; while a post-*Survey* redo added a sleek
lounge, the "great salad bar" continues to be the highlight
of the "pedestrian" fare.

Cheesecake Factory ◐S　　　　21 | 21 | 19 | $25
*Pavilion at King of Prussia Mall, 570 Mall Blvd. (Allendale Rd.),
King of Prussia, 610-337-2200*
■ "It's finally here, yahoo!" – the "extremely popular"
American chain has descended upon King of Prussia, and
with its "endless waits", "bustling" room, "frazzled" staff

Philadelphia   F | D | S | C

and "enormous portions" of "obscenely good food", including an "incredible variety" of the eponymous cake, this outpost is certainly "fulfilling its reputation."

Chef Charin ⑤   21 | 12 | 20 | $28
126 Bala Ave. (bet. City & Montgomery Aves.), Bala Cynwyd, 610-667-8680

■ Bala balloteers are "always happy to eat" at this "tiny, tiny" BYO bistro where the "well-prepared" Continental dishes are "not spectacular but perfectly pleasant" before or "after the movies"; though a "competent" staff gets you to the show on time, "reservations are important" when a "popular" flick is running at the theater across the street.

Cherry Street Vegetarian ◐⑤   ▽ 20 | 14 | 20 | $17
1010 Cherry St. (bet. 10th & 11th Sts.), 215-923-3663

■ It's "hard to believe it's all vegetarian" at this "reliable" Chinatown BYO, a "great refuge" for "kosher" and "gluten-friendly folks" who can't wait to dig into "exciting" "textured and flavored" specialties; even carnivores claim "the faux meat rocks!"

Chestnut Grill & Sidewalk Cafe ⑤   18 | 16 | 18 | $24
Chestnut Hill Hotel, 8229 Germantown Ave. (Southampton Ave.), 215-247-7570

■ The "affable" staff does its darnedest to "make your stay a blast", but the dining room "downstairs is a dungeon" nevertheless, so get a seat on the "deliciously sunny porch" and "people-watch" "the parade going by on Germantown Avenue" while you munch on a "nice, light" American meal at Chestnut Hill's "neighborhood staple."

Chez Colette ⑤   18 | 19 | 17 | $39
Sofitel Philadelphia, 120 S. 17th St. (Sansom St.), 215-569-8300

◪ The Sofitel's New French in a "terrific", "airy" space along Sansom Street has the charms of a "Parisian cafe", down to "indifferent" service; though the kitchen's "step up from normal hotel fare" is worth "trying", when diners describe the dishes as "Toulouse-style", they may be thinking of Lautrec, since portions are as "small" as the diminutive painter himself.

Chickie's & Pete's Cafe ◐⑤   20 | 14 | 17 | $21
4010 Robbins Ave. (Frankford Ave.), 215-338-3060
Roosevelt Plaza, 11000 Roosevelt Blvd. (bet. Red Lion & Woodhaven Rds.), 215-856-9890

■ The "hot" "crabs are as juicy as the local gossip" at these "upbeat" Northeast Philly "sports bars", where "picking" crustaceans and slurping "cold beer" in front of the "large TVs" is "more Philly than *Rocky*"; they're "always crowded", so they "must be good" – "just wear a gas mask" if you're a non-smoker.

vote at zagat.com

Philadelphia F | D | S | C

Chlöe ⌀ 23 | 17 | 22 | $31
232 Arch St. (bet. 2nd & 3rd Sts.), 215-629-2337
■ For "BYO at its finest", try this "tiny", "unpretentious" New American bistro across from the Betsy Ross House, "where the husband-and-wife chefs really care" to impart "genuine warmth and quality" with a "creative", "seasonal" menu featuring "so many good flavors" "it's hard to make a choice" – "if you can get a seat"; especially when area galleries throw their monthly "First Friday" party, the "no-reservations policy is a huge pain in the butt."

Chops S – | – | – | VE
401 City Ave. (Monument Rd.), Bala Cynwyd, 610-668-3400
Alex Plotkin, the longtime general manager of the Palm at Center City's Bellevue hotel, has resurfaced in a City Avenue office building to give Bala Cynwyd power brokers and Main Line swells what they sorely lacked: an upscale traditional steakhouse whose behemoth portions, top-notch wine list and chummy, knowledgeable servers seem transported straight from downtown.

Christopher's ●S 15 | 15 | 16 | $24
108 N. Wayne Ave. (Lancaster Ave.), Wayne, 610-687-6558
◪ On Wayne's "Main Street USA", this New American "hometown meeting place" is so "kid-friendly" that tykes vie "noisily" for stools with "all sorts of businesspeople who hang after work"; "lunch is hoppin'" too 'cause "the prices are right", even though foodies fuss that "cardboard has more flavor" than most of the eats here.

Chun Hing S 19 | 11 | 19 | $18
Pathmark Shopping Ctr., 4160 Monument Rd. (City Ave.), 215-879-6270
◪ "Always packed with people" of the "senior" variety, this strip-mall Chinese behind the Adam's Mark is an "old, reliable", "convenient" spot for a "dirt cheap, decent" meal with the folks; snobs sniff at "minimal decor" and dishes in "need of a makeover", cracking "can you say Chung King?"

Cibucán S 19 | 17 | 18 | $29
2025 Sansom St. (bet. 20th & 21st Sts.), 215-231-9895
◪ "Bring friends, and you'll have a blast" downing "killer martinis" and "bumping and grinding" in your seats in the "trendy" upstairs lounge at this "fun-loving" Center City Nuevo Latino; let the "friendly staff guide you as you pick tasty morsels" for "nibblers and sharers" off the tapas menu – that is, if you're not one of the sober wallet-watchers who "liked it better as a BYO."

CINCIN S 24 | 19 | 21 | $30
7838 Germantown Ave. (Springfield Ave.), 215-242-8800
◪ Call it "SinSin" cry Chestnut Hillers clamoring for a "sumptuous" "culinary adventure" at Michael Wei's

Philadelphia

"vibrant" "Chinese-French hybrid", regarded along with its sibling YangMing as the "best" of the suburbs for "delicious, delicate" dishes served in a "pretty pink dining room"; at peak hours, "steel yourself for the noise assault" and remember "they honor reservations like a doctor's office", i.e. "waits can be long."

circa ⬛ | 21 | 23 | 20 | $40 |
1518 Walnut St. (bet. 15th & 16th Sts.), 215-545-6800

The "high-ceilinged", "beautiful old bank building on Restaurant Row" is "wonderful", dining in the vault is a "great" "gimmick" and the "sexy" "staff is suitable for paparazzi"; so if the "mood is melancholic" at this Center City New American, perhaps it's because fare that garners comments ranging from "outstanding" to "disappointing" is "not always a good investment" "during a recession."

Citron Bistro ⬛ | – | – | – | M |
818 W. Lancaster Ave. (Bryn Mawr Ave.), Bryn Mawr, 610-520-9100

The Wakim brothers have transformed Marbles, their noisy, family-friendly Bryn Mawr favorite into this handsome, more subdued Spanish-slanted Mediterranean bistro that's entirely smoke-free; to accompany the heady cream of fennel soup and scallops in saffron broth, select a bottle from the Iberian-focused wine list.

Citrus ⌀ | ∇ 29 | 17 | 20 | $24 |
8136 Germantown Ave. (bet. Abington Ave. & Hartwell Ln.), 215-247-8188

Sometimes, it seems as if all of Chestnut Hill is "lining up" for the "fabulous", "farm-fresh" veggie fare "with flair" and "creative, delicious" seafood specialties at this "excellent" BYO where the prices are as "light" as the "innovative cuisine"; it's "worth the wait" for a table in the "tiny", "pretty" place, though don't sport your mink 'cause the only fur they allow here is faux.

City Tavern ⬛ | 18 | 23 | 19 | $36 |
138 S. Second St. (Walnut St.), 215-413-1443

"Journey back to the days of our Founding Fathers" at this replica of a 1773 tavern in Society Hill, where "cute, costumed people" proffer pepperpot soup and other "old-time" American dishes to "tourists"; if you "quaff enough brews made from George Washington's recipes", "you're sure to meet Ben Franklin here", but ye olde dude might point toward your "overpriced" meal and remind you a penny saved is a penny earned.

Cock 'n Bull ⬛ | 17 | 18 | 18 | $29 |
Peddler's Village, Rtes. 202 & 263, Lahaska, 215-794-4010

"A favorite with the tour-bus crowd", this Traditional American in Peddler's Village is "good for a shopping

Philadelphia | F | D | S | C |

break", though the "hearty", "standard fare" is served in such "generous helpings", you'd be advised to "fast for three days" and "arrive hungry"; "dumpy" doesn't so much describe the Martha Washington impersonator on special 'Colonial Kitchen' Mondays (during the winter) as it does the "*Little House on the Prairie*-ish" decor that "hasn't changed in years."

CONTINENTAL, THE S | 23 | 19 | 18 | $30 |
138 Market St. (2nd St.), 215-923-6069

☑ "Come for the scene, stay for the food" at Stephen Starr's "retro" diner in Old City, where "sultry waitresses" have stepped out of "*Vogue*" to serve the "fabulous crowd" "a plethora of martinis to go along with" "trendy" Eclectic tapas that are "as good as bar grub gets", though "the cool kids" "have to yell" for their orders to be heard; anti-trendoids throw shade at divas "dressed in black" "trying to act too cool", sniping "*Shallow Hal* could have been filmed here."

Copabanana ●S | 17 | 11 | 14 | $19 |
344 South St. (4th St.), 215-923-6180

☑ It's "loud, crowded, smells like stale beer", "you have to whistle to get attention" and "there's more metal on your waitress' body than on your table", but Philly folks "keep going back" to this "cheap" Ameri-Mex "hangout" on South Street if only to "kick back", check out the "people parade" and "suck down the best margaritas east of Texas"; sometimes they even "forget to eat", though you shouldn't, 'cause the burgers and Spanish fries are "awesome."

Copa Too ●S | 16 | 10 | 13 | $18 |
263 S. 15th St. (bet. Locust & Spruce Sts.), 215-735-0848

☑ Copabanana's "funky" younger bro is a Center City "student's dream" for "potent" margaritas, "yummy fries" and what "was, is and always will be a really good burger", but when they tell ya to get "your tough skin on" before you enter, they may be thinking of a wet suit, 'cause it's a "down 'n' dirty" "dive"; are the "cloud-headed waiters" suffering from oxygen deprivation?

Cosi S | 15 | 16 | 12 | $14 |
325 Chestnut St. (4th St.), 215-399-0214 ●
8605 Germantown Ave. (Evergreen Ave.), 215-753-1707
215 Lombard St. (2nd St.), 215-925-4910
235 S. 15th St. (Locust St.), 215-893-9696 ●
140 S. 36th St. (bet. Sansom & Walnut Sts.), 215-222-4545 ●
1128 Walnut St. (12th St.), 215-413-1608 ●
1720 Walnut St. (bet. 17th & 18th Sts.), 215-735-2004
Bryn Mawr Plaza, 761 W. Lancaster Ave. (Morris Ave.), Bryn Mawr, 610-520-5208 ●

☑ The "collegiate" crowd, "business lunchers" and "12-year-olds on cell phones" all consume "chic sandwiches" on "excellent" bread with "good coffee" or, if they're old

Philadelphia | F | D | S | C |

---

enough and have had a rough day, "great mocha martinis" at this "multiplying" chain; "make-your-own s'mores" and "comfy chairs" leave some campers happy, but the "pricey" fare and "slow", often "clueless" service have tempestuous types asserting "it's enough to make you storm out."

Country Club S | 15 | 11 | 16 | $17 |
1717 Cottman Ave. (Summerdale Ave.), 215-722-4880
■ Despite its goyish moniker, this Northeast Philly "favorite" is a "fine" "old" diner with a distinctly "Jewish twist" where you can get "everything under the sun, hon", particularly "amazing cheesecake"; go in for a "nosh and gossip" delivered by a "friendly" staff, and note that the food rating doesn't reflect the post-*Survey* addition of ex Cafe Nola and Marcos Cafe chef Marco Carrozza, who is consulting on modernizing the "stuck-in-the-'50s" fare.

Coyote Crossing S | 20 | 20 | 17 | $27 |
800 Spring Mill Ave. (8th Ave.), Conshohocken, 610-825-3000
☒ You'll "feel like you're somewhere else", "like in Mexico" for instance, when you dine on the "enchanting garden" patio at this "hideaway" in Conshohocken, where the south-of-the-border eats are "authentic" and "delicious"; "awesome" margaritas lure packs of "singles" to the "bustling" bar, causing critics to howl over the "fraternity-style environment", not to mention the "annoying no-res policy" and a staff that "needs to get a clue."

Creed's Seafood & Steaks | ∇ 21 | 19 | 20 | $39 |
499 N. Gulph Rd. (Pennsylvania Tpke.), King of Prussia, 610-265-2550
■ "Good steak and seafood" is the creed at this surf 'n' turf house, a "vast improvement" over the Baron's Inne that formerly occupied the King of Prussia site; the "refurbished" spot is "lovely" and "bright", with patio dining, a raw bar and "quiet" entertainment in the piano bar.

Cresheim Cottage Cafe S | 18 | 19 | 20 | $30 |
7402 Germantown Ave. (bet. Allens Ln. & Cresheim Valley Dr.), 215-248-4365
☒ This "delightfully historic" "restored cottage" on the Mount Airy–Chestnut Hill border should be a "picture-perfect" spot "to take your grandmother or aunt"; the "patio is delightful in the spring, summer and fall" and dining by the "fireplace is warm and comfortable in winter", so the old gal will probably "keep wanting to love it" – if only the New American fare didn't "disappoint."

Crier in the Country S | 19 | 20 | 20 | $37 |
Crier in the Country, 1 Crier in the Country Ln. (off of Rte. 1, east of Wilmington Pike), Glen Mills, 610-358-2411
☒ Lydia "the ghost is nice" for ambiance at this "romantic" New French in an "elegant, historic" Glen Mills "mansion";

vote at zagat.com

Philadelphia F | D | S | C

the "beautiful setting" includes a glass conservatory perfect "for a prom" or some other "special time", but most folks in this part of the country cry that the "pretty place has pretty average food."

CUBA LIBRE S   19 | 26 | 19 | $38
10 S. Second St. (bet. Chestnut & Market Sts.), 215-627-0666

■ "*Pirates of the Caribbean* meets Old City" at this Cuban "stage set" where the "decor makes you believe" you're "on the streets of Havana", "amazing mojito" in hand; the "smashing" atmo and "gorgeous", "hip" crowd having "hoppin' fun" "make everything taste better" than *los críticos* claim it is – they say "surprisingly tasteless" describes both the fare and the "snobby" service.

Cucina Forte S   ▽ 22 | 18 | 23 | $27
768 S. Eighth St. (Catharine St.), 215-238-0778

■ The "fabulous" ricotta gnocchi from chef-owner Maria Forte (formerly of Alla Letizia and Mezza Luna) is the main draw at her attractive South Philly Italian BYO, though other "very good, interesting" dishes also make this spot a "find"; the chandelier and 100-year-old embossed gold ceiling exude an old-timey "class."

Cuisines S   ▽ 21 | 17 | 19 | $33
200 Wilmington-West Chester Pike (Naamans Creek Rd.), Chadds Ford, 610-459-3390

☑ Despite its plural name, there's only one type of cuisine served at this "quiet", "consistent" Chadds Ford eatery, and it's straightforward Continental; most of the surveyors who've eaten here find, "surprisingly", that most "everything works" on the "limited menu", despite the fact that trendies label it "tired."

Cuttalossa Inn   17 | 23 | 18 | $41
3487 River Rd. (Cuttalossa Rd.), Lumberville, 215-297-5082

☑ The "grounds are gorgeous" at this "romantic" "local wedding spot" north of New Hope: the "restored mill" sports a "fabulous" patio "next to a stream" and a "footbridge crossing to stone-walled ruins", beside which is an outdoor bar; unfortunately, the "pure magic" of the "spectacular natural decor" is sullied by "so-so" American fare.

Dahlak S   23 | 15 | 18 | $16
4708 Baltimore Ave. (bet. 47th & 48th Sts.), 215-726-6464
5547 Germantown Ave. (Maplewood Ave.), 215-849-0788

■ It's "another world", all right, at this Ethiopian-Eritrean in West Philly, and it's a world "with no ambiance"; but that doesn't matter when "a family as loyal as their customers" serves a "cheap, fun", "tasty change" of pace in such "heaping portions" that it "makes everything else seem boring" in the area.

Philadelphia F | D | S | C |

Dalessandro's Steaks ●≠ 23 | 7 | 16 | $10 |
600 Wendover St. (Henry Ave.), 215-482-5407
■ As the ratings would have it, this Roxborough "corner" sandwich "nirvana" cooks up the local manna, i.e. the "best Philly cheese steaks, period, no discussion", so of course, "patrons are packed like sardines in the little shop" – even "the dilapidated state of the place will never keep 'em away"; plus, "humorous, tough but friendly", "truck driver–style waitresses" are miles ahead of the grumps at the other "joints."

D'Angelo's Ristorante Italiano ● 21 | 17 | 20 | $40 |
256 S. 20th St. (bet. Locust & Spruce Sts.), 215-546-3935
■ A "power" "club of locals" wonders "how they make that red sauce sooo good", "just like mama used to" "during the Rizzo administration", at this "upbeat" Italian "classic" off Rittenhouse Square; the "old boys" say "it can do no wrong", even given "Restaurant Row prices."

Dante & Luigi's S 20 | 14 | 18 | $28 |
762 S. 10th St. (Catharine St.), 215-922-9501
■ Despite "attempts to appeal to a more upscale clientele", Italian "food at its non-fancy best" is still dished up for a "fair price" at this "South Philly landmark", a centenarian "red-gravy" "time capsule"; though it "seems like the staff has to know you to give decent service", it's renowned as the joint where Nicky Scarfo took a bullet in the '80s, so it draws jokers who ask for a seat in the "no-shooting section."

Darbar Grill S ▽ 22 | 14 | 19 | $16 |
319 Market St. (4th St.), 215-923-2410
■ "Finally, a restaurant in Old City where you don't have to mortgage the house to eat at" exclaim wallet-watchers at this Indian BYO "oasis" on Market Street, where the "tasty" "daily changing buffet" is considered "simply the best" of its kind on the "fringes of the First Friday area."

Dark Horse Pub, The S – | – | – | M |
(fka Dickens Inn)
421 S. Second St. (Lombard St.), 215-928-9307
This "cozy" British pub in Society Hill has "changed hands", and many see "improvement" under the crew from the Black Sheep across town; while the new talented chef, Ben McNamara (ex New Wave Café), brings serious skill to the kitchen, the "excellent beers" and football on the telly continue to make it a good bet for "after-work get-togethers" and "out-of-town Anglophile friends."

Dave & Buster's ●S 12 | 16 | 13 | $22 |
Pier 19 N., 325 N. Columbus Blvd. (bet. Callowhill & Race Sts.), 215-413-1951
◪ If your idea of "fun, fun, fun" with that special someone is "skee-ball" and "weak drinks", "but not a romantic dinner",

vote at zagat.com

Philadelphia | F | D | S | C |

this "busy" American "adult playground" on Columbus Boulevard is "great for a date"; you and your sweetie will probably "feel like you're stuck in a circus" enduring the arcade franchise's "assault on all senses", and the "sports bar"–style grub is "an afterthought", but it does "give you the energy to keep on playing" the games.

Davio's S | 22 | 21 | 22 | $45 |
111 S. 17th St. (bet. Chestnut & Sansom Sts.), 215-563-4810
■ "Got an expense account, you'll fit right in" at this "top-shelf" Northern Italian chophouse upstairs in an "elegant" "high-ceilinged bank" building in Center City; "privacy between tables", "attentive service" and "beautifully presented", "consistently delicious" dishes make it "nice for a business lunch", though your more claustrophobic clients might not like the "odd feeling of isolation" they get from "entry via elevator."

Day by Day | 20 | 13 | 17 | $16 |
2101 Sansom St. (21st St.), 215-564-5540
■ "Day in and day out", "very reliable", "tasty lunches brighten the work" week of the Center City office pool at this "unpretentious", long-running corner Traditional American with a catering division; "amazing soups", "large salads" and other "attractive, fresh" items are "never a letdown", but the "no-weekend", no-evening hours are.

Delmonico's Steakhouse S | 22 | 20 | 18 | $46 |
Hilton Philadelphia City Avenue, 4200 City Ave. (50th St.), 215-879-4000
■ As Gertrude Stein might have written, "a steakhouse is a steakhouse is a steakhouse", but this "throwback" in the Hilton Philadelphia City Avenue "unexpectedly" "rivals the big" downtown chop shops with "melt-in-your-mouth" meat that "costs less"; still, with "slow service" "taking longer to get your steak than it does for the place to age it", you may find yourself quoting a more obscure line from the lady bard: 'please be the beef.'

Denim Lounge ●S | – | – | – | E |
1712 Walnut St. (bet. 17th & 18th Sts.), 215-735-6700
Too cool to actually hang a sign out front, this high-style, second-story Restaurant Row nightspot is well worth seeking out (look for the velvet rope and doormen) thanks to Scott McLeod's Asian-accented New American dishes; those who stick around for drinks in the assorted lounge areas can groove to the DJ's thumping sounds and ogle celebrities partying in the upper-level VIP room.

DEUX CHEMINÉES | 27 | 27 | 26 | VE |
1221 Locust St. (bet. 12th & 13th Sts.), 215-790-0200
■ Culinary "king" Fritz Blank's prix fixe "shrine to haute" French is "straight out of a Victorian novel" marvel

Philadelphia F | D | S | C

devotees; amid the "sumptuous old-world setting" of this "charming mansion" in Center City, disciples willingly "sacrifice dieting" to "savor" the "indulgence" of "superior" fare brought forth by an "impeccable" staff; some say it's "a bit stuffy", but what do they expect from "a real special-occasion place?"

Devon Seafood Grill ◐ S 21 | 20 | 19 | $37
225 S. 18th St. (Chancellor St.), 215-546-5940
■ "Happening singles" cop a "just-above-chain feel" at this oceanic playground on Rittenhouse Square, where "packs" of sharks cruise "on Friday nights"; "if you're not there for the scene", try the "solid seafood" – fin fans claim there's "nothing fishy" about it.

D'Ignazio's Towne House S 15 | 17 | 18 | $28
117 Veterans Sq. (Baltimore Pike), Media, 610-566-6141
■ "Delco natives" "have been going off and on for years" to this "blue-hair hangout" in Media, and they claim it's "still good" for "big portions" of "classic" Italian-American eats served by "old-school waiters" amid "trinkets galore"; gastronomes gripe that the grub "tastes like a TV dinner", and neat freaks "wouldn't want to be responsible for dusting this place."

DILWORTHTOWN INN S 26 | 26 | 25 | $50
1390 Old Wilmington Pike (bet. Pleasant Grove & Street Rds.), West Chester, 610-399-1390
■ "For an inn from Revolutionary times, it sure is hip" says the "horsey set"; "an evening of absolute class" dining on a "sophisticated" meal in one of the "small, beautiful, candlelit dining rooms" or outside in the "lovely stable ruins" at this "romantic" New American in the "stately" "colonial" survivor of the Battle of Brandywine is "hard to beat" – it's so "very special", you "feel like you're visiting the elite of Chester County", but, thankfully, "without the stuffiness."

DiNardo's Famous Seafood S 20 | 13 | 17 | $30
312 Race St. (bet. 3rd & 4th Sts.), 215-925-5115
■ "If you're in the mood" to "get messy", the "meaty hardshells" at this "classic" Old City seafooder do the trick; "genuine '70s-style" Philly dining includes "hustle-bustle" amid "tacky decor", "long waits" for tables that make you "feel like a sardine" and "staff rudeness that's almost entertaining", but crustacean bingers say the "big" blue bruisers here are "wonderful, hon"; critics crab "it may be famous, but that doesn't mean it's good."

DiPalma 22 | 23 | 21 | $45
114 Market St. (bet. Front & 2nd Sts.), 215-733-0545
■ With "talent, technique and a great appreciation for flawless food", "young chef-on-his-way" Salvatore DiPalma

vote at zagat.com

Philadelphia F D S C

cooks "creative" Northern Italian at his "attractive" place; a "quiet" meal paired with "top service" is a "serene" counterpoint to Old City's overheated scene, though the "Euro-sleek downstairs bar" might lure younger lounge lizards after all.

DJANGO S 27 | 20 | 23 | $32
526 S. Fourth St. (South St.), 215-922-7151

■ Bryan Sikora and Aimee Olexy's "little gem of a BYO" off South Street "already rivals many other favorite" destinations "in the hearts" of Brotherly Lovers for its "mind-boggling", "monthly menu", which highlights local, "seasonal produce" with European flavors in "inventive combinations"; the "exquisite cheese plate" and "bread in the flower pot" are alone "worth a trip", and the setting "is so warm and inviting" that soothsaying surveyors suggest the spot is "a keeper for years to come."

DMITRI'S S 25 | 14 | 20 | $27
795 S. Third St. (Catharine St.), 215-625-0556
2227 Pine St. (23rd St.), 215-985-3680

■ "It doesn't pay to cook at home" when "the stuff dreams are made of" is plated for you at Dmitri Chimes' "minimalist" Med seafooders in Queen Village and Fitler Square, where the fare is "mouthwateringly fabulous"; though they're as "crowded" and "noisy as airports", with equally "hurried" service, "you won't mind the wait" when you're taking a trip to "heaven and Santorini all at once."

Down Home Diner 17 | 11 | 15 | $16
Reading Terminal Mkt., 51 N. 12th St. (bet. Arch & Market Sts.), 215-627-1955

☒ "Down-home" transplants find "comfort in the midst of the chaos" at Reading Terminal Market gittin' an "old-fashioned" "tummy"-ful of "artery-cloggin'-good" "diner" dishes at telegenic owner Jack McDavid's "Southern-style" "sit-down" spot; given the location, those who complain it's "like dining on a subway platform" aren't far from accurate.

Drafting Room S 18 | 15 | 18 | $25
Colonial Shops, 635 N. Pottstown Pike (Ship Rd.), Exton, 610-363-0521
900 Bethlehem Pike (Norristown Rd.), Spring House, 215-646-6116

☒ "Mingle with the young" over sips from the "awesome beer selection" at these "pub-like" New Americans in Exton and Spring House; fans of the "fun" say the "well-executed", "inventive" eats make the joints "more than just watering holes", and you don't have to "trek to Center City" for a "super Sunday brunch" buffet; killjoys complain that the "shabby" spots are "schizo" — "are they trying to be sports bars or family restaurants?"

Philadelphia | F | D | S | C |

DULING-KURTZ HOUSE & COUNTRY INN S | 22 | 25 | 23 | $42 |
Duling-Kurtz House & Country Inn, 146 S. Whitford Rd. (Lincoln Hwy.), Exton, 610-524-1830

■ "Save" this "beautiful country inn" "overlooking lovely gardens" in Exton for a "treat, and reward" "your significant other" with a table in "the private alcove" and an "elegant", "traditional" meal of American-Continental specialties; "when appearing on *QVC*, Joan Rivers" dines here, so one can conclude that the "experienced owner knows how to please an upscale" clientele.

East of Amara S | 20 | 13 | 18 | $23 |
700 S. Fifth St. (Bainbridge St.), 215-627-4200

■ For a "good quick fix" of bold "flavor", head straight to Wallapa Suksapa's "tranquil", "friendly" Siamese "oasis" off South Street, where "yummy" pad Thai and "scrumptious duck" highlight a "wonderful, modestly priced" menu; just note that if you want to "Thai one on" here, you'll have to BYO.

East Side Mario's S | 12 | 15 | 14 | $20 |
180 Old Lincoln Hwy. (Pottstown Pike), Exton, 610-363-0444

◪ "Lunch with the kids is ok" at these Italian chain links in Exton and Clementon, NJ, because the "large portions" are "cheap enough", but be forewarned that the "adorable" "pseudo-alfresco decor" seems to encourage the tykes to use their outdoor voices, so the rooms get "noisy enough to give you a headache"; mature diners demure with a simple "yuck."

Effie's S⌀ | 21 | 16 | 20 | $24 |
1127 Pine St. (Quince St.), 215-592-8333

■ "Bring your own bottle" (but not your credit cards) to Effie Bouikidis' "casual" Greek "bargain" standby quartered in "cute" Center City "row houses", where you always "get a warm reception" and "authentic" fare in "large portions"; for a "romantic" treat, "ask to sit in the garden" in summer or "in the carriage house with the fireplace on a cold night."

El Azteca | 18 | 11 | 17 | $17 |
714 Chestnut St. (bet. 7th & 8th Sts.), 215-733-0895
1710 Grant Ave. (Bustleton Ave.), 215-969-3422 S

◪ The "decor is from the dollar store", but amigos say given how "insanely cheap, plentiful" and "well prepared" the "mildly spiced" Mexican meals are, "lunch rocks" at this trio of "shacks"; gastronomes gripe that the grub seems "microwaved", though "margaritas make it taste better", so since only the Northeast Philly outpost has a liquor license, "bring your own tequila" to Center City and South Jersey and the "staff will mix up a pitcher" for you.

---

vote at zagat.com

Philadelphia | F | D | S | C |

Elephant & Castle ●S | 11 | 13 | 13 | $21 |
Crowne Plaza Philadelphia Center City, 1800 Market St. (18th St.), 215-751-9977

☒ "Maybe they're trying to be too English" say surveyors who don't yet realize that dining on the bonny old isle has evolved beyond the "mediocre service" and "bland" bites available at this "British twist on TGI Friday's"; plenty of folks "have a drink" at the chain "pubs" in Center City and Cherry Hill, but expats who remember the bombing of London say they'd eat here "only under war conditions."

El Sombrero S | ▽ 21 | 14 | 19 | $21 |
295 Buck Rd. (bet. Holland & Rocksville Rds.), Holland, 215-357-3337

☒ "Party" post-game with the "rowdy soccer moms" at this "no-frills", "family-owned" fiesta set in a Bucks "strip mall", where gaggles of gals "celebrate" the kids' big win over "awesome", "inexpensive", "hard-to-find Mexican" meals; though it's BYO, the friendly servers will "gladly put your bottle on ice for you."

Engine 46 Steakhouse ●S | 13 | 14 | 14 | $26 |
10 Reed St. (Columbus Blvd.), 215-462-4646

☒ "Hope ya like dalmations" dish design divas, because the "goofy" decor at this renovated 19th-century South Philly firehouse has gone to the dogs; the "loud", "kid-friendly" steak place may be convenient to "the Riverview movies", but disappointed beefaholics feel burned by the "greasy, gristly meat."

Epicurean, The S | 19 | 16 | 19 | $30 |
902-8 Village at Eland (Kimberton Rd.), Phoenixville, 610-933-1336

☒ "What a beer list" burp imbibers bellied up to the bar at this "casual" New American in a Phoenixville "shopping center", where 200-plus brews upstage what epicureans call "good" but "uneven" eats; with a "super staff" and "local music on weekends", it does show its "enthusiasm."

Ernesto's 1521 Cafe S | ▽ 23 | 18 | 21 | $31 |
1521 Spruce St. (bet. 15th & 16th Sts.), 215-546-1521

■ Center City slickers "sweet" on this "Euro-style" trattoria say that "when the Kimmel Center" crowd finds it, "it'll be a mob scene"; for now, though, regulars can "hang out" at this "lovely", "little" Italian scarfing down "very creative dishes" like the vegetable napoleon, not to mention a "wonderful weekend brunch" and Ernesto's mama's homemade desserts.

Esca S | - | - | - | E |
18 W. Mechanic St. (Main St.), New Hope, 215-862-7099

It's a treat snuggling by the fireside bar at this homey, romantic newcomer on the towpath in New Hope, but

Philadelphia F | D | S | C

the real draw is Wayne Surline's Latin-influenced New American dishes (such as pulled pork empanadas and chipotle-braised short ribs) and the raw bar area evocative of the Caribbean; neighbors already embrace it as a favorite for a refined lunch and take advantage of the weeknight 'locals' menu', three courses for only $15.

Eulogy Belgian Tavern S – | – | – | M
136 Chestnut St. (bet. Front & 2nd Sts.), 215-413-2354
Sudsheads save their highest praise for the brews poured at this comfortable, anti-hip Belgian newcomer in Old City, which features 15 beers on tap plus more than 100 by the bottle (including such oddballs as Hoegaarden and Stone Arrogant Bastard ale); if you're looking for some nourishment to soak up the hops, note that the pub grub has a better reputation than the dinner menu served upstairs.

EVERMAY ON THE DELAWARE S 24 | 25 | 26 | $62
EverMay On The Delaware, 889 River Rd. (Headquarters Rd.), Erwinna, 610-294-9100
■ "What a treat" squeal "romantics" about this New American prix fixe "getaway" stashed in a "beautiful" Upper Bucks B&B where "a weekend and dinner is the ultimate luxury"; it's so "lovely", "delicious" and "expensive", it's like having a "celebratory feast" "in a classy, private home with warm friends", and "everything is perfect until you get the check"; N.B. Friday–Saturday, 7:30 PM seating only.

Fadó Irish Pub S 16 | 19 | 17 | $22
1500 Locust St. (15th St.), 215-893-9700
■ "What do you expect from an Irish pub?" – it's "rowdy, with good Celtic music", "Guinness, noise" and "new college graduates in suits"; tuck into a "dark", "cozy nook" at Center City's "faithful reproduction" chainster for a nibble of "straightforward fare", but if you're looking for gourmet grub, then "Fadón't [stay] for dinner."

Famous 4th Street Delicatessen S 19 | 9 | 14 | $15
700 S. Fourth St. (Bainbridge St.), 215-922-3274
■ "Gimme my sandwich now!" – stressed out "political bigwigs" go to "the source for comfort", David Auspitz's Queen Village "institution" where "some items are truly delicious even if eating there is a little yucky"; sure, the "grungy" decor "needs updating", but given "great pastrami", "superb lox" and "heavenly chocolate chip cookies", it's no wonder "one of the few remaining real Jewish delis" in town is "still famous after all these years."

Fatou & Fama S – | – | – | M
4002 Chestnut St. (40th St.), 215-386-0700
Senegal-born chef Fatou N'Diaye has turned this bright University City storefront into a vibrant melting pot of West Indian, West African and American soul food flavors; the

vote at zagat.com

Philadelphia | F | D | S | C |

helpful (if not speedy) staff will steer you toward tasty Senegalese specialties such as *pastels* (savory pastries filled with spiced fish or meat) and *chebujen* (mackerel stew), while African storytellers make an occasional appearance; N.B. alcohol is not permitted.

Fayette Street Grille S | 22 | 14 | 21 | $29 |
308 Fayette St. (bet. 3rd & 4th Sts.), Conshohocken, 610-567-0366
■ Conshy connoisseurs concur on the "excellent bargain" "three-course prix fixe" at this "imaginative" New American BYO; it's "loud", "cramped" and with the "door opening directly into the dining area, on a cold winter day Jack Frost is your unwelcome guest", but after "delicious" dinners "worth sinning for", regulars bet you'll "leave satisfied."

Felicia's S | 22 | 16 | 20 | $35 |
1148 S. 11th St. (Ellsworth St.), 215-755-9656
■ Incredulous Italophiles say the "gnocchi is unbelievable" at Nicholas Miglino's "traditional" "treasure" where the "authentic" specialties from The Boot are "nice, very nice" indeed; amid "jolly" surrounds peopled by "witty" waiters, South Philly fills up "before going to the game"; N.B. its grand new interior outdates the above Decor score.

Fellini Cafe Trattoria S | 21 | 13 | 16 | $22 |
31 E. Lancaster Ave. (bet. Cricket Ave. & Rittenhouse Pl.), Ardmore, 610-642-9009
14 E. Eagle Rd. (W. Darby Rd.), Havertown, 610-446-6669
106 W. State St. (Olive St.), Media, 610-892-7616
3541 West Chester Pike (Newtown Street Rd.), Newtown Square, 610-353-6131
Olde Sproul Shopping Village, 1188 Baltimore Pike (east of I-476), Springfield, 610-338-9900
■ Big bellies of the western suburbs "take a walk on the wild side" to these "gaudy", "get 'em in, get 'em out", "red-gravy" BYOs; with "huge portions" of "delicious", "basic" Italian at "low prices", they're the "epitome of value dining", though the "overbooked" "mob scene" means Fellini-esque "chaos" and "long waits"; N.B. a new takeout branch just opened in Havertown.

Fergie's Pub ●S | ∇ 15 | 16 | 19 | $16 |
1214 Sansom St. (12th St.), 215-928-8118
■ The "bicycle-riding" "smart crowd" "is as comfortable as at home" when they "hang" at this "jolly Irish" joint; "no TV" plus "lots-of-fun Quizo nights" are "welcoming" to eggheads, while an eclectic menu of "good grub" to soak up the "cheap beer" keeps sudsheads happy.

Fez Moroccan Cuisine S | ∇ 20 | 22 | 20 | $27 |
620 S. Second St. (bet. Bainbridge & South Sts.), 215-925-5367
■ Such a "fun-filled adventure may not be for everyone", so "go with friends" willing to "lose their inhibitions" in the

subscribe to zagat.com

Philadelphia   F | D | S | C

"dark", "eating with their fingers, sitting on the floor" and "lounging on pillows" at this off–South Street "cultural experience"; "delicious" Moroccan meals, "crowd-pleasing belly dancers" and "gorgeous decor" have Philly folks "feeling like tourists in their own hometown."

Figs S   24 | 17 | 21 | $29
2501 Meredith St. (25th St.), 215-978-8440

☒ "Save your airfare to Morocco" and stay close to home at this "super neighborhood bistro" in Fairmount, where the "creative" Mustapha Rouissiya "does it all – cooks, waits tables and gives excellent recommendations" on "exotic", "delightful" dishes like lamb tagine or an ice cream made with the eponymous roasted fruit.

Finnigan's Wake S   12 | 14 | 16 | $20
537 N. Third St. (Spring Garden St.), 215-574-9240

☒ "Bachelor-party heaven" for Northern Liberties' "cops and firefighters" just might be this "friendly" "Irish corner pub" where the "banquet facilities are excellent"; it's "great for hanging out and listening to a band", and "whichever floor you're on" in the "spacious" quadruplex, the "barkeeps are the nicest", but with the possible exception of the "wonderful" shepherd's pie, the grub just "doesn't qualify."

FORK S   24 | 22 | 22 | $39
306 Market St. (bet. 3rd & 4th Sts.), 215-625-9425

■ "The ultimate in casual cool" might be this "respectably mod" New American in Old City, which is a bit "New York", but not too much, because "you can sit at the bar and enjoy the lack of scene", the staff is "cordial" and the "affordable", "seasonal" "fare is innovative without being weird"; surveyors "savoring every delicious bite" at dinner, lunch or the "pleasant" Sunday brunch mix metaphors, sighing "stick me with a fork, I'm in heaven", even if it's "noisy" and "cramped" up there.

FOUNDERS S   26 | 27 | 25 | $57
Park Hyatt at the Bellevue, 200 S. Broad St. (Walnut St.), 215-790-2814

■ "They treat you like royalty" at the Park Hyatt's "elegant" "institution" where patrons "ride the elevator" up to a "memorably" "exquisite" Asian-accented New French meal with weekend "ballroom dancing", "a lovely touch to an [almost] lost dining experience"; with "outstanding" floor-to-ceiling city views, this "special room" "screams class all the way"; N.B. jacket required Friday and Saturday.

FOUNTAIN RESTAURANT S   29 | 29 | 29 | $66
Four Seasons Philadelphia, 1 Logan Sq.
(Benjamin Franklin Pkwy. & 18th St.), 215-963-1500

■ "It's hard to overpraise" this "smashing" Logan Square "landmark", though supporters certainly try, burbling with

Philadelphia F | D | S | C

superlatives about the Four Seasons' "perfect-in-every-way" New French–New American dining experience, No. 1 in this *Survey* for Food, Service, Decor and Popularity; top toque Martin Hamann performs "triumphant culinary" feats that are "guaranteed to impress", the staff is "terrific" and the decor is drop-dead "gorgeous", so the "super-high" tariff is "worth every gilded penny."

Fountain Side S – | – | – | M
537 Easton Rd. (Meetinghouse Rd.), Horsham, 215-957-5122
"Don't let the tacky entrance scare you" from this Horsham Italian-American BYO advise "regulars" who "return often"; the "well-disciplined kitchen" puts out "consistently" "great" dishes, while the front of the house is "maintained" by a "friendly owner."

Four Dogs Tavern S 15 | 17 | 16 | $25
1300 W. Strasburg Rd. (Telegraph Rd.), West Chester, 610-692-4367
◪ This "charming tavern" "in the rolling woods of Chester County" warrants "a drive" for lunch in the "gorgeous bar" or "lovely" garden; despite middling ratings, the "creative" New American fare and "nice" staff set some tails wagging, though bashers bark the chow's merely "average."

Franco & Luigi's S – | – | – | M
1549 S. 13th St. (Tasker St.), 215-755-8900
For couples who think "opera is cool", a "great date place" is this "intimate" Italian BYO in a South Philly row house attached to a same-named corner pizzeria; "in between waiting on tables", seemingly everyone on the "wonderful staff" joins in the musical "fun", and ya know, they're a bunch of "great singers" – oh, and the food is "pleasant."

Frederick's S 23 | 21 | 20 | $46
757 S. Front St. (Fitzwater St.), 215-271-3733
■ "Take a date" to this "lively" Italian stalwart that's akin to "sitting in mama's dining room"; the "alabaster columns" and "old-time pianist" may strike sophisticates as all-too-appropriately Queen Village, but those in on the "secret" whisper it's the "hearty portions" of "top-notch" fare and "great", "professional" servers who make bananas Foster "at your table" that keep them in *la famiglia*.

FRIDAY SATURDAY SUNDAY S 22 | 19 | 21 | $35
261 S. 21st St. (bet. Locust & Spruce Sts.), 215-546-4232
■ A survivor of the city's "'70s restaurant renaissance", this now-"classic" Rittenhouse Square American-Continental feels like "an old friend" for "homey", "lip-smacking" fare, a "reasonably priced wine list" and "dependable" service; the "intimate" setting may be a "time warp", but "after all these years", the "amazing fish tank" in the "very sexy bar" upstairs can still "spark" up a "date."

Philadelphia

| F | D | S | C |

FuziOn S   22 | 17 | 20 | $29
Center Point Shopping Ctr., 2960 Skippack Pike (Valley Forge Rd.), Worcester, 610-584-6958

■ "You'll go back" to the suburbs for "inventive" Asian fusion fare from chef Michael Ly at one of Montco's BYO "favorites"; "nicely prepared seafood" and "don't-miss desserts" stand out, and though even city slickers suffer conFuziOn over the "noisy" ambiance, more insist the food "makes up for it"; N.B. check out its new patio.

Gables at Chadds Ford S   – | – | – | E
423 Baltimore Pike (Brintons Bridge Rd.), Chadds Ford, 610-388-7700

You "find out why the parking lot is so crowded" when you pull into this brassy Chadds Ford New American in a "great looking" converted dairy barn with "lovely patio dining"; with an upscale menu featuring seafood specialties like Chinese-style calamari, plus brisk service and a serious focus on martinis, it's an anomaly in staid Wyeth country.

Garnian Wa S   ▽ 19 | 11 | 18 | $18
Paoli Plaza, 1776 E. Lancaster Ave. (Bear Hill Rd.), Paoli, 610-889-1761

◪ An "inexpensive" BYO Chinese option in a Paoli strip mall, this longtimer garners an assortment of assessments when it comes to the food, ranging from "consistently good", "well prepared" and "fresh" to "run-of-the-mill"; the staff, however, is "very nice", and it's "great for takeout."

General Lafayette Inn & Brewery S   16 | 18 | 17 | $26
General Lafayette Inn, 646 Germantown Pike (Church Rd.), Lafayette Hill, 610-941-0600

◪ "After work", this "rustic" Montco Traditional American in a "historic building" provides a "comfortable" "meeting place" to get a little R&R over a fine batch of "microbrews"; the "yummy" "bar food" outranks the "adequate" mains, but after a few "exceptional lambics", "you won't notice."

General Warren Inne   ▽ 27 | 22 | 26 | $48
General Warren Inne, Old Lancaster Hwy. (Warren Ave.), Malvern, 610-296-3637

■ Who knows what the meals were like in 1745, but today's clientele is "never disappointed" by this "charming" colonial in Malvern serving American-Continental cuisine; beef Wellington, Châteaubriand and other standards are "melt-in-your-mouth" "excellent"; it's an oldie but a goodie that's "expensive but well worth it."

Genji S   23 | 16 | 18 | $32
1720 Sansom St. (bet. 17th & 18th Sts.), 215-564-1720

■ Ardent admirers tell tales of "fresh, fresh sushi" at this Center City Japanese where the "gifted chefs" roll out

vote at zagat.com

Philadelphia

F | **D** | **S** | **C**

some of the "best" and "prettiest" fin fare in town in a "soothing atmosphere"; the service can be "slow" but is "pleasant" enough, and the prices are "decent", so it's no wonder that it can get "crowded."

Geno's Steaks ◐ S ⌀   19 | 9 | 14 | $9
Italian Mkt., 1219 S. Ninth St. (Passyunk Ave.), 215-389-0659

■ "Assume the position to avoid staining shirt" and "take a bite" of the indi-geno-us "savory" "soul food" at this 24/7 South Philly cheese steak stand where "you'd better know how to order, or be mocked"; whether it's better than the competition across the street is open to debate – it might come down to "which line is shorter" – but most agree it's a "must-do for tourists" and pub crawlers "after midnight."

Gilmore's   ▽ 27 | 24 | 27 | $43
133 E. Gay St. (bet. Matlack & Walnut Sts.), West Chester, 610-431-2800

■ "Spectacular", "innovative" French fare has 'em flocking to this "gem in West Chester" helmed by "talented" chef Peter Gilmore (ex Le Bec-Fin); the "lovely", "intimate" townhouse setting and "charming", "impeccable service" elicit bravos, while its BYO policy and moderate prices earn ovations, so of course, "book way ahead."

Girasole Ristorante S   20 | 17 | 18 | $36
1305 Locust St. (bet. Broad & 13th Sts.), 215-985-4659

◪ "A good choice" before a show, this "sophisticated" Center City Italian is celebrated for its "excellent homemade pasta" and the "best pizzas this side of Napoli"; bashers, however, boo the "noisy" atmosphere and "disorganized", "inattentive" service, adding "watch the pre-theater timing" to ensure you make your curtain.

Gnocchi S ⌀   21 | 16 | 19 | $25
613 E. Passyunk Ave. (bet. Bainbridge & South Sts.), 215-592-8300

■ "Dishes to make mama proud" include a "fabulous" "variety" of the eponymous "homemade" potato dumplings, pasta and "beyond" at this "cute" "neighborhood" Southern Italian BYO off South Street; the "large portions" teeter on "teensy tables", and because it's so "affordable", the joint gets "crowded as hell", but it still "radiates warmth."

Goat Hollow S   19 | 16 | 17 | $23
300 W. Mt. Pleasant Ave. (Lincoln Dr.), 215-242-4710

◪ "Quaint" and "diverse", with a "'60s hippie touch" and a "kid-friendly staff", this "faithful" "corner pub" is a "very Mount Airy" "hangout"; the "unpretentious" New American menu is "nice" enough, and in-house art exhibits are "funky" "fun", but the local herd bleats "don't go when they have live music if you care about your eardrums."

Philadelphia   F | D | S | C

Golden Pheasant Inn ⑤   ▽ 21 | 22 | 20 | $46
Golden Pheasant Inn, 763 River Rd. (13 mi. north of New Hope), Erwinna, 610-294-9595

▣ The setting for this "beautiful" Pheasant is certainly "pleasant" – in fact, "attractive greenhouse dining" in the former barge stop on the Delaware Canal is a "romantic's dream"; however, the inn's "good" "classic Country French cuisine" isn't golden to all gourmands, as some "bored" birds say "you're paying for the atmosphere."

Goose Creek Grill ⑤   18 | 14 | 17 | $21
840 E. Street Rd. (Wilmington Pike), West Chester, 610-399-9800

▣ "You have to love the geese", in the "park and stream" in season and in the "fun" decor year-round, at this "casual" American in West Chester that's "great for kids", who make their own "brick-oven" pizzas; grown-ups, who honk over a "noisy" interior that's "much less inviting than it looks from outside", "prize" the "nice" veranda seating.

Gourmet ⑤   23 | 16 | 23 | $36
3520 Cottman Ave. (Frankford Ave.), 215-331-7174

▣ "The shops of Northeast Philly" are the "unexpected site" for this "unusually fine" New French "gem", an "old, great standard" that fans feel "deserves a lot of credit" for 20 some years of "consistently excellent" fare like signature rack of lamb; modernists blurt out "blah", dissing dishes that "haven't changed very much in years."

Grasshopper   22 | 18 | 21 | $34
4427 Main St. (Carson St.), 215-483-1888

■ "Amid the hubbub" of Manayunk is this "unassuming" "nouveau" French where the "attentive" staff "aims to please and succeed"; given "lovely, imaginative but not silly food" and a "cozy" vibe, diners would bring "dates" here "a lot more often if parking weren't such a pain."

GRILL, THE ⑤   23 | 26 | 23 | $53
(fka Paris Bar & Grill)
Ritz-Carlton Philadelphia, 10 S. Broad St. (Chestnut St.), 215-735-7700

▣ Suspicious surveyors suspect "they play favorites" because while some "expense-accounters" who visit this Avenue of the Arts hotel's "clubby", "lovely" New American find the "exquisite" fare and "French"-influenced service "you would expect from the Ritz", others feel the "average" dishes and "slow service" are "not consistent with the reputation" of the "opulent" outfit.

Grill Restaurant ⑤   ▽ 21 | 21 | 21 | $42
Westin Philadelphia, 99 S. 17th St. (bet. Chestnut & Market Sts.), 215-563-1600

■ The Ritz-Carlton moved out of Liberty Place, and with it went the restaurant buzz, but the few surveyors who've

vote at zagat.com

Philadelphia   F | D | S | C

tried the Westin's "quiet" New American think "more people should take advantage" of this "sophisticated" hotel dining room because the "excellent" fare and service come as "a very pleasant surprise."

Gullifty's ◐S   13 | 12 | 14 | $20
1149 E. Lancaster Ave. (bet. Franklin & Montrose Aves.), Rosemont, 610-525-1851

◪ Main Line moms and dads take the "family" for a "night out" at this "sentimental favorite from their high school days", a "reasonably priced" New American in Rosemont "teeming" with screaming "loud" tykes; regulars "wouldn't recommend straying too far from chicken fingers, burgers" and "tasty pizzas", and don't expect "attentive" service from the "distracted" "sorority sister" servers, even if the "college kids" who "love it" here think the staff is "hot."

Gypsy Rose S   17 | 16 | 18 | $30
505 Bridge Rd. (bet. Gravel Pike & Gypsy Ln.), Collegeville, 610-489-1600

◪ "The best thing is the country setting" overlooking the Perkiomen River at this New American in a bicentenarian building in Collegeville; foodies suggest "trying the grilled-Brie appetizer" and "great crab cakes", but otherwise they find the fare a burlesque in "high mediocre", while design divas strip points for the "worn-out decor."

Hadley's Bistro S   ▽ 19 | 18 | 18 | $37
Sheraton Society Hill, 1 Dock St. (Walnut St., bet. Front & 2nd Sts.), 215-238-6656

◪ It's "good for a business lunch" or a "burger before a movie" at the Ritz, but the Sheraton Society Hill's New American is "almost empty" at other times; they do "deserve an 'E' for effort" for keeping it "pretty and quaint" inside.

Half Moon Saloon   ▽ 20 | 15 | 16 | $26
108 W. State St. (Union St.), Kennett Square, 610-444-7232

■ "There's something for everyone" at this "pub-like" Eclectic in Kennett Square: "a comfortable, unpretentious atmosphere", live bands, 17 "good beers" on tap and an "interesting menu" sporting everything from signature grilled wild game to "crab nachos and cheese fries to die for"; you can "sit and enjoy all night", perhaps up on the new rooftop deck.

Hank's Place S⊄   18 | 12 | 18 | $14
Baltimore Pike & Creek Rd., Chadds Ford, 610-388-7061

◪ "You might see a Wyeth", and you'll definitely "catch some local gossip", at this "fast", "cheap" "greasy spoon" that Chadds Ford "local yokels call their joint" for "farm fresh–wholesome, all-American, cholesterol-enhancing chow" that's especially "great for breakfast", starting at

Philadelphia

| F | D | S | C |

6 AM; there's "no decor", unless you take the "long lines" of Brandywine "characters" for some sort of design scheme.

Happy Rooster   21 | 15 | 19 | $43
118 S. 16th St. (Sansom St.), 215-963-9311

▄ A happy flock made of "half the lawyers in town" clucks that the New American fare at this "clubby" coop in Center City "just keeps getting better" since the former roosters have flown and "welcoming" owner Rose Parrotta took charge; the other half argues that the "uneven" eats and cocky "attitude" are "nothing to crow about"; N.B. a roomy second dining room opened post-*Survey*.

Hard Rock Cafe ●S   13 | 18 | 15 | $21
1113-31 Market St. (12th St.), 215-238-1000

▄ They ain't exactly dancing in the street over this "touristy" "rock 'n' roll" "nostalgia" chainster in Center City, where the music would be sweet if it weren't so "ear-piercing"; it's "great for kids and kids-at-heart" 'cause it doesn't matter what you wear, and the "typical" American fare is "teenage-perfect", but diners yawning "same ol', same ol'" are ready for a brand-new beat.

Harmony Vegetarian S   19 | 12 | 18 | $19
135 N. Ninth St. (bet. Cherry & Race Sts.), 215-627-4520

■ The "skillfully prepared" "mock meat" is "sure to please even the most avowed carnivore" at this Chinatown Vegetarian "classic" known for "fast", "courteous" service; though visitors "would prefer nicer decor", the moderate prices help compensate.

Havana S   16 | 16 | 16 | $26
105 S. Main St. (bet. Mechanic & New Sts.), New Hope, 215-862-9897

▄ Grab a seat on the "great patio" to savor the "crowds floating" along Main Street at this "popular" Caribbean-American in New Hope, 'cause it makes the "decent" "food taste better"; inside, the "funky younger crowd" gets "noisy" to "hip music", though a few naysayers aren't Havana good time with the "touristy" airs.

Hibachi S   19 | 17 | 19 | $26
Pier 19, 325 N. Columbus Blvd. (Callowhill St.), 215-592-7100
261 Old York Rd. (Township Line Rd.), Jenkintown, 215-881-6814
145 S. State Rd. (Sproul Rd.), Springfield, 610-690-4911

▄ "If you don't mind getting food tossed at you" and "eating with strangers" at "shared tables", this expanding chain of Japanese sushi-and-steakhouses in PA and DE is "great fun" for the family; the teppanyaki can be "tasty" when the "right chef" grills it "in front of you", but critics who think it's "all show business" pan the "knife act" as "tired."

vote at zagat.com

Philadelphia   F | D | S | C

High Street Caffe S ▽ 29 | 21 | 25 | $31
322 S. High St. (Dean St.), West Chester, 610-696-7435
■ "You'd never guess from the outside" that this "non-smoking" Cajun-Creole BYO in downtown West Chester serves "outstanding" grub with a "gourmet twist"; insiders go for the "lunchtime bargain", while at night, N'Awlins meals and music "at their finest" lure a "hip" crowd that debates whether the purple digs are "tasteful" or "bizarre."

Hikaru S 20 | 16 | 19 | $29
4348 Main St. (Grape St.), 215-487-3500
◪ With all their "great gimmicks", the "*Iron Chef*"–wannabe sushi and hibachi guys sure have "personality" at this "fail-safe" Japanese in Manayunk, but the "standard" fare isn't quite as exciting; however, you do get a "nice view" of the neighborhood "looking out on the sidewalk."

H.K. Golden Phoenix ●S 20 | 12 | 18 | $18
911 Race St. (bet. 9th & 10th Sts.), 215-629-4988
■ "The food carts keep coming" loaded down with "yum-yum dim sum" at this Chinatown Chinese "favorite" where "typical Hong Kong"–style "chaos" and "Pepto Bismol–pink walls" only add to the charm; the staff is always "willing to help", but given their "weak English", you're never sure what "tantalizing" morsel you're biting into.

Horizons Cafe – | – | – | M
Moreland Plaza, 101 E. Moreland Rd. (Old York Rd.), Willow Grove, 215-657-2100
Former flesh-eaters "don't know how they make tofu and seitan taste and look like steak, scallops and sausage, but they do" at this "artful", "affordable" BYO Vegetarian in Willow Grove; it's all so "delicious" that even carnivores say it's "oftentimes better than the real thing."

Hoss's Family Steak & Sea House S 14 | 12 | 12 | $17
6 N. Pottstown Pike (Lincoln Hwy.), Exton, 610-594-8171
See review in the Lancaster/Berks Counties Directory.

Hosteria Da Elio S – | – | – | M
615 S. Third St. (bet. Bainbridge & South Sts.), 215-925-0930
"One of the better of the new wave of BYOs", Elio Sgambati's "cozy", romantic trattoria off South Street offers all the basics for casual Italian dinners at their best; regulars recommend signature cannelloni and insist you don't miss the chocolate dessert.

Hotel Du Village S ▽ 22 | 24 | 22 | $48
Hotel Du Village, 2535 River Rd. (Phillips Mill Rd.), New Hope, 215-862-9911
■ For "country elegance sans airs", get "warm" and "cozy" by one of the "lovely fireplaces" at this "romantic" mom-

Philadelphia | F | D | S | C |

and-pop French lodged in a turn-of-the-century New Hope manor house; the inn's fare may be a bit "unimaginative" for esoteric eaters, but it's "delicious" nonetheless, even though diners complain you "can't see" how "beautifully prepared" it all is because the rooms are "so dark."

House of Jin S | ▽ 20 | 16 | 19 | $19 |
234 W. Chelten Ave. (Pulaski Ave.), 215-848-7700
■ This Chinese-Japanese in Germantown just might be "too good not to have already been discovered"; adherents agree "amazing" meals like signature lobster with black-bean sauce "never disappoint", the "staff is friendly and attentive" and terrace dining adds to the "attractiveness" of the setting.

Hunan S | 20 | 14 | 20 | $22 |
47 E. Lancaster Ave. (Rittenhouse Pl.), Ardmore, 610-642-3050
◪ "They've stood the test of time" at this long-running Chinese BYO in Ardmore, where regulars rate the "solid", "authentic" fare "still worthy in spite of much competition"; detractors agree the "pedestrian" place is "consistent", i.e. "consistently mediocre", but at least it's "a relative bargain" for the area.

Hymie's Merion Deli S | 17 | 8 | 13 | $16 |
342 Montgomery Ave. (Levering Mill Rd.), Merion Station, 610-668-3354
◪ In the battle of the "suburban" "Jewish delis", this Merion "classic" is an old warhorse where "big-haired waitresses" "in pancake" makeup sling "insults" along with "all the garlic kosher pickles you can eat and a good sandwich"; the digs are "dreary", but "schmoozy" Main Liners "go for the news" on the neighborhood and a "heapful" of "corned beef heaven, hon", so go ahead – "break the diet" and "get back to your roots."

Il Cantuccio ⌀ | 21 | 15 | 20 | $24 |
701 N. Third St. (Fairmount Ave.), 215-627-6573
■ The room is "tiny", and the fare, "served piping hot to your table", is so "wonderful" that dining at this "homey" BYO "gem" is like "eating in an Italian grandma's kitchen", albeit with more "chaos"; Northern Libertarians say "show up early, bring a nice Chianti" and you're in for a "hearty", "fair-priced" meal that's "more than red-gravy" typical.

Illuminare S | – | – | – | E |
2321 Fairmount Ave. (bet. 23rd & 24th Sts.), 215-765-0202
Lawyer/foodie Brian Augustine had a dream, and he's seeing it to fruition at this storefront Italian that's lighting up Fairmount with a winning menu of seafood, pastas and brick-oven pizzas in cozy environs complete with open kitchen and fireplace; neighborhood romantics are particularly taken with the twinkling courtyard.

vote at zagat.com

Philadelphia
F | D | S | C

Il Portico ⑤   21 | 21 | 20 | $48
1519 Walnut St. (bet. 15th & 16th Sts.), 215-587-7000
☑ "What's the exchange rate here?" wonder "expense-accounters" "reminded of Florence" when dining on "unusual treats like boar" beneath the "crystal chandeliers" at this "gorgeous", "formal" Northern Italian on Walnut Street's Restaurant Row; "if the boss is treating", "wear your best jewelry" and go for it, but surveyors "are not sure they would splurge" out of pocket to swallow the "sarcasm" of the "arrogant" staff.

Il Sol D'Italia ⑤   21 | 18 | 19 | $34
255 N. Sycamore St. (Durham Rd.), Newtown, 215-968-5880
☑ Bucks Countians count on this "good yuppie [Southern] Italian" in Newtown for signature crab ravioli with lobster cream sauce and other "tasty" entrées; the "busy bar" gets "loud" and "crowded on weekends", and staffers are "big on regular customers", but mere acquaintances agree that "even the rest of us feel welcome."

Il Tartufo ⑤∌   20 | 16 | 18 | $34
4341 Main St. (Grape St.), 215-482-1999
■ "It's worth battling Manayunk parking" for the "yummy" ("but not always available") Jerusalem artichokes, "warm, soft" "housemade matzo" and other "interesting" Judeo-Roman offerings at this "solid", cash-only Northern Italian by Alberto Delbello of Il Portico and Tira Misu; the decor's "cosmopolitan feel" extends to servers who, like so many Vespas about a piazza, "frantically run around."

Imperial Inn ●⑤   20 | 13 | 18 | $21
146 N. 10th St. (bet. Cherry & Race Sts.), 215-627-5588
☑ The "dim sum is where it's at" in this "reliable" spot in Chinatown where the Chinese fare may lack "originality" but is "favored" among traditionalists who "really enjoy the old standards", and it's "affordable enough for frequent dining"; there's nothing imperial about "tired" decor in "need of remodeling", though the "upstairs is less crowded, sunny" and pleasant enough.

Independence Brew Pub ⑤   14 | 17 | 15 | $21
1150 Filbert St. (bet. 11th & 12th Sts.), 215-922-4292
☑ When you're looking for a "place to meet a fun 25–35 crowd", the "noisy sports-bar" scene at this brewpub under the Convention Center is "fine"; with "grown-up happy hours" and "above-average" house-concocted suds, it's a "nice place" to drink, but the American grub "needs a little work."

Indonesia ⑤   – | – | – | M
1029 Race St. (bet. 10th & 11th Sts.), 215-829-1400
Fans of the eponymous country's cuisine make regular visits to fill up on the "wonderful flavors" of excellent gado

60   subscribe to zagat.com

Philadelphia　　　　　　　　　　F | D | S | C

gado and satays, both hot and mild, at this plain-Jane BYO in Chinatown; the "accommodating" staff is only too happy to help neophytes make their selections.

INN AT PHILLIPS MILL S ⊘　　26 | 26 | 24 | $46
Inn at Phillips Mill, 2590 N. River Rd. (Phillips Mill Rd.), New Hope, 215-862-9919
■ "In New Hope but away from the hustle", this "romantic" BYO "country inn" in a mid-18th-century house is "a joy to visit" for "delicious" French bistro dinners and service so "phenomenal" and "unpretentious" that "every request is fulfilled, and with good cheer" to boot; but the kicker is probably the "absolutely charming" setting featuring four fireplaces and a "delightful courtyard garden"; green here doesn't mean just foliage, though – it's cash-only.

Inn on Blueberry Hill S　　22 | 22 | 22 | $45
1715 S. Easton Rd. (Almshouse Rd.), Doylestown, 215-491-1777
■ At this "charming" New American in a "lovely" circa-1800 inn near Doylestown, chef William Kim "pairs flavors extremely well" on a "creative, beautiful" menu featuring "exotic game", albeit in "small portions"; the front of the house "does it right" also, and the "interior is charming", even if "the view of Sears is hardly enchanting" from the back of the dining room.

Inn Philadelphia, The S　　21 | 24 | 21 | $38
251 S. Camac St. (bet. Locust & Spruce Sts.), 215-732-2339
◪ "Sweethearts" who are swell on this "cozy" "oasis" in two "wonderful old houses" in Center City swear it's "the gold standard for romantic" restaurants, where the "secret garden" is a "slice of heaven" for a "quiet dinner" and the piano bar is "a hoot"; as for the New American fare, some surveyors' "top-notch" is simply others' "blah."

Io E Tu Ristorante S　　22 | 14 | 22 | $31
1514-20 S. Ninth St. (bet. Dickinson & Tasker Sts.), 215-271-3906
■ "Bring your appetite" to this "wonderful", "family-run" trattoria because you're sure to "overeat" chef-owner Giovanni Varallo's "superb" "Italian cooking"; the joint is so "legitimately authentic" that "the decor screams South Philly and sometimes the servers scream at each other", but they're so "welcoming" to diners that you "feel like the king or queen" of "the neighborhood."

Iron Hill Brewery & Restaurant S　　17 | 17 | 18 | $24
30 E. State St. (bet. Church & Monroe Sts.), Media, 610-627-9000
3 W. Gay St. (High St.), West Chester, 610-738-9600
See review in the Wilmington/Nearby Delaware Directory.

vote at zagat.com

Philadelphia   F | D | S | C

Isaac's Restaurant & Deli S   17 | 13 | 16 | $13
Crossroads Sq., 630 W. Uwchlan Ave. (Pottstown Pike), Exton, 484-875-5825
309 Lancaster Pike (bet. Conestoga Rd. & Rte. 202), Frazer, 610-647-3450
66 E. Street Rd. (Wilmington Pike), West Chester, 610-399-4438
See review in the Lancaster/Berks Counties Directory.

Italian Bistro S   16 | 16 | 17 | $24
211 S. Broad St. (bet. Locust & Walnut Sts.), 215-731-0700
2500 Welsh Rd. (Roosevelt Blvd.), 215-934-7700
◪ "Yummy for my tummy" say parents and "children" at the various branches of this "basic", "family-friendly" Italian chain; the meals might be "predictable", but "large portions" make it "one of the best buys around", even though critics turning up their noses at "Chef Boyardee"–style fare sniff "if this is Italian, then I'm a Martian."

Izzy & Zoe's S   18 | 13 | 14 | $11
Hamilton Village Shops, 224 S. 40th St. (bet. Locust & Walnut Sts.), 215-382-2328
■ "What's not to like?" ask University City slickers digging into "terrific sandwiches" and other "wonderful Jewish soul food" at this "cute" "little deli" "right on the edge of Penn's campus"; even though study-breaking coeds enduring "long waits" admit "it's not New York", "free dill pickles boost their votes."

Jack's Firehouse S   19 | 19 | 19 | $38
2130 Fairmount Ave. (bet. 21st & 22nd Sts.), 215-232-9000
◪ "How many people really eat buffalo and ostrich?" – given the longstanding popularity of TV chef Jack McDavid's "intriguingly" "nouvelle" "Southern comfort" spot in a "cool" turn-of-the-century firehouse across from the "old state pen" in Fairmount, the answer is quite a few "adventurous" sorts; however, not everyone's hot on the "weird food combos", and phobes sound the "alarm" over "slow", "snooty" service, imploring the man to "lose the camera" and concentrate on running his house.

JAKE'S S   26 | 22 | 24 | $47
4365 Main St. (bet. Grape & Levering Sts.), 215-483-0444
■ Bruce Cooper's "stylish" New American "started it all in Manayunk" back in the '80s, and "it hasn't lost anything" in the ensuing years – in fact, "lots of regulars" agree that "on all fronts" it "just gets better and better, like fine wine"; "choose anything on the menu, and nothing will disappoint", though standouts include the "sinful crab cakes" and "must-try cookie taco dessert"; it's "pricey", but it's a "nabe" "fave", so "don't plan to just drop in" – "reservations are a must."

Philadelphia | F | D | S | C |

Jamaican Jerk Hut ⑤   21 | 11 | 16 | $17
1436 South St. (15th St.), 215-545-8644

■ "No pretenses" at Nicola Shirley's "affordable" Jamaican BYOR (that is, bring your own rum) near Broad and South; while some of "the best jerk outside of Negril" and the "friendly" staff are "authentic" enough to "transport you" to "the islands", it "looks like a dump" indoors, so for a truly "idyllic summer experience", dine on the "incredibly quaint veranda" out back and "relax" to the musicians' irie tunes.

Jasmine Thai   23 | 22 | 21 | $28
314 S. Henderson Rd. (Pennsylvania Tpke.), King of Prussia, 610-337-5986

■ "Contemporary" cooking in "wonderful layers of flavor" is "not what you would expect from a shopping center" spot, but that's just what you get with signature macadamia shrimp and other "fantastic" fare at this "romantic" Thai in King of Prussia; it's "a little pricey", but design ideas are thrown in for no extra charge, i.e. the setting is "so lovely" you may be inspired "to run home and redecorate."

Jenny's Bistro ⑤   – | – | – | M
Peddler's Village, Rte. 263 & Street Rd., Lahaska, 215-794-4003

A "wonderful alternative to the New Hope madness" is this "charming" New American in Peddler's Village, with a "varied menu" served amid French country decor inside or out on the patio; on weekend nights, the vibe really gets mellow with live piano music and cocktails until midnight.

Jim's Steaks ●⑤   22 | 10 | 14 | $10
431 N. 62nd St. (bet. Callowhill St. & Girard Ave.), 215-747-6615
Roosevelt Mall, 2311 Cottman Ave. (Bustleton Ave.), 215-333-5467
400 South St. (4th St.), 215-928-1911
Stony Creek Shopping Ctr., 469 Baltimore Pike (Sproul Rd.), Springfield, 610-544-8400

■ "These places will go down in history" for "defining the Philly cheese steak" say "local-flavor" aficionados; from Cottman Avenue to Springfield, from South Street to West Philly, "if you need to spike your cholesterol level", "watch the mound of beef get piled on a roll with Cheese Whiz" and dig in – it's so "honest-to-goodness kick-ass", it's "worth the parking ticket" you'll get waiting in the "long line."

Joe's Peking Duck House ⑤   20 | – | 16 | $20
925 Race St. (bet. 9th & 10th Sts.), 215-922-3277

◪ "All the atmosphere is on the plate" at this "good little duck house" in Chinatown, where the "solid family Chinese" eats "never change" and "never disappoint" according to some regulars; others disagree, opining the food is "not quite what it used to be", though a post-*Survey* spruce-up means it's not quite as ugly a duckling as it once was.

vote at zagat.com

Philadelphia | F | D | S | C |

John Harvard's Brew House ◐S | 14 | 15 | 16 | $21 |
Springfield Sq. S., 1001 Baltimore Pike (Lincoln Ave.), Springfield, 610-544-4440
629 W. Lancaster Ave. (Old Eagle School Rd.), Wayne, 610-687-6565
◪ "Yuppies on the make" "go for an easy night out" at these "warm, fun" chain brewpubs in the suburbs and Wilmington; "the beers can be quite delicious", and if gastronomes gripe that the New American grub is "so-so", guzzlers remind them "this isn't a fancy place, so don't order anything fancy" – just "good fish 'n' chips", "decent" burgers and "meatloaf fit for a king", all at "decent prices."

Johnny Mañana's ◐S | – | – | – | M |
4201 Ridge Ave. (Midvale Ave.), 215-843-0499
Behind the giant chile pepper hanging outside this East Falls Mexican lurks a fun menu of excellent made-from-scratch treats and a serious rotating list of 150 tequilas to fuel the happy mood stoked by live weekend music.

Jolly's S | ▽ 18 | 17 | 18 | $34 |
Latham Hotel, 135 S. 17th St. (Walnut St.), 215-563-8200
■ Given the "classy ambiance" at this "sleek" steak joint in the Latham, "power-lunchers" say they'd "expect higher prices"; as it is, most carnivores consider the meals to be "as good as at the Prime Rib", but it's also "cool" enough to be "great" for a jolly good "burger and beer at the bar", so well-wishers wonder why it's "often a ghost town."

Jones ◐S | – | – | – | M |
700 Chestnut St. (7th St.), 215-223-5663
High-concept king Stephen Starr's new comfort-food haven in the Historic District merits wows all around, from the retro-chic decor that merges Howard Johnson's orangey interior with *The Brady Bunch* den and an alpine ski lodge to the homespun American menu to the ever-chipper servers; brace yourself, though, for the high decibels, especially when a DJ lays down the groove.

Joseph Ambler Inn S | 20 | 22 | 21 | $40 |
Joseph Ambler Inn, 1005 Horsham Rd. (bet. Stump & Upper State Rds.), North Wales, 215-362-7500
■ It's "nice to stroll around outside after dinner" on the "beautiful grounds" of this "charming" "country inn" on a "restored farmstead" in North Wales; "corporate travelers" appreciate sitting "in a well-renovated barn" amid "old Americana" to dine on New Americana like "rarely found game" and other "wonderful" "exotic" stuff.

Joseph Poon S | 22 | 15 | 20 | $28 |
1002 Arch St. (10th St.), 215-928-9333
■ The "unofficial mayor of Chinatown", "funny guy" Joe Poon, "provides a good floor show", and his cooking is

subscribe to zagat.com

Philadelphia

F | D | S | C

"definitely a circus for the mouth" say "entertained" patrons of his "mind-bogglingly" "creative" "Asian fusion" cuisine; it's a "bit of a madhouse", but you'll "leave the restaurant flying high off the good vibes."

Joy Tsin Lau ●S   19 | 13 | 16 | $20
1026 Race St. (bet. 10th & 11th Sts.), 215-592-7226
■ Sure, the "cavernous rooms" and the "dragon" decor can be a "little overwhelming", but you "can't beat" the "fun" "vibes" at this "lively" Chinatown standby where even Chinese customers come for the "super dim sum selection"; "go with a group" and "get there early to get a good table", the better to snatch the "tasty" "treats" from the rolling carts.

Judy's Cafe S   22 | 13 | 20 | $28
627 S. Third St. (Bainbridge St.), 215-928-1968
☑ "It's all about the meatloaf and mashed potatoes" at this "perennial favorite", a "heartwarming", "offbeat American" that dishes up "delicious" "home cooking in Queen Village" for a "fab gay and straight mix"; the "playful" "waiters in heels" make "everyone feel welcome" at "one of Philly's friendliest spots", though design divas dish that the digs could use a "redo."

Kabul S   21 | 16 | 20 | $23
106 Chestnut St. (bet. Front & 2nd Sts.), 215-922-3676
■ The "fresh", "flavorful food", "an intriguing mix of the humble and the exotic" "made with pride and love", draws Old City "regulars who have packed" this "no-frills" BYO "in solidarity", "showing their support" during Afghan "crises"; the "pleasantly quiet" room is "dark but relaxing", and what's more, the staff is "engaging and delightful."

Kansas City Prime S   23 | 20 | 21 | $52
4417 Main St. (bet. Carson & Gay Sts.), 215-482-3700
☑ "Kansas City never looked or tasted this good" bellow beef-eating buddies of this "upscale" temple of meat in "hip" Manayunk, where "huge", "succulent steaks" "cooked to perfection" are brought to table by an "attentive" staff; however, detractors cut down the "inconsistent" fare and "spotty service", claiming "there's nothing prime about" this "clip joint"; N.B. a post-*Survey* expansion, including a wine cellar and a piano bar, may outdate the Decor score.

Kawabata S   18 | 15 | 17 | $29
2455 Grant Ave. (Roosevelt Blvd.), 215-969-8225
☑ Loyalties are divided over this "old reliable" Japanese off the Boulevard in Northeast Philly, with the faithful fawning over "fresh, tasty" sushi that's "served nicely" by a "very friendly" staff, while bashers balk at the "pricey" menu and complain that they "never feel welcome."

vote at zagat.com

Philadelphia

| F | D | S | C |

Keating's ⓈⓈ ▽ 21 | 21 | 18 | $38
Hyatt Regency at Penn's Landing, 201 N. Columbus Blvd. (Walnut St.), 215-928-1234

◪ It's an "exceptional entrant on the waterfront" exclaim worshipers wowed by the "excellent" Traditional American fare and "beautiful fine wood decor" at this Hyatt Regency destination on Penn's Landing; even those less enamored of a "kitchen that needs some improvement" are taken by a location where on a clear day you can catch a "great view of Camden."

KENNEDY-SUPPLEE MANSION Ⓢ 22 | 25 | 22 | $48
Valley Forge Nat'l Historical Park, 1100 W. Valley Forge Rd. (County Line Expwy.), King of Prussia, 610-337-3777

◪ "It's hard to return to reality" after "treating" yourself to an "exquisite" evening at this "beautifully restored" nine-room 1850s mansion in Valley Forge National Historical Park, where some diners delight in "outstanding" Continental cuisine and "unobtrusive" service; battling naysayers turn up noses at staffers who have theirs "in the air", as well as at fare "that's not good enough to justify the location."

Khajuraho Ⓢ 23 | 16 | 17 | $24
Ardmore Plaza, 12 Greenfield Ave. (Lancaster Ave.), Ardmore, 610-896-7200

◪ The "delectable" Indian dishes at this Ardmore Plaza BYO are "fit for a king", but "bring an extinguisher" because they sure are "zesty"; the "sensual" decor, complete with "erotic sculptures", is "as spicy as the food", though surveyors suggest that someone should light a fire under the "maddeningly slow" servers.

Kimberton Inn Ⓢ 22 | 23 | 23 | $40
Kimberton Rd. (Hares Hill Rd.), Kimberton, 610-933-8148

■ Get "warm and cozy" at "a table by the fireplace" at this "gorgeous" 1796 Chester County fixture, just "what a country inn should be"; the "owner is a perfectionist, and the customers reap the benefits", including "all-around excellent" "upscale comfort food" and an "incredibly attentive staff" that makes sure "you never have an empty water glass", despite the "chaos" of "simultaneous weddings" and "rehearsal dinners."

Kimono Sushi Bar Ⓢ ▽ 19 | 11 | 18 | $20
Lafayette Hill Shopping World, 519 Germantown Pike (Church Rd.), Lafayette Hill, 610-828-6265

◪ "Some of the best sushi in town" and "great" udon to boot, with a few "decent Chinese" dishes thrown in for good measure, lure Lafayette Hill Shopping World bargain hunters and "neighborhood" regulars to this modest Japanese BYO longtimer; sophisticates snipe "I've had better", but even they concede that at these "fair prices", the joint "has potential."

subscribe to zagat.com

Philadelphia | F | D | S | C |

Kim's ▽ | 25 | 9 | 18 | $18 |
5955 N. Fifth St. (Champlost St.), 215-927-4550

■ "It's worth the trip" to this BYO "family place" in Olney, where the "wonderfully authentic Korean BBQ", including the "delicious" house specialty of bulgogi (marinated beef), is "cooked right at your table" in "breathtaking proportions"; the setting is "pleasantly" "unpretentious", as are the tariffs.

Kingdom of Vegetarians ▽ | 20 | 13 | 20 | $15 |
129 N. 11th St. (bet. Arch & Race Sts.), 215-413-2290

■ Its loyal subjects aver there's an "overwhelming array" of yum-yum dim sum for "joyful noshing" at this "excellent Vegetarian" in Chinatown that's kosher to boot; the "faux-meat dishes please even die-hard carnivores", the all-you-can-eat buffets are a "steal" and the "friendly" service makes everyone feel royal.

King George II Inn | 20 | 21 | 20 | $37 |
102 Radcliffe St. (Mill St.), Bristol, 215-788-5536

☑ Revolutionaries are "glad we won the war" so we get the spoils: this "classic" inn, serving since 1681 in Lower Bucks; its "beautiful setting" includes "lovely Delaware views", and the American-Continental fare is "delicious" and "creative"; Georgians adjudge the service "solicitious", but a few seditious sorts snort it's "snooty" and "slow."

Kisso Sushi Bar | 23 | 19 | 20 | $31 |
205 N. Fourth St. (Race St.), 215-922-1770

☑ For an "inventive" meal, "let them choose" for you at this "minimalist" Old City Japanese BYO known for "fresh", "sumptuous sushi"; despite the "good vibe", some kisso and tell of "leisurely" pacing and "meager" portions that leave you "going home hungry."

Knave of Hearts ●◐ | 20 | 18 | 18 | $32 |
230 South St. (bet. 2nd & 3rd Sts.), 215-922-3956

☑ "Don't ever leave us!" is the heartfelt entreaty of "hippies" and nostalgic nibblers who've "loved" this "funky" Eclectic "oasis on South Street" for more than a quarter-century; the "scrumptious" chicken coco loco may be the "longest running dish in town", and the "strawberry soup rocks"; though knaves slam the "spaced-out" staff and "crowded" room, sentimental hearts gush that it's "still worth a visit after all these years."

Knight House ▽ | 22 | 20 | 19 | $41 |
96 W. State St. (Clinton St.), Doylestown, 215-489-9900

■ A passel of vassals vows this "undiscovered treasure" in an "elegant converted house" with a "wonderful garden" in Doylestown offers "blue-ribbon dining"; the New American fare is "exceptional", with "unusual presentations" of "interesting but not strange" dishes, and even those who lance it as "pricey" have to admit it's "special."

vote at zagat.com

Philadelphia F | D | S | C

Kobe ▽ 19 | 19 | 20 | $32
Hilton Valley Forge, 251 W. DeKalb Pike (Henderson Rd.), King of Prussia, 610-337-1200
◪ It's "fun with a group" or the "kids" when you hunker 'round the hibachi and watch the "entertaining chefs" do their thing at this long-standing King of Prussia Japanese steakhouse in the Hilton Valley Forge; the food's "good" and service is "excellent", but the jaded jeer it's "too much dough for the show."

KOCH'S DELI S⊄ 26 | 8 | 21 | $11
4309 Locust St. (43rd St.), 215-222-8662
■ New York, Schmew York: this takeout-only "West Philly institution" is a "prototypical deli" "champ" dishing up "witty" "repartee" to go with "delicious chopped liver"; though there's always a "long wait", it's "made tolerable by the free samples" passed out by the "friendly" staff, and the payoff is that "fabulous", "mammoth sandwich."

Korea Garden S ▽ 22 | 20 | 20 | $27
Center Sq., 732 DeKalb Pike (Skippack Pike), Blue Bell, 610-272-5727
■ This "authentic" Korean barbecue BYO in a Blue Bell shopping center is "off to a good start" according to avid grazers who go for the "attentive" service, "interesting" decor and "awesome" hibachi fare cooked up on "real charcoal grill tables"; pleased parents proffer posies of praise, as "kids love it."

KRISTIAN'S RISTORANTE S 25 | 21 | 22 | $43
1100 Federal St. (11th St.), 215-468-0104
■ "Bravos" abound for the Leuzzi family's "elegant" South Philly Italian, deemed a "delight" thanks to chef Kristian's "great osso buco" and other "top-notch" dishes; the "charming" staff and "welcoming" surroundings make this "favorite" "worth every penny", as well as every minute spent "waiting for reserved tables."

La Boheme S⊄ ▽ 23 | 16 | 21 | $27
246 S. 11th St. (bet. Locust & Spruce Sts.), 215-351-9901
■ "You'll sing arias after tasting the food" at this "sweet", "stylish" French corner in Center City near the Forrest Theatre; most feel it's "far superior to its more pretentious counterparts", citing a "Mediterranean flair" to the fare, "friendly" service and "unbeatable prices" that are abetted by a BYO policy.

LA BONNE AUBERGE S 25 | 26 | 25 | $66
Village 2 Apartment Complex, 1 Rittenhouse Circle (Mechanic St.), New Hope, 215-862-2462
◪ "What a night out!" cry Francophiles of this "special-occasion" French "classic" in New Hope that's been "consistently superb" since 1972; the "excellent cuisine",

Philadelphia　　　　　　　　　　F | D | S | C

"voluminous wine list", "wonderful service" and "romantic", "church-quiet" ambiance are *très bonne* indeed; however, "much-too-expensive" tariffs and a "difficult" location "tucked away in a condo complex" that's grown up around its 1750 farmhouse have critics exclaiming *sacré bleu*!

La Collina　　　　　　　　　　21 | 19 | 20 | $47
37-41 Ashland Ave. (Jefferson St.), Bala Cynwyd, 610-668-1780
☑ "Older Main Liners" tout this "classic", "upscale" Bala Northern Italian specialist as a "credit" to Cynwyd, offering "authentic" fare and "attentive" service; that's only "if they know you", the less "politically connected" complain, and though everyone enjoys the "wonderful view" of the river, modernists simply "yawn" over the "tired warhorse."

La Colombe Panini S⌿　　　　24 | 18 | 18 | $11
4360 Main St. (bet. Grape & Levering Sts.), 215-483-4580
La Colombe Torrefaction S⌿
Rittenhouse Sq., 130 S. 19th St. (bet. Sansom & Walnut Sts.), 215-563-0860
☑ The "best cappuccino on the planet" might just be sipped at one of these "chic" coffeehouses, voted the *Survey*'s No. 1 Bang for the Buck; Rittenhouse Square java junkies can't get enough of the "superior" brews, "tasty" panini and other "light bites", or the "glamorous" "European" ambiance, while Manayunk morning mavens only wish their spot would open earlier than 7:30 AM.

Lacroix at the Rittenhouse S　　─ | ─ | ─ | VE
Rittenhouse Hotel, 210 W. Rittenhouse Sq. (bet. Locust & Walnut Sts.), 215-790-2533
Acclaimed chef Jean-Marie Lacroix has been given carte blanche to live his culinary dream at this *très* elegant classic French grande dame with a wonderful treetop view of Rittenhouse Square; legions of loyalists marvel over his sumptuous, ever-changing prix fixe menus, accompanied by a 31-page wine list and proffered by a professional service team amid luxe environs with a hushed ambiance.

LA FAMIGLIA S　　　　　　　26 | 24 | 25 | $57
8 S. Front St. (bet. Chestnut & Market Sts.), 215-922-2803
■ A "memorable" experience awaits at the Sena family's "grand" Italian "jewel" in Old City, but "be prepared to spend big bucks" for it; while wallet-watchers warrant it "obnoxiously" "overpriced", the "remarkable" fare, a wine list that "reads like a telephone book", "*bella*" decor and a staff that "fawns" over you "like you're a king" make this "class act" a "favorite" for big-purse "special occasions."

Lai Lai Garden S　　　　　▽ 25 | 27 | 25 | $30
1144 DeKalb Pike (Skippack Pike), Blue Bell, 610-277-5988
■ It's no lai that this "lavish Chinese-Japanese" "suburban" in Blue Bell is a "winner" for "excellent sushi", signature

vote at zagat.com

Philadelphia F | D | S | C

honey-walnut shrimp and other "beautifully presented" "gourmet" goodies; as befits a place with a "fancy attitude", "service is attentive" and it's "classy looking" as all get out, so "take a good look at the decor because you're paying for it."

Lakeside Chinese Deli S⊄ — | — | — | M
207 N. Ninth St. (Race St.), 215-925-3288
So the setting screams "White Castle" – this Chinatown Chinese is still "amazing" for "absolutely" "fabulous", "cheap" dim sum ferried by a "friendly" staff, and though the "setting is unappealing", at least it's "clean"; regulars say you'll definitely want to "repeat" the experience, but don't try it on a Thursday, because that's when it's closed.

La Locanda del Ghiottone S⊄ 24 | 17 | 20 | $29
130 N. Third St. (Cherry St.), 215-829-1465
■ Groupies who "miss" the late, "beloved" chef Giuseppe swear his "spirit lives on" at this "cozy" Italian trattoria in Old City, where current toque Franco Lombardo's "authentic", "rustic" dishes, served in "large portions" amid a "romantic" setting, help ease the loss; "long lines" irk the impatient, but most think it's "worth the wait."

La Lupe ●S — | — | — | I
1201 S. Ninth St. (Federal St.), 215-551-9920
In the heart of South Philly's cheese steak country, this plain-looking Mexican taqueria set up shop in a black-and-white-tiled former garage in the Italian Market, and it's drawing wide notice for its authentic tacos, enchiladas and simple breakfast items (notably tortillas grilled to order); not only is it one of the best places in the area to trot out your high school Spanish (to the chuckles of the unfailingly helpful staff), but it's open till late at night.

Lamberti's Cucina S 18 | 16 | 18 | $27
212 Walnut St. (bet. 2nd & 3rd Sts.), 215-238-0499
Feasterville Plaza Shopping Ctr., 1045 Bustleton Pike (Street Rd.), Feasterville, 215-355-6266
◪ There's "nothing cutting-edge", just "ample quantities" of "pasta you can count on" at this Southern Italian clan of "homey", "affordable" "family spots" where "attentive" servers enhance the "pleasant atmosphere"; however, unimpressed purists put off by the "run-of-the-mill" eats sigh "ho-hum."

Landing, The S 18 | 20 | 18 | $36
22 N. Main St. (Bridge St.), New Hope, 215-862-5711
◪ Those extolling this "New Hope tradition's" "beautiful location overlooking the Delaware" and "cozy", "relaxing" "dining room with two fireplaces" have landed on solid ground, but discussion of the New American fare gets choppy: pros praise the "greatly improved", "innovative"

Philadelphia

L'Angolo ⑤ ▽ 24 | 19 | 24 | $26
1415 Porter St. (Broad St.), 215-389-4252
■ "Shhh – don't tell anyone" about this shoebox-size South Philly secret plead in-the-know noodle nuts who "treasure" the "memorable" homemade pastas and other "fabulous" Italian dishes loaded with the bulb that makes the joint a "garlic lovers' haven"; a BYO policy enhances the "value" at this "cute", "bright", "comfortable" spot.

Langostino ⑤ ▽ 17 | 10 | 18 | $30
100 Morris St. (Front St.), 215-551-7709
■ The "neighborhood" raves about this small-fry Italian BYO off I-95 in South Philly due to its "excellent" pastas, "very fine" mussels and eponymous signature crustacean, served by a "particularly friendly" staff in a cozy space.

La Padella ⑤ 19 | 18 | 19 | $36
Grant Plaza II, 1619 Grant Ave. (bet. Bustleton Ave. & Krewstown Rd.), 215-677-7723
☑ "Downtown style and class" is "a most welcome surprise in a shopping mall" in Northeast Philly, where pals praise "delicious", "high-end" Italian cooking; critics pan "choppy service" and dishes they deem "slightly above average" at "well-above-average prices."

La Pergola ⑤ 18 | 12 | 15 | $21
42 Shewell Ave. (Main St.), Doylestown, 215-230-9936
726 West Ave. (Old York Rd.), Jenkintown, 215-884-7204
■ "What more could a boychik ask for" than these Jewish-Mediterranean twins in Doylestown and Jenkintown, where "ample portions" of "simple", "yummy" grub come at "reasonable prices"?; the "atrociously pink" decor "could use sprucing up", but believe the "bubbies" when they say "only I make better brisket."

Las Cazuelas ⑤ 23 | 17 | 21 | $23
426 W. Girard Ave. (bet. 4th & 5th Sts.), 215-351-9144
■ "Holy mole!" rave amigos about this "numero uno" Mex BYO where both the "amazing", "authentic", "affordable" south-of-the-border fare and the "desolate" Northern Liberties block have surveyors saying "run, don't walk" to the door; a "friendly" staff makes it "cheery" indoors, and despite the "dicey" location, it's "becoming popular", so expect "long waits."

La Terrasse ⑤ 20 | 20 | 19 | $38
3432 Sansom St. (bet. 34th & 36th Sts.), 215-386-5000
☑ So it "ain't like the old days", but this reincarnation of the "collegey" "favorite" on Penn campus remains a "solid standby" for "well-prepared" French fare, including a "best-

Philadelphia　　　　　　　　　　　F D S C

deal" bar menu served by "quick, funny" mixologists; today's "wealthy students" grab a seat "under the tree" in the "lovely" space and ignore the glum alums who wonder "what happened" to their undergrad haunt.

Latest Dish, The ◐S　　　　21 16 17 $28
613 S. Fourth St. (bet. Bainbridge & South Sts.), 215-629-0565

◪ The latest dish has it that the "bar scene resembles a floor show" at this "fun-loving", "late-night" bistro set in the "middle of biker hell" off South Street; while the "younger crowd" finds the New American–Eclectic eats as "tasty" as the action, foodies frown at options that they consider "ordinary", but everyone gets their boogie on afterward at the upstairs nightclub, Fluid.

Lauletta's Grille S⊄　　　　▽ 22 15 21 $28
1703 S. 11th St. (Morris St.), 215-755-5422

■ Tucked away on a block of understated row houses, this "out-of-the-ordinary" BYO "find" "should make South Philly proud"; it's a labor of "love" by chef-owner and hometown boy Joe Lauletta, who "makes to order" "simple" but "delicious" Italian-Mediterranean dishes in a "very small" space that retains the spirit, and the "great" value, of the luncheonette it once was.

La Veranda S　　　　22 21 19 $47
Penn's Landing, Pier 3, N. Columbus Blvd. (bet. Arch & Market Sts.), 215-351-1898

◪ "Romantics" "sit outside" at this "upscale" Italian "treat" perched right "on the water" at Penn's Landing; "politicians" and "wise guys" alike ignore the "gorgeous view" of the Delaware to focus on "wonderful antipasti", "fabulous fish dishes and delicious pastas", but while "expense-account types" may be made to "feel like royalty", commoners are ready to revolt over "high prices" and "plenty of attitude", crying "forget it if you're not important."

La Vigna S　　　　22 17 21 $36
1100 S. Front St. (Federal St.), 215-336-1100

■ "Big portions" of "old-fashioned" Northern Italian "standards" at "sensible prices" draw a "steady" stream of customers to this veteran "in the heart of South Philly" that's so "comfortable" it's "almost like eating in someone's home"; even though "there are better places" around, the "friendly" servers "aim to please and they really care", which results in a "consistently fine" experience; N.B. check out the chef's table in the wine cellar.

LE BAR LYONNAIS　　　　29 24 26 $49
1523 Walnut St. (bet. 15th & 16th Sts.), 215-567-1000

■ "When you want" the "Le Bec-Fin touch" at a fraction of the cost, follow the lead of those in-the-know and "slum"

Philadelphia · F | D | S | C

it at this "plush yet unstuffy" "baby bistro" nestled below chef-owner Georges Perrier's Center City flagship; it's a "real find" for "exceptional" French fare served by a "gracious", "knowledgeable" staff, and you're guaranteed "great conversation with whoever's eating at the bar."

LE BEC-FIN — 29 | 28 | 28 | $85
1523 Walnut St. (bet. 15th & 16th Sts.), 215-567-1000

■ Georges Perrier's French "star" on Restaurant Row continues to turn out "perfection on a plate", dazzling patrons with "stupendous" French dinners and a "magical" dessert cart; though its "formal" Louis XVI–style space has recently been redone to re-create a circa-1900 Paris salon, it's still a "world-class" setting for "impeccable" service, adding up to a "memorable experience" that's "as close to heaven as you can get" in Philadelphia.

Le Bus S — 19 | 14 | 16 | $21
4266 Main St. (bet. Green & Shurs Lns.), 215-487-2663
Rittenhouse Sq., 135 S. 18th St. (bet. Sansom & Walnut Sts.), 215-569-8299

☑ A "good choice" for "kid-friendly" dining in Manayunk is this "frenetic" American where "homestyle sandwiches" on some of the "best breads in town" are "piled high" with "wholesome" stuff and "dreamy banana-nut pancakes" have folks flipping for their "favorite brunch", even though those who knew it when feel it's "losing its luster."

Le Castagne — ∇ 25 | 25 | 25 | $44
1920 Chestnut St. (20th St.), 215-751-9913

■ "Walk in and you're in Milan" at this "surprising" Northern Italian, "another winner from the Sena family" of La Famiglia; in a "chic" setting with "knockout" decor, the kitchen sends forth "inventive" fare, which "shines" so bright that stellar "pastas like these are near-impossible to find outside of Italy"; the "fabulous bar" and a "polite" staff help make it "worth the walk to the fringes of Center City."

Lee How Fook S — 23 | 7 | 18 | $20
219 N. 11th St. (bet. Race & Vine Sts.), 215-925-7266

■ "Don't be deceived by the decor (or lack thereof)" at this "spartan", "family-run" Chinese BYO 'dump' 'cause the fare is some of Chinatown's "finest"; "everything" on the extensive menu is "unbelievably great", but the highlights are its "phenomenal" hot pots and "awesome salt-baked squid"; tack on "efficient" service and "cheap" tabs, and you get one of Philly's "perennial downscale favorites."

LE MAS S — 23 | 25 | 22 | E
Spread Eagle Vlg., 503 W. Lancaster Ave. (Eagle Rd.), Wayne, 610-964-2588

☑ Le Bec-Fin's Georges Perrier "has done it yet again" with this "stylish" Main Line charmer whose South-of-

vote at zagat.com

Philadelphia F | D | S | C

France spirit makes you "feel like you're dining" in a Provençal "farmhouse" complete with vaulted ceilings, walk-in stone fireplaces and a sunny indoor courtyard; devotees concede that it "can't compete with the original" but insist that "everything" "clicks" on the "sensational" menu at "much more affordable" prices; "disappointed" detractors throw barbs at the "awkward" service.

Lemon Grass Thai S   22 | 16 | 18 | $24
3626-30 Lancaster Ave. (36th St.), 215-222-8042
■ At this "cozy" University City Thai, the "awesome" prix fixe "lunch special" is a "bargain" "treat" that "can't be beat", particularly for herbivores, as it includes "lots of vegetarian" options; "great names like 'evil jungle princess'" bespeak the "lively flavors", though a few also wonder if they refer to the staff, noting "service needs improvement"; N.B. there's a BYO outpost in Lancaster.

LE PETIT CAFÉ S   24 | 18 | 22 | $31
7026 Terminal Sq. (Market St.), Upper Darby, 610-352-8040
■ "Good things" really do come in petite packages, as habitués of this "cute" French "pearl" "hidden" away in Upper Darby can attest; "tiny" in space but "big in taste", it appeals with "excellent" cooking that's "well seasoned and presented" by a "warm" staff that's "generous to a fault"; even if it gets a "tad crowded" and "parking can be a challenge", a meal is "always almost perfect, and your wallet will still have money in it."

Liberties ●S   18 | 16 | 17 | $26
705 N. Second St. (Fairmount Ave.), 215-238-0660
◪ The "young crowd" grooving to live jazz at this "fun neighborhood joint" in Northern Liberties claims the "neat spot" turns out New American fare that's "better than expected" for a "pub"; others say the "inconsistent" kitchen takes too many liberties with quality, turning out dishes that "vary from excellent to mediocre."

Little Fish S⊄   22 | 12 | 19 | $26
600 Catharine St. (6th St.), 215-413-3464
■ Schools of afishionados swim into John Tiplitz's "funky" "shoebox" "three blocks from South Street" to savor a "limited menu" of "big flavors" and watch as the "fabulous" fin fare is "made in front of them"; it's "like eating in someone's home" (albeit a "cramped" one), but "that's half the charm" – just make a "reservation" and BYO.

Little Marakesh S   – | – | – | M
1825 Limekiln Pike (Twining Rd.), Dresher, 215-643-3003
Run by a sweet family from Casablanca, this Moroccan BYO casbah transports diners out of its Dresher strip mall with authentic decor, belly dancers and outstanding tagines and couscous; it's groovilicious for group functions.

Philadelphia | F | D | S | C |

Little Pete's S | 14 | 7 | 15 | $13 |
1904 Chestnut St. (bet. 19th & 20th Sts.), 215-563-2303
219 S. 17th St. (Chancellor St.), 215-545-5508 ●⇄
The Philadelphian, 2401 Pennsylvania Ave. (bet. 24th & 25th Sts.), 215-232-5001

◪ "A million citizens can't be wrong" about these "always-packed" "old-fashioned diners" in Center City and the Art Museum area; chickadees on the run chirp that "cheap" "hash-house" grub and service like "lightning" make them "better than fast food", and even if the "ambiance is beyond-belief" "divey", 17th Street is 24/7 and "you gotta eat breakfast somewhere" when you're "desperate at 3 AM."

Loie ●S | – | – | – | M |
128 S. 19th St. (bet. Sansom & Walnut Sts.), 215-568-0808
Two vibes coexist at this stylish, art nouveau newcomer set in a former Rittenhouse Square deli; while the kitchen turns out competent, reasonably priced French brasserie fare for the masses seated in the sumptuous booths, young hipsters gravitate toward the pool table in the back (late at night, when the DJ spins, it's all nightspot).

Lombardi's S⇄ | 20 | 13 | 16 | $18 |
132 S. 18th St. (Sansom St.), 215-564-5000

■ "It's the oven that makes this pizza one of the best in the area" say pie-happy patrons of this Center City parlor; the brick-baked crusts are "good" and "thin", the toppings are "delicious" and the "servers remember you", but the "down 'n' dirty" vibe might make the cash-only 'za "better to eat at home" via takeout or delivery.

London Grill ●S | 20 | 18 | 18 | $33 |
2301 Fairmount Ave. (23rd St.), 215-978-4545

■ In a "convenient location" for a "great post–Art Museum" meal, this "popular" Fairmount feedery serves up "bohemian gourmet" New American fare to culture vultures and "after-work" "neighborhood" folk; the "friendly bar" has "happy happy-hour" power with "super-incredible" deals, and the "bright, cheerful sunroom" exudes a "congenial" warmth – bummer the staff's attitude leaves some feeling cold.

Long's Gourmet Chinese S | 19 | 13 | 18 | $22 |
2018 Hamilton St. (bet. 20th & 21st Sts.), 215-496-9928

■ "Who needs Chinatown" when "top-quality" "fancy Chinese" can be had without the "overwhelming parking" problems at this "low-key" joint near the Art Museum?; the surroundings are as "tasteful" as the "pretty dishes", which "no gloppy brown sauces" dare grace.

Los Catrines/Tequila's S | ▽ 23 | 26 | 21 | $34 |
1602 Locust St. (16th St.), 215-546-0181

■ The decor is "much nicer after its move" to "spectacular" quarters in Center City, and the "authentic" "regional

vote at zagat.com 75

Philadelphia

F | D | S | C

Mexican cooking" is as "*delicioso*" as ever; with this casa "inspiring obsession in its devotees", addicted amigos are simply advised to go easy on the "great selection" of "exotic tequilas."

Lourdas Greek Taverna ⑤ ⊄   20 | 15 | 19 | $27

50 N. Bryn Mawr Ave. (Lancaster Ave.), Bryn Mawr, 610-520-0288

■ Opa! – what a "welcome addition" this Greek taverna is to Bryn Mawr opine epicureans eager for "refreshing" "basics" like signature moussaka and a "fantastic octopus"; the room is "noisy", "bright" and rather "spartan", but sages say it's "pleasant" enough; "too bad you need reservations – it would be nice to just drop in" for a BYO "excellent value."

L2 ⑤   19 | 18 | 20 | $30

2201 South St. (22nd St.), 215-732-7878

■ "Be prepared for a lot of velvet", plus loads of "sweet attention" and "good, homey", "reasonably priced" plates, at this "delightfully" "quirky" American "out of the way" near Graduate Hospital; if a staff and a setting "full of character" aren't "charming" enough for you, perhaps a "yummy" 'yodel' or fudgy 'mocha rash' for dessert is.

Lucy's Hat Shop ⑤   17 | 16 | 16 | $28

247 Market St. (bet. 2nd & 3rd Sts.), 215-413-1433

☑ "Hats come off and sometimes more" during the "don't-miss" Drunkin Monkey Sunday buffet brunch (offered during football season), complete with make-your-own Bloody Marys and bottomless mimosas, at this boozy Old City Continental; "hip, young" "people-watchers" "hang out" here for "definitive drinking with friends", but though some of them find the fare "decent", others say they "would rather eat their chapeau."

Ludwig's Garten ⑤   19 | 20 | 19 | $25

1315 Sansom St. (bet. 13th & 14th Sts.), 215-985-1525

☑ "If you're up for kraut and sausages", reach out for "a touch of Bavaria right on Sansom Street", where "lots of pork products" highlight a "wild" German menu and there are "more beers on tap than you can count or pronounce"; though "waitresses in costume", "loud" "oompah music" and "way-kitschy" decor are a bit too "tacky"-Teutonic for trendoids, "sometimes, like before a *Sound of Music* sing-along, you need" to strive for your wurst.

Maccabeam ⑤   19 | 6 | 14 | $15

128 S. 12th St. (bet. Sansom & Walnut Sts.), 215-922-5922

■ Tasters who don't eat *trayf* testify that "one of the best bargains in town" is found at this "sparsely" adorned "kosher Middle Eastern" in Center City; "delicious soup", "good falafel", a "great vegetarian platter" and other

Philadelphia | F | D | S | C |

"basic fare" make for "unbeatable" cheap eats, except of course from Friday to Saturday sundowns.

Mad 4 Mex ●S | 13 | 13 | 11 | $17 |
Shops at Penn, 3401 Walnut St. (34th St.), 215-382-2221
■ "Especially after they've consumed a few" "big-ass margaritas", the "Penn students" who "hang" at this University City Tex-Mex chainster "don't care about the quality of food" that's "never more than ok", and they "stop noticing" the "tacky frat-house" decor and "space-cadet service" – they're just looking "to score a date" and fuel their mad "all-nighters"; but ya know, with "lots of vegan options", the "humble" grub can actually be "healthy."

Magazine | – | – | – | E |
2029 Walnut St. (21st St.), 215-567-5000
Peter Dunmire, who banged pots at some of the better restaurants in town, has returned to the kitchen with this hip though cozy Francophilic comfort-fooder with sidewalk seating in Center City; local trendies lap up dishes such as lobster and shrimp dumplings followed by chocolate tart in antique-filled environs with original art gracing the walls.

Maggiano's Little Italy S | 20 | 20 | 18 | $27 |
1201 Filbert St. (12th St.), 215-567-2020
King of Prussia Mall, 205 Mall Blvd. (Gulph Rd.), King of Prussia, 610-992-3333
■ "Abbondanza!" – it's a "family-style" "food orgy" at this chain Italian near the Convention Center, where the eating's "surprisingly delicious" and you "waddle out satisfied", "doggy bag" with "tomorrow night's dinner" in tow; the shtick is "all about Sinatra", red-checked tablecloths and other "typical" motifs, and frankly, the Chairman of the Board might agree that the service needs "some help."

MAINLAND INN S | 26 | 23 | 25 | $45 |
17 Main St. (Sumneytown Pike), Mainland, 215-256-8500
■ When the city's got you down, take a "charming" "country ride" "far from the rat race" to this "top-drawer" New American near Lansdale for "classic, "restrained dining"; "consistently beautiful" dishes are delivered at "no rush" by a "respectful", "knowledgeable" staff across "creaky floors" in "old-fashioned" rooms that bespeak a "formal" yet "cozy" "quaintness."

Main-ly Café/Bakery S | 19 | 15 | 17 | $19 |
4247 Main St. (Rector St.), 215-487-1325
■ At this "cute little" Continental BYO, the sweets are "dangerously good" but the tables are dangerously "close" for the kind of gossip in which the "Manayunk girls who lunch" indulge; since it switched its name from Main-ly Desserts, word is that "practically everything" is "tasty" on the "expanded dinner menu."

vote at zagat.com

Philadelphia   F | D | S | C

Mallorca ⑤   19 | 21 | 22 | $39
117-119 South St. (bet. Front & 2nd Sts.), 215-351-6652
◪ "What is there to say but 'flaming sausage'?" ask carne-craving compadres of this Spanish-Portuguese chainster on South Street; well, you could say "fantastic tapas", "*estupendo*" paella and "good sangria", and you should add "generous portions" as an aside; the "old-world charm" of the "pretty surroundings" and "friendly staff" soothe some, but a few who've visited locations elsewhere say this "commercial" "stepchild" "tries hard but misses."

Mama Palma's ⑤⌀   21 | 14 | 18 | $18
2229 Spruce St. (23rd St.), 215-735-7357
■ It's "worth the parking woes" of Center City to scarf down the "dream pizza" at this Southern Italian "brick-oven" "favorite" where the "thin crust" is "fabulous" and the "toppings are unusual" "but come together spectacularly"; needless to say, ya gotta "go early" or battle the "yuppie" "families" who frequent the joint.

Ma Ma Yolanda's ⑤   ▽ 17 | 17 | 20 | $30
746 S. Eighth St. (bet. Catharine & Fitzwater Sts.), 215-592-0195
◪ The jury is out on this "homey" South Philly Italian "filled with antiques" and "church statues"; some think of it as an "accommodating", "old family favorite" with "good" takes on "red-gravy" standards, but even given a big-production signature steak stuffed with spinach, prosciutto and cheese and topped with a mushroom-wine sauce, others can only muster a "yawn."

Mamma Maria ⑤   19 | 15 | 21 | $42
1637 E. Passyunk Ave. (bet. 11th & 12th Sts.), 215-463-6884
◪ "Plan to spend the evening" and "don't eat for two days before", because you're in for a "fixed-price, multicourse, homemade Italian" meal plus "all-you-can-drink" vino at this South Philly feastery; if the "expensive" fare is just "ok" and the decor is a bit "shabby", when you "sit back and let mamma do it all", it's still a "great place to feel spoiled."

Manayunk Brewery & Restaurant ⑤   15 | 17 | 15 | $23
4120 Main St. (Shurs Ln.), 215-482-8220
◪ An "old textile mill" in Manayunk is the site of this "reliable all-American" brewpub "aimed at twentysomething" "frat boys" "wearing black" or, if they're a bit more conservative, "J. Crew and Banana Republic"; most head for the "fun summer deck" and "go for the drinks, not the food" or the "dark basement" dining.

Mandarin Garden ⑤   23 | 15 | 20 | $24
91 York Rd. (Davisville Rd.), Willow Grove, 215-657-3993
◪ Sinophiles use "wonderful", "outstanding", "delicious", "innovative" and other bits of mandarin prose to describe

78   subscribe to zagat.com

Philadelphia F | D | S | C

the "dependably" "creative" fare at this "eager-to-please" Willow Grove Chinese, a "fave" in the "northern suburbs"; "joking waiters" "make the dining fun" here, but no one's chuckling at the "somewhat worn" garden-variety decor.

Manila Bay Bar & Grill S ▽ 18 | 9 | 16 | $18
6724 Castor Ave. (bet. Kerper & Knorr Sts.), 215-722-7877

■ If you're seeking "something a bit different", this family-run place in Northeast Philly provides an "excellent intro to Filipino" cuisine with "simple" yet "delicious" dishes like signature grilled pork marinated in vinaigrette; all of it, including the pricing, is so "good" that you can almost ignore the "very casual" "luncheonette aesthetics."

Marabella's S 16 | 17 | 16 | $26
602 Skippack Pike (Penllyn-Blue Bell Pike), Blue Bell, 215-641-9100

☑ "Where are they all going?" nostalgic noshers ask about the once-numerous outposts of this Italian standby; the "cool-looking" survivor in Blue Bell is still "very crowded on weekends" with "whole families" making way later on for "wild", "noisy pickup" crowds; as for the grub, some find the dishes "dependably" "decent", while others turn up their noses at the "tired" "red-sauce" "basics."

Marathon Grill 18 | 12 | 15 | $16
1339 Chestnut St. (13th St.), 215-561-4460
Commerce Sq., 2001 Market St. (bet. 20th & 21st Sts.), 215-568-7766
1818 Market St. (18th St.), 215-561-1818
121 S. 16th St. (Sansom St.), 215-569-3278 S
Suburban Station, 1617 John F. Kennedy Blvd. (16th St.), 215-564-4745

■ "The lawyer's McDonald's", the "hangout for the regional crowd", "the Palm for middle management" – whatever you label these "popular" New American delis, you "can't go wrong" with their "huge-portioned" sandwiches and "tasty", "healthful" salads; moreover, with a host of other offerings, they may merit mention for the "most variety of any menu in the city", so if service is "rush 'em in, rush 'em out", what can you expect when so many folks find them "lovely for lunch"?

Marathon on the Square ●S 19 | 17 | 16 | $24
1839 Spruce St. (19th St.), 215-731-0800

☑ "Between informal and formal, gourmet and casual", there is a happy medium, and this "trendy/comfy" New American off Rittenhouse Square seems to "have finally solved its identity crisis" by "reducing the swank factor" and focusing on "huge", "reasonably priced" sandwiches and "lots of comfort food"; while there's a "good vibe" at brunch, "unreliable" service overall leads some to wonder "where is my waiter?"

vote at zagat.com

Philadelphia

| F | D | S | C |

Marco Polo ⑤   20 | 15 | 18 | $30
Elkins Park Sq., 8080 Old York Rd. (Church Rd.), Elkins Park, 215-782-1950

☒ "Fish is my wish" wail "locals" at this Italian seafooder where it seems that "whirlwind" "chef Lo is doing a great job" luring in Elkins Parkers, as reports are that "some eat here nightly", dining on "delicious everything", including "fresh whole" fin fare "filleted at the table"; the less-enchanted feel that service is "distracted" and the "pricey" "gourmet food doesn't fit in with the Bennigan's decor."

Margaret Kuo's ⑤   – | – | – | M
175 E. Lancaster Ave. (Wayne Ave.), Wayne, 610-688-7200

The eponymous restaurateur, who has kept the Main Line well-fed for three decades, has opened this handsome bi-level Asian in downtown Wayne; while the downstairs room offers enough variety of Chinese dishes to satisfy most tastes, true adventure seekers go upstairs (past a stunning waterfall) to the Japanese section, which features a sushi bar, intimate booths and private tatami rooms.

Margaret Kuo's Mandarin ⑤   21 | 17 | 19 | $24
190 Lancaster Ave. (Morehall Rd.), Frazer, 610-647-5488

☒ It's "not a chop suey joint" assert adherents who've "eaten many times a year for many, many years" at this "dependable" Chesco Chinese BYO; they point for evidence toward the "excellent" "Peking duck for two prepared tableside", for which they're willing to endure "unfriendly" service; a post-*Survey* redo not only dispels any old notions about "nondescript" decor, but it has also added a sushi bar to the premises.

Marigold Dining Room ⑤   ▽ 20 | 22 | 22 | $22
501 S. 45th St. (Larchwood Ave.), 215-222-3699

■ Owner Richard DeMatt's "personal" approach seems to be "improving" this Eclectic sixtysomething BYO in an "old, cheerful house", as surveyors say that the West Philly "institution's" "home cooking" is "getting better and better"; in other words, chowing down on a plate of meatloaf or digging into Sunday brunch here is "like eating at your grandmother's, but grandmom didn't cook this good."

Marker, The ⑤   21 | 21 | 20 | $43
Adam's Mark Philadelphia, 400 City Ave. (Monument Rd.), 215-581-5010

☒ A klatch of commoners "feels like royalty" at the "posh, pricey" Continental "hidden" inside the Adam's Mark, where despite "elegant" decor and "beautiful presentations", you "aren't uncomfortable if you're not wearing your best clothes"; "Sunday brunch is a fabulous" "treat", with a "piano player included as part of the deal", but fussy foodies feel that the "ordinary hotel dining room fare" doesn't do justice to the place's "pretensions of grandeur."

80   **subscribe to zagat.com**

Philadelphia

F | D | S | C

Marmont Steakhouse S   – | 19 | 18 | $31
222 Market St. (bet. 2nd & 3rd Sts.), 215-923-1100

◪ "If you're in your 20s", "dress in black" and "join the party" at this "delicious" Old City boîte, which morphed post-*Survey* into a modest-priced steakhouse; groupies say it's a "great place for a date or hanging out with your friends" over stunningly presented prime cuts and "cool" "cocktails that speak for themselves."

Marrakesh S∄   20 | 22 | 21 | $31
517 S. Leithgow St. (bet. 4th & 5th Sts.), 215-925-5929

■ "Aladdin meets fine dining" at this cash-only, "family-run" Moroccan "bargain" down a "back alley" off South Street; it's so "dark" and "sensual" inside, it's "a great place to seduce and be seduced", though when you dip "your fingers" into your meal it's "a little scary, since you can't see what you're eating"; still, after a "delightfully different" seven-course dinner, your hands will emerge with your "thumbs up."

Marra's S   20 | 11 | 15 | $19
1734 E. Passyunk Ave. (bet. Moore & Morris Sts.), 215-463-9249

■ Where "the waitresses' popping gum is deafening" and it seems like "the gravy's been simmering for decades", the "rat-pack" "masses flock in for a reason": "salad and pizza and a cannoli, the perfect cheap meal" "South Philly style" at this "true" Southern Italian "favorite" that's been around since 1927.

Mayfair Diner ●S   16 | 13 | 19 | $15
7373 Frankford Ave. (Bleigh Ave.), 215-624-8886

■ Those who appreciate "old values" say this Northeast Philly "classic" is "just what a neighborhood diner should be"; it's "bright and clean", with a meatloaf-and-mashed-potatoes cuisine that makes you "feel like a kid again" and a "sensibly priced", "delicious" breakfast served 24 hours a day – what else is there to say except "more coffee, hon?"

McCormick & Schmick's S   20 | 22 | 20 | $39
1 S. Broad St. (Penn Sq.), 215-568-6888

■ "You can order anything from a sardine to a shark" at this "seafood lover's delight" on the Avenue of the Arts, so "power brokers" "swim in from all over" to sample the "good basic fish"; if gourmet guppies gripe about a "run-of-the-mill" "chain experience", even "landlubbers" dive into the "amazing" "happy-hour" nibbles.

McFadden's S   – | – | – | M
461 N. Third St. (bet. Spring Garden & Willow Sts.), 215-928-0630

Fun-seekers in droves have found this dark, woody Celtic pub chainster near Northern Liberties; though the bar, 17

vote at zagat.com   81

Philadelphia | F | D | S | C |

TVs and DJ are the big draws, some say it's ok to settle into love seats and booths for burgers and desserts, including smashed cookie ice cream made on the premises.

McGillin's Olde Ale House ● | 15 | 16 | 16 | $17 |
1310 Drury St. (bet. Chestnut & Sansom Sts.), 215-735-5562
■ Grab some "fun" "friends" and "step back in time" at this "big, noisy" Drury Lane bar, "still happening" after 140-plus years; it's a "great place to get drunk" on "cheap beer" and gnaw on "Tuesday-night wings" and other American "pub grub" specials.

Melrose Diner ●S⊅ | 16 | 12 | 18 | $14 |
1501 Snyder Ave. (15th St.), 215-467-6644
☑ If "*Alice* was your favorite show", visit this South Philly "landmark" 'cause she "still lives here"; the "waitresses are cranky", you have to "share a booth with strangers" and they "charge for a second cup of coffee", pal, but you can gorge yourself 24/7 on the "quintessential" "local flavor" of the joint; "yech", gasp gourmands, "too bad you can't eat the mystique."

Melting Pot S | 19 | 17 | 18 | $32 |
8229 Germantown Ave. (Southampton Ave.), 215-242-3003
☑ "A whole new generation" is "playing with their food" thanks to this "entertaining" fonduery in Chestnut Hill, where you're bound to "gain about 10 pounds" at each "delicious" seating; it's an "icebreaker", for sure, though jaded palates suggest all that "dipping" can get "monotonous" and "kind of expensive."

Mendenhall Inn S | 22 | 22 | 22 | $43 |
Mendenhall Inn, Kennett Pike (1 mi. south of Rte. 1), Mendenhall, 610-388-1181
■ "Bring mom" for a night of "pure pleasure" straight out of the "old school" at this "staid but sophisticated Chesco standby" for New American fare "impeccably presented"; the "setting is gorgeous", the service is "classy" and the "blue-haired" gal will "feel like a queen" gobbling up bananas Foster made "tableside."

Mexican Post ●S | 18 | 13 | 17 | $20 |
104 Chestnut St. (Front St.), 215-923-5233
☑ "It's not fancy, it's just fun" slurs the "rowdy after-work crowd" at this Mexican fiesta "in the heart of Old City"; in the afterglow of the "strong margaritas", the eats seem all the more "tasty", though *los críticos* crack that the "joint" is "so crowded" only "'cause the mediocre food is so cheap."

Mezza Luna S | 23 | 18 | 21 | $35 |
763 S. Eighth St. (Catharine St.), 215-627-4705
■ *Amici* call it the "gravy de la gravy" of South Philly, where "melt-in-your-mouth" ricotta gnocchi with Gorgonzola

Philadelphia F | D | S | C

sauce and other "lovely" Italian "indulgences" are "to die for", but they're "not for the calorie-conscious"; the staff is "friendly" and "full of personality", and with a "warm atmosphere" "to match", this "rather sophisticated" "gem" gives off the vibe that "everybody's family."

Michael's Ristorante S | 20 | 17 | 20 | $38
824 S. Eighth St. (Christian St.), 215-922-3986
"If you're in South Philly at mealtime", this "family" feedery "in the heart of Italian country" is "not bad" for all your "typical red-sauce" "favorites", and if you're really hungry, ya "gotta go" for the signature veal chop because healthy appetites insist it's the "largest they've ever had"; if you're out of the area, "disappointed" diners dish "don't bother" making the trip.

Mikado S | ∇ 24 | 21 | 19 | $27
66 E. Lancaster Ave. (Simpson Rd.), Ardmore, 610-645-5592
"Nothing beats the volcano roll" boast boosters boiling over with praise for Thai Pepper's Japanese cousin next door in Ardmore; "first-rate" fish sliced by "experienced chefs" makes for "excellent sushi" to sample along with a "decent selection of sakes" in "beautiful" duplex digs.

Minar Palace | 21 | 6 | 14 | $12
1605 Sansom St. (bet. 16th & 17th Sts.), 215-564-9443
"Overlook the cafeteria trays" and the "dreary dining room" for "absolutely" "killer" chow "at rock-bottom prices" at this Center City Indian; it's "not just your standard chicken tikka masala", but boy, is the place a "dump" – no wonder "they do a lot of take-out business."

Mirna's Cafe S | 21 | 14 | 17 | $30
Center Sq., 758 DeKalb Pike (Skippack Pike), Blue Bell, 610-279-0500
417 Old York Rd. (West Ave.), Jenkintown, 215-885-2046
While the "quieter", newer Blue Bell location is "much roomier", "you can almost taste the food at the table next to you" in the close, "hectic" Jenkintown quarters – but that's ok because all the "bountiful" Med-Eclectic meals are "fab" at these "inventive" BYOs; now if you could only "hear yourself chew" over the "suburban moms and screaming tots", the "surly" servers' "rude" remarks and the "people raving about the fare."

Mixto S | – | – | – | M
1141 Pine St. (bet. Quince & 12th Sts.), 215-592-0363
The folks from North Philly's humble Tierra Colombiana are rocking Wash West with this highly polished Cuban-Colombian addition spread over adjoining row houses; while the exposed brick, wooden beams and massive skylight are highly pleasing (as is the vibe at the upstairs

vote at zagat.com   83

Philadelphia   F | D | S | C

bar), some are not as impressed with the food (filling, if somewhat bland) or the service (slow).

Mokas   – | – | – | M
3505 Lancaster Ave. (35th St.), 215-222-4410
Founded by a veteran of Dmitri's, this new Greek taverna in University City fills the need for homestyle moussaka, lamb kebabs and other Mediterranean delights in civilized surroundings near Drexel U; the crackling fireplace and nightly live piano music stoke the romance level indoors, while the grapevine-covered patio beckons outdoors.

Monk's Cafe ◐ S   21 | 15 | 17 | $23
264 S. 16th St. (Spruce St.), 215-545-7005
■ A "legendary selection" of suds in the bottle and on tap makes this "funky" yet "upscale" Center City Belgian a "beer-experimenter's paradise", but the clientele also gets "crazy cravings" for the "excellent" pommes frites, "superb mussels, burgers" and other "hearty fare"; the "jumpin', joyous" joint is "packed" with "boisterous" "worshipers" who've "taken a vow of loudness", so if you're into quiet contemplation, don't go on weekends.

MONTE CARLO LIVING ROOM   25 | – | 23 | $56
150 South St. (2nd St.), 215-925-2220
■ "Top-notch all around", this "upscale" Italian on South Street is garnering even more kudos nowadays thanks to new chef Robert Capella's (ex Founders) wizardry in the kitchen and the elegantly redone front of the house, which is now appointed with a French country look; regulars say the "gracious", "professional" staff hasn't lost its touch, while the Tony Maneros in the crowd still appreciate the opportunity to work off their "fabulous" meal at the club "upstairs that feels like *The Last Days of Disco*."

Moody Monkey S   ▽ 17 | 19 | 17 | $23
2508 W. Main St. (Egypt Rd.), Jeffersonville, 610-631-1233
◪ Surveyors swing over to this Eclectic in Montco for its "fantastic beer selection" and they also go ape for the "lively", "surprisingly hip" decor, but they're split over the "ambitious" menu, with supporters going bananas for the "varied menu" of "affordable" eats, including "great appetizers", and protesters proclaiming this primate "needs to get the kinks out."

Moonstruck S   23 | 22 | 22 | $38
7955 Oxford Ave. (Rhawn St.), 215-725-6000
■ "Loved from day one", this "fabulous, glamorous" spot serving Northern Italian delicacies in Northeast Philly is "improving all the time"; mealsters moon over "fresh", "first-rate cooking", "very friendly" service and a "marvelous" setting, which is "separated into intimate dining alcoves" for optimum "romance."

Philadelphia F D S C

More Than Just Ice Cream S 20 | 13 | 15 | $16
1119 Locust St. (11th St.), 215-574-0586

Sure, sugar, "desserts are queen" at this "fun, gay hangout" in Center City, where coneheads concur that the "ice cream rocks" and the "spectacular deep-dish apple pie" in "ridiculously large portions" proves that size really does matter; devotees who delight in the "tasty salads, sandwiches" and other "light" New American fare insist the "joint" "is so much more" than just sweet, though it takes its licks for "slow service."

Moriarty's ●S 16 | 14 | 16 | $20
1116 Walnut St. (11th St.), 215-627-7676

"Good before or after the theater for a quick bite", this "busy, youthful" Center City pub dishes out "meaty" "wings beyond belief" and "sandwiches and burgers to go with" the "great beer" selection; the "noisy", "cramped" *Cheers*-meets–TGI Friday's atmosphere makes you feel like you're being "jammed in with a shoehorn", but whaddya expect from your "standard" "frat boy" "hangout"?

Morimoto S – | – | – | VE
723 Chestnut St. (bet. 7th & 8th Sts.), 215-413-9070

Iron Chef Masaharu Morimoto and golden boy Stephen Starr "rock Philly" with their "cool" Japanese joint on Jewelers Row; amid a "wonderfully lit" "gorgeous interior" by Karim Rashid, diners embark on an "extraordinary" culinary cruise to "sushi heaven" and other heights with the eponymous captain "in action" and "making the rounds to all the tables"; the only catch is "it's so pricey, you can't go often" enough.

Morning Glory Diner S⌀ 23 | 14 | 17 | $15
735 S. 10th St. (Fitzwater St.), 215-413-3999

What's the story with this "upscale" South Philly diner "convenient to the Italian Market"? – it's small, "too popular and thus too crowded", creating "unbearable waits", but nevertheless, it's "worth it", especially at "weekend brunch", for "glorious" "twists on traditional breakfasts" gobbled with "great cups of java"; when the sun goes down, nightingales tell tales of "hearty" "home cooking."

MORTON'S OF CHICAGO S 24 | 21 | 23 | $55
1411 Walnut St. (bet. Broad & 15th Sts.), 215-557-0724
Pavilion at King of Prussia Mall, 500 Mall Blvd. (DeKalb Pike), King of Prussia, 610-491-1900

"If you want to dress up, eat a steak, drink a bottle of red wine, maybe have a cigar", perhaps "impress clients", this pair of "sophisticated" meat "lovers' paradises" in Center City and King of Prussia "is the place"; the "mouthwatering" "choice cuts" and "unbelievable sides" come in "gigantic portions" (no, "you won't starve"), and it's all toted to table by an "enthusiastic" staff; "add some taste to the size" beef

vote at zagat.com

Philadelphia

F | D | S | C

bashers, who also find the "he-man prices" and "fawning service off-putting."

Moshulu S
– | – | – | E
401 S. Columbus Blvd. (Delaware River), 215-923-2500
First launched in 1904, this 394-foot, four-masted bark – the oldest and largest still afloat in the world – is about to resurface at press time on Penn's Landing after a tragic pier collapse in 2000; lavishly restored, it now gives off a sultry South Seas feel, providing a transporting Polynesian backdrop for chef Ralph Fernandez's New American cooking; needless to say, book a window table or sit out on the deck to take in a stellar view of the Delaware River waterfront; N.B. jacket required.

Mothers' S
16 | 15 | 17 | $28
34 N. Main St. (bet. Bridge & Randolph Sts.), New Hope, 215-862-9354
☑ Offering "homestyle" fare that tastes "just like mom's" but in slightly more "unusual combinations", this "nothing fancy ol' reliable" American in New Hope "keeps 'em coming back"; "it's not growing old gracefully" squawk snipers estranged by the "formulaic" fare and "slow" service, though ironists find the staff "a riot", "tossing" food "on the table" like "they're doing you a favor."

Mr. Martino's Trattoria S≠
22 | 18 | 21 | $26
1646 E. Passyunk Ave. (bet. Morris & Tasker Sts.), 215-755-0663
■ "Travel back in time for a great Italian meal" at this South Philly BYO in an "intimate" storefront "that's deliciously dark and old-world", just the "romantic atmosphere for a date"; the "chef makes the most of a small menu" that includes "outstanding pasta", the "staff makes you feel at home" and the "unbelievably reasonable" prices enhance the comfort level; N.B. dinner only, Thursday–Sunday.

Murray's Deli S≠
18 | 9 | 15 | $16
285 Montgomery Ave. (Levering Mill Rd.), Bala Cynwyd, 610-664-6995
☑ One "warring" faction of Jewish soul food aficionados insists that this Bala deli "king" leaves the competition "in the dust" with the Main Line's "only remaining decent corned beef on rye", plus "they know what they're doing" with "wonderful chopped liver" and borscht; those who refuse to take sides say it boasts the same "crabby service" and "dumpsville" decor as the other joint – the "only difference" is that the "diners dress better with nicer jewelry" to "see and be seen."

Mustard Greens S
23 | 16 | 20 | $26
622 S. Second St. (bet. Bainbridge & South Sts.), 215-627-0833
■ The "fresh, flavorful" and "healthful" takes on Chinese cuisine offered at this "contemporary" "alternative" near

Philadelphia   F | D | S | C

South Street are "always a pleasure" to "repeat" customers, who can't get enough of its "heavenly garlic noodles" and other "clean, light" dishes, all prepared "with flair" and served with "personality"; it's a "different kind of cooking" from the standard, but it's "reliable time after time."

My Thai S   21 | 16 | 19 | $23
2200 South St. (22nd St.), 215-985-1878

■ Attracting a "devoted cult following" for good reason, this "tiny", "homey" South Street "find" "never disappoints" with its "tantalizing" Thai "comfort food", "beautifully presented" in "calm" surroundings by an "unobtrusive" staff; factor in "reasonable prices" and the result is a "wonderful surprise."

Nais Cuisine S   23 | 12 | 20 | $32
13 W. Benedict Ave. (Darby Rd.), Havertown, 610-789-5983

✌ You can "count on" "marvelous" New French–Thai fare at this family-owned BYO "hole-in-the-wall" in Havertown, a "favorite old" "gem that improves with age" according to those who "always have a good meal here", especially if they order the "best roast duckling in the suburbs"; dissenters say it's "nothing special", citing "unexciting" fare and "out-of-date" "rec room" decor that "won't turn any heads."

NAN   26 | 18 | 22 | $33
4000 Chestnut St. (40th St.), 215-382-0818

■ It might "look like a corner store from the outside", but inside there's a "diamond in the rough" – a "pleasant", if "spartan", setting allows University City diners to focus on chef-owner Kamol Phutlek's "fabulous", "artistically presented" "fusion" of New French and Thai flavors that positively "sparkle"; it's a "great" BYO "bargain" staffed by "lovely people" and "quiet enough to actually talk", leading scores of smitten sorts to urge "don't miss it."

New Delhi S   20 | 12 | 16 | $15
4004 Chestnut St. (bet. 40th & 41st Sts.), 215-386-1941

✌ "You know what you're getting" at this "authentic" Indian in University City, considered by wallet-watching freshmen a "perfect college restaurant" for its "cheap" lunch and dinner buffets featuring fare that's "excellent for beginners"; it's "not the best in town, but it's pretty darn good", despite the "dingy" digs.

New Orleans Cafe S   22 | 21 | 18 | $31
1 W. State St. (Jackson St.), Media, 610-627-4393

✌ "Everything's delicious" and there's "lots of it" at this "posh" Cajun-Creole cafe, so fans "save on airfare" to the Big Easy and savor the "spice" in Media instead; purists gripe about "hit-or-miss" fare that "falls short" of the real

vote at zagat.com

Philadelphia | F | D | S | C |

deal and warn that the "spotty", "uninterested" service is an even "weaker link."

New Wave Café ●S | 24 | 12 | 19 | $27 |
784 S. Third St. (Catharine St.), 215-922-8484

☑ "Don't let" the "dumpy" "taproom" quarters "fool you", because "friendly" "bar scene meets fine dining" at this "unique" New American "surprise" in Queen Village, where appreciative locals can "eat well without having to dress up", or dress New Wave; new chef Jason Seraydarian picks up where Ben McNamara left off, tempting with "truly outstanding" cooking (and you won't "pay a lot of money"), so naturally, there's a "long wait for a table" at this no-reservations spot.

Nifty Fifty's S⊄ | 17 | 18 | 17 | $12 |
2491 Grant Ave. (Roosevelt Blvd.), 215-676-1950
2555 Street Rd. (Knights Rd.), Bensalem, 215-638-1950
1900 MacDade Blvd. (Kedron Ave.), Folsom, 610-583-1950

☑ "Only the carhops are missing" from these "entertaining", "neon"-bedecked "diner re-creations" that "bring back" the "retro" "fun" foods of the "'50s – "greasy burgers", "freshly made" fries and "phenomenal milkshakes"; it's such a "cool blast from the past" that you almost "expect to see the Fonz" out on a "cheap date", though he's probably got "Excedrin" in the pocket of his leather jacket, because the atmosphere "is a zoo."

Nodding Head Brewery & Restaurant ●S | 17 | 14 | 16 | $19 |
1516 Sansom St., 2nd fl. (bet. 15th & 16th Sts.), 215-569-9525

■ Guzzlers nod in agreement that this "dark", second-floor Center City brewpub is "heads above" the pack for "worthy" handcrafted beers and American "bar food" like "great burgers" and the "hottest wings", as well as vegan options, served in a "friendly" atmosphere at "amazingly low prices"; even if it's "in need of a broader menu", regulars say it's "as much fun to hang out here as to eat."

Noodle Heaven S | 15 | 11 | 15 | $18 |
224 S. Broad St. (Locust St.), 215-735-6191

☑ "Conveniently" located near the Academy of Music, this Avenue of the Arts Chinese BYO serving "run-of-the-mill" chow "could be fancier", but at least the "zippy" staff gets you in and out "quickly", so it's "adequate" for an "inexpensive" "fix" before a show, though goodness knows, it's "not heaven."

North by Northwest S | 19 | 21 | 20 | $25 |
7165 Germantown Ave. (bet. Mt. Airy & Mt. Pleasant Aves.), 215-248-1000

☑ What becomes of "old Woolworth's" stores? – they morph into "lively" nightclubs with "plenty of room", "good"

Philadelphia   F | D | S | C

"vibes" and "great" "live acts" to "breathe life" into local scenes; thus is the story of this Mount Airy American, and even if the "upscale comfort food" is "under par" and the service "inconsistent", residents embrace it as a "welcome addition" to an "underused part of the city", hoping this "ambientious undertaking may help revive the neighborhood."

North Sea ◐S   ▽ 24 | 14 | 20 | $22
153 N. 10th St. (Race St.), 215-925-1906

■ "Really fresh" seafood plucked from "the tank" reels fin fanatics into this unassuming Chinatown Chinese; insiders suggest "don't order from the menu – point to what others are eating and you'll get authentic" Cantonese food, including the "essential salt-baked soft-shell crabs."

N. 3rd ◐S   – | – | – | M
801 N. Third St. (Brown St.), 215-413-3666

Perfectly pitched for up-and-coming Northern Liberties, this dark, arty bar serves ribs, mac 'n' cheese and other hearty, modest-priced American comfort food from a blackboard menu, with a welcoming vibe and people-watching on the side; N.B. an adjacent space presents live music in cozy quarters.

Novelty S   21 | 23 | 21 | $42
15 S. Third St. (bet. Chestnut & Market Sts.), 215-627-7885

■ In the "oh-so-cool" former crib of a toy and gags shop, "Jake's little brother" is a "novel", "stylish" spot in Old City; the "inventive", "well-executed" New American menu offers "trendy" "fun" to the "cacophonic" "twentysomething crowd" that goes to "hog heaven" over the tasty fare, in particular the "always interesting" 'novelty box' sampler, which changes daily.

Oasis S   19 | 21 | 18 | $30
1709 Walnut St. (17th St.), 215-751-0888

◪ With its waterfalls and dim lighting, this "beautiful" Center City oasis is a "soothing" refuge that has retooled its "eclectic Asian menu" to "focus more" on Japanese cuisine; the consensus is the "sushi is good", but "other menu selections vary" in quality and are "unadventurous" "for the price", plus service trickles more "slowly" than the aquaceous decor feature.

Ocean Harbor ◐S   20 | 12 | 15 | $20
1023 Race St. (bet. 10th & 11th Sts.), 215-574-1398

■ "Take a group of people" to this "chaotic" Chinatown "classic" for dim sum and "be adventurous", easy to do when the little plates are so "superb", "authentic" and "cheap"; the "huge variety" of dinner offerings are "above the norm" too, especially the "delightful" "Hong Kong"– style whole fish that's "not to be missed."

vote at zagat.com   89

Philadelphia

| F | D | S | C |

Odette's ⑤   20 | 19 | 19 | $43
S. River Rd. (Rte. 32), New Hope, 215-862-2432

◪ "Dinner and cabaret" or the "fun sing-along piano bar" "makes for a very pleasant 'something different' evening" while the gazebo is "great for a nice luncheon overlooking the river" at this "charming" New Hope Continental set in a 1794 tavern; but you may want to just "go for a drink" poured by an "old-fashioned bartender", since the fare gets mixed reviews, ranging from "great" to "average."

Old Guard House Inn   23 | 21 | 22 | $44
953 Youngsford Rd. (Righters Mill Rd.), Gladwyne, 610-649-9708

■ "Nothing has changed here in 20 years", and "you can bet your blue blazer" that Gladwyners are glad; "preppies past" and present giddyap for "super-super food" and "atmosphere galore" to this "dark", "refined" American-Continental in an "18th-century stagecoach stop", and if you think the joint's for "snobs" only, visit on "a blustery night" to get a load of the "WASP retirees shoulder-to-shoulder with Main Line's tree surgeons" in the "most diverse bar" crowd in the big-money suburbs.

Ooka Japanese ⑤   ∇ 19 | 16 | 20 | $26
1109 Easton Rd. (Fitzwatertown Rd.), Willow Grove, 215-659-7688

◪ The "swordsmen" put on "a show preparing intriguing entrées" at the hibachi tables at this Willow Grove Japanese BYO where the "grill food is very tasty" but the sushi seems to be "hit or miss" – fans flip for "first-rate" fish, while foes find the "average quality" a flop; monolinguists lament "waitresses who don't understand American."

OPUS 251 ⑤   24 | 24 | 22 | $48
Philadelphia Art Alliance, 251 S. 18th St. (bet. Latimer & Locust Sts.), 215-735-6787

◪ It's an "artful alliance" at the Art Alliance; this New American "tucked" into the "mansion" off Rittenhouse Square pairs "scrumptious" fare, a "charming" "jewel box" of a room and a "gracious" garden for "transporting European"-style dining; too bad too many say there's "too little" food and too much "attitude" "for the price."

Ortlieb's Jazzhaus ●⑤   17 | 15 | 17 | $25
847 N. Third St. (Poplar St.), 215-922-1035

■ The "food won't kill you" at this "relaxed" Northern Liberties "speakeasy", but really "nothing matters but the great jazz"; home to "hot live" beats and "decent Cajun" eats, the former Ortlieb's cafeteria is a "Philly classic", though it's certainly "not the place for a quiet dinner."

Otto's Brauhaus ⑤   18 | 16 | 18 | $27
233 Easton Rd. (Pine Ave.), Horsham, 215-675-1864

■ It's "German – what more can we say" except "you won't go away hungry" after "good beer and bratwurst" in the

Philadelphia   F | D | S | C

biergarten at this "suburban stomach-stuffer" in Horsham; they're "unfortunately attired" in "traditional garb", but the "friendly fräuleins" hold their heads up nonetheless, adding "a lot to the spirit of things."

Outback Steakhouse S   17 | 14 | 16 | $27
3240 Tillman Dr. (Street Rd.), Bensalem, 215-633-8228
322 W. Ridge Pike (Chemical Rd.), Conshohocken, 610-828-8931
675 Lancaster Ave. (Rte. 202), Frazer, 610-407-9444
Glen Eagle Square Shopping Ctr., 561 Glen Eagle Sq. (Wilmington Pike), Glen Mills, 610-558-0644
2520 York Rd. (Rte. 263), Jamison, 215-918-2019
610 Old York Rd. (Baeder Rd.), Jenkintown, 215-886-5120
202 Marketplace, 411 Doylestown Pike (Horsham Rd.), Montgomeryville, 215-855-1060
Olde Sproul Shopping Village, 1162 Baltimore Pike (Sproul Rd.), Springfield, 610-544-9889

☒ "Oh, that bloomin' onion" squeal devotees of this "fake Australian" steak chain that "attracts the masses" for "big portions" of "ok", "high-cholesterol" fare and "perky", "dependable" service; just take the "beeper" and "go out back, out front, wherever" to endure a "wait that seems to take forever", despite negativists nattering "take your Rolaids with you."

OVERTURES S   25 | 22 | 23 | $44
609 E. Passyunk Ave. (bet. Bainbridge & South Sts.), 215-627-3455

■ "Bring your Château Margeaux" to this "elegant and affordable gourmet BYO" off South Street, where you and "that special person" will be "pampered and pleased" by French-Med "perfection" on a plate presented by a "wonderfully friendly and capable" staff; just "don't go after you get a tattoo across the street" lest it clash with the "beautiful trompe l'oeil" decor.

Pace One S   21 | 21 | 20 | $40
Pace One Country Inn, 341 Thornton Rd. (Glen Mills Rd.), Thornton, 610-459-3702

☒ "A guaranteed hit to take visitors" "to impress, or just treat yourself to a real night out" is this Traditional American in a "romantic old farmhouse with a cute terrace" in Thornton; fans say the "fresh seafood bar can't be beat" and the rest of the "interesting" offerings are "tasty" as well, though fans find the "chef needs hints on presentation."

Paganini Pizza & Cafe S   ▽ 18 | 13 | 14 | $22
72 W. State St. (Clinton St.), Doylestown, 215-348-9600

☒ It may not be virtuoso, but this "casual" Italian offshoot of the same-named trattoria across the street in Doylestown hits some "nice" notes for a "light bite" of "great pizzas and salads"; the decor is "nothing to look at", so it's best

Philadelphia

F | D | S | C

to hang out on the patio and try not to be bugged by the "unfriendly service."

Paganini Trattoria S 19 | 19 | 16 | $32
81 W. State St. (Clinton St.), Doylestown, 215-348-5922
A "limited selection" of "fresh pasta dishes is prepared and presented innovatively" at this "casual" but "classy" Doylestown Italian; architecturally inclined auditors say an "irrational layout" leads to "somewhat noisy acoustics inside", but it's "fun" to take in the "sidewalk views" from the "great patio."

Palace of Asia S 20 | 17 | 18 | $27
Best Western Inn, 285 Commerce Dr. (bet. Bethlehem Pike & Susquehanna Rd.), Fort Washington, 215-646-2133
"The place is usually crowded with Indians", and that "confirms" the "reliability" of this "first-rate" subcontinental "near an industrial park" in the Fort Washington Best Western; it "looks like a dive from the outside, but inside awaits" a "delicious discovery", despite the fumblings of a "well-meaning but confused staff."

PALM S 24 | 19 | 22 | $49
Park Hyatt at the Bellevue, 200 S. Broad St. (Walnut St.), 215-546-7256
It's "like a high school reunion" with "all the glitterati" and "wanna-bes" "aisle politicking" in "show-off jewelry and designer duds" at this "noisy" "boys' club" at the Bellevue; "when you're in the mood for steak" as monstrous as "Wilma Flintstone served" or "a prehistorically sized lobster", take a few gulps of a "big, wonderful martini", "get a cigar" and wrap your mind around the fact that "table-hopping egomaniacs" and the "snobby" staff that serves them are simply "part of the allure."

Paloma ▽ 26 | 20 | 24 | $43
6516 Castor Ave. (bet. Hellerman St. & Magee Ave.), 215-533-0356
"Why go into town" when Adan Saavedra turns out an "artfully presented", "sophisticated blend" of French and Mexican cuisines at this "rare find" right on Castor Avenue?; with an "absolutely charming" interior and "service that's attentive but not intrusive", the Northeast "is fortunate to have a restaurant like this", so if you haven't been, surveyors insist "go now!"

Pantheon S – | – | – | VE
Ritz-Carlton Philadelphia, 10 S. Broad St. (Chestnut St.), 215-735-7700
The Ritz-Carlton has retooled the menu of its Italian eatery into a decent American comfort-food list that's going over like gangbusters among business diners fleeing the Avenue of the Arts crush; there's no denying the elegant setting,

Philadelphia

F | **D** | **S** | **C**

which opens onto the most smashing lobby in the city, with a dome that re-creates that of its Roman namesake; N.B. breakfast and Sunday brunch only.

Paradigm
19 | 22 | 17 | $37

239 Chestnut St. (bet. 2nd & 3rd Sts.), 215-238-6900

▨ Trying hard to fulfill its "hip" paradigm, this "lively" American-Continental in Old City "rocks at night" with a "fun, sexy" vibe, and it's not just because of the "magical bathroom doors" that "fog" when locked (or provide a "free show" when they're not!) – it's also the "ultra-trendy" crowd sipping "great apple martinis" served by "scantily clad help"; diners find the fare is "actually pretty good", though it "doesn't live up to the decor."

¡PASIÓN! S
26 | 24 | 24 | $50

211 S. 15th St. (bet. Locust & Walnut Sts.), 215-875-9895

■ Passion runs high for Guillermo Pernot's "cutting-edge" cooking at this Center City Nuevo Latino where "everything is superlative", from "tantalizing" seviches to "orgasmic" grilled meats; add in "sexy" decor that "tells the story without being a theme park", plus "flawless" service from a staff "with loads of personality", and the experience equals a "splurge" "worth writing home about."

Passage to India S
18 | 15 | 18 | $20

1320 Walnut St. (Juniper St.), 215-732-7300

▨ "If you live or work nearby", "try the lunch buffet", or go for an "inexpensive", "quick bite before the orchestra" at this "reliable", "white-tablecloth" Indian in Center City, where the meal is enhanced by the "piano player's ABBA" tunes; one diner's "relaxed" is another diner's "tired", however, with detractors dissing the "bland" bites.

PASSERELLE S
24 | 25 | 23 | $52

175 King of Prussia Rd. (Lancaster Ave.), Radnor, 610-293-9411

■ With "large windows overlooking a peaceful scene", the "pond and swans are included in the price" of a "first-class" meal at this "dreamy" Main Line Franco-American in a "refurbished farmhouse", where "luscious" dishes are delivered by "vigilant but unintrusive servers"; it may be *très cher,* but "take mom" anyway, use your "expense account" and "celebrate anything" you can think of.

Pat's King of Steaks ●S≠
19 | 8 | 13 | $9

1237 E. Passyunk Ave. (9th St.), 215-468-1546

▨ When you find yourself at "3 AM, cheese running down your arms", at the possible "ground zero of the cheese steak universe" "with lots of other drunk people", and the "pigeons are cleaning up after you", "don't be afraid" – just enjoy the "quintessential Philadelphia" feast of "gooey, greasy, yummy junk food with attitude" at this 24-hour South

vote at zagat.com 93

Philadelphia F D S C

Philly stand; whether the king deserves its self-selected crown is a hot debate, however, with insurgents insisting it's "not all it's cracked up to be."

Pattaya Grill S 21 | 15 | 19 | $23
4006 Chestnut St. (40th St.), 215-387-8533

◪ For those who "always enjoy" getting a "treat for a reduced price", the "great early-bird" at this University City Thai "reliably" fits the bill; at other times, the offerings are "good but not particularly memorable", though if you think "spice" is nice, you "may request more zest in any dish", and the "sunroom is lovely" for a meal.

Peacock on the Parkway 19 | 17 | 19 | $28
1700 Benjamin Franklin Pkwy. (17th St.), 215-569-8888

■ This "proud" bird struts its stuff on the Parkway with one of the "best lunch deals in town"; "inventive but not out of this world", the "wide selection" of American-Med dishes is as "consistently" "pleasant" as the "lovely" atmosphere created by a "friendly family" that pitches in – "papa cooks, mama is the hostess" and their daughter manages the place.

Peking S 24 | 20 | 21 | $27
Granite Run Mall, 1067 E. Baltimore Pike (Middletown Rd.), Media, 610-566-4110

■ It's "a shock to find such a gem in the middle of Granite Run Mall" marvel surveyors sweet on Margaret Kuo's "beautiful" "linen-tablecloth" Chinese-Japanese; though the signature duck, "excellent fish specials" and other "fantastic" fare might lead you to "think you're in NYC", "very fair prices" remind you that this is Delaware County.

Penang ●S≠ 22 | 18 | 19 | $23
117 N. Tenth St. (bet. Arch & Cherry Sts.), 215-413-2531

◪ An "eclectic crowd" sits "elbow to elbow" in Chinatown on an "adventure without fear" at this "bustling" Malaysian, "taking chances on" "delicious", "exotic" "treasures" from the "huge menu"; if you're too timid for "some of Philly's most unusual entrées", "you can't go wrong with the noodle dishes", though the "eye-catching industrial" "metal decor" makes the room so "loud" that if "you don't know what you ordered", your server might not either.

Penne S – | – | – | M
Inn at Penn, 3611 Walnut St. (36th St.), 215-832-6222

There's more than just a pun at work in the name of the Inn at Penn's Italian addition in the heart of University City, as patrons can see for themselves the pastas handmade by Roberta Adamo in her open so-called pasta lab stationed right in the dining room that's done up with faux stone walls and Roman busts; what's more, the wine bar offers an exemplary list of 50-plus wines by the glass as well as a selection of flights.

Philadelphia   F | D | S | C

Pepper's Cafe ∌   21 | 9 | 20 | $16
2528 Haverford Rd. (Eagle Rd.), Ardmore, 610-896-0476
■ For "drive-by pasta or a sandwich" when you "just don't want to cook", pull up to this BYO "shack" "wedged between auto-body shops" in Ardmore; while locals "don't expect fine dining", Kate Rapine's Italian dishes "could pass for mom's", and she prepares them "right in front of you" in the "smallest restaurant around"; needless to say, "there's very limited seating, but it's excellent for takeout."

Persian Grill S   20 | 11 | 18 | $25
637 Germantown Pike (Joshua Rd.), Lafayette Hill, 610-825-2705
■ "Insiders know to ask for the 'crispy' rice" at this Middle Eastern in Montco; "it looks like a diner", and like a diner, "it's always packed", but the servers aren't sending out eggs over easy – "outstanding", "aromatic" dishes like "fresh hummus", "fabulous chicken" and signature lamb attract devotees, as do "great flavored vodkas" and an "excellent beer list."

Philadelphia Fish & Co. S   21 | 18 | 20 | $34
207 Chestnut St. (2nd St.), 215-625-8605
■ Get "everything you want without the Walnut Street price tag", "pomp and circumstance" at this "dependable" Chestnut Street seafooder; the "fish is fresh and the servers aren't – just as it should be", plus the "owners make the rounds" to keep an eye on the "pleasant" dining room and make sure your meal goes "swimmingly well."

Philly Crab & Steak House S   21 | 15 | 19 | $31
Grant & Academy Shopping Ctr., 3334 Grant Ave. (Academy Rd.), 215-856-9510
355 York Rd. (Street Rd.), Warminster, 215-444-9208
◪ "I loved the steak, she loved the crab" he said of the "good" meal they consumed at one of these surf 'n' turf twins in Northeast Philadelphia and Warminster; like our hero and heroine, if you "stick to the basics, you'll be satisfied", despite Grant Avenue's "dark", "odd decor" and "lousy location."

Pho 75 S∌   22 | 7 | 15 | $11
823 Adams Ave. (Roosevelt Blvd.), 215-743-8845
1122 Washington Ave. (12th St.), 215-271-5866
◪ "For restaurants that serve only soup, there's no better place" to load up on the stuff than this South Philly/Northeast Vietnamese duo where the "comfort" comes "fast", "cheap" and "tasty"; for your "in-pho", despite "sub-zero" "grocery store" decor, these "joints" "rule."

Pho Xe Lua S   ▽ 21 | 9 | 20 | $15
907 Race St. (9th St.), 215-627-8883
■ The "decor is diner-style, but don't let that fool you", since "throngs" of "locals can't be wrong" about this Thai-

vote at zagat.com   95

Philadelphia

F | D | S | C

Viet "hangout" in Chinatown; the "staff loves to suggest", so "be adventurous" and you'll be "rewarded" with "treasures" like lemongrass soup and "unbeatable milkshakes" made with mango or, for really esoteric appetites, the assertive durian, a pungent Southeast Asian fruit.

Pietro's Coal Oven Pizzeria S 18 | 14 | 16 | $21
1714 Walnut St. (bet. 17th & 18th Sts.), 215-735-8090
121 South St. (bet. Front & 2nd Sts.), 215-733-0675

◪ The "standard brick-oven" pies and "giant salads" are made to share "with a bunch of friends" at these "upscale" twins on South Street and off Rittenhouse Square; though it's "not McPizza", it's "good, not great", and a cost-conscious clientele crabs it "always ends up costing more than it should"; service that ranges from "efficient" to "lousy" doesn't always improve the value.

PIF S 25 | 14 | 20 | $33
Italian Mkt., 1009 S. Eighth St. (bet. Carpenter St. & Washington Ave.), 215-625-2923

◪ "A destination for wine aficionados" toting prized *vins*, this BYO French bistro in South Philly is "still finding its way" but is certainly off to a "good beginning"; chef-owner David Ansill shops for "fresh ingredients from the Italian market" for his "limited" but "wonderfully" "creative", "daily changing menu", served in a "tiny" room with French countryside decor.

Pigalle S – | – | – | E
702 N. Second St. (Fairmount Ave.), 215-627-7772

This handsome brasserie is helping to place Northern Liberties on the map; hipsters and foodies go for hearty French-Euro dishes like duck confit and classic desserts like profiteroles, plus an excellent wine list and low-key service; *tout est magnifique!*

Pink Rose Pastry Shop S 24 | 19 | 18 | $12
630 S. Fourth St. (Bainbridge St.), 215-592-0565

■ The award for "best place for tea with a friend to cry over being dumped" goes to this "dessert destination" off South Street, where "scrumptious" "noshes" "make your mouth water" as much as your lovelorn eyes; "sugar, fat and caffeine – what could be better?" ask "pastry" "pigs"; "the aroma alone adds calories", but "it's worth it."

Pizzicato ●S 17 | 15 | 17 | $26
248 Market St. (3rd St.), 215-629-5527

◪ For those who aren't too picky, "a glass of wine, a green salad, a Pizzicato pizza and a Ritz movie make a great Philadelphia evening"; however, pie aficionados pluck at this Old City Italian where the "uneventful" eats aren't nearly as "lively" as the "people-watching" – "keep the salt shaker handy", they razz, as "it's the only flavor here."

Philadelphia | F | D | S | C |

Places! Bistro S ▽ 23 | 21 | 21 | $37
People's Light & Theatre Co., 39 Conestoga Rd. (Lancaster Pike), Malvern, 610-647-8060
■ It's hard to tell what a post-*Survey* chef change will mean at this "comfortable" Eclectic "hidden" in the People's Light & Theatre Company in Malvern, but so far it's going "excellent" places!; its "highly competent preparations" are "delightful even if you're not going to a show", and connoisseurs coo "sit in the garden in warm weather" for an "idyllic" "alfresco" experience.

Plate S – | – | – | M
Suburban Sq., 105 Coulter Ave. (Anderson Ave.), Ardmore, 610-642-5900
David Mantelmacher, the owner of circa on Center City's Restaurant Row, has branched out into the suburbs with this brand-new venture in Ardmore's Suburban Square; the moderately priced American comfort-food menu promises something for everyone, including heart-healthy fare for the diet-conscious, while late-night DJs are expected to attract the scene-conscious.

Plough & the Stars ●S 19 | 20 | 18 | $30
123 Chestnut St. (2nd St.), 215-733-0300
☒ "Even the bartenders are imported from Ireland" at this "chichi" Celtic-Continental in "beautiful" duplex digs in Old City, where "inventive takes on traditional fare" can be ploughed through from brunch to afternoon tea to late into the night; the "young, hip" "scene" is "great for single women" who dig "suburban" faux-bikers, since you'll "never see more black leather jackets on a Friday night", though if you're working a pickup line, your would-be date "must be able to read lips" above the "blasting music."

Plumsteadville Inn S 21 | 23 | 21 | $35
Plumsteadville Inn, Rte. 611 & Stump Rd. (4 mi. north of Doylestown), Plumsteadville, 215-766-7500
■ "A lovely place to spend" a "very Bucks County" evening is this "homey" "old-time favorite" lodged in an 18th-century carriage stop; while "not very imaginative", the Traditional American menu offers "superb" "prime rib and the like" to savor to the strains of a "nice piano player", and the "great Sunday brunch" comes "at a reasonable cost."

POD S 22 | 24 | 20 | $43
Inn at Penn, 3636 Sansom St. (bet. 36th & 37th Sts.), 215-387-1803
■ "The mess hall on the *Star Trek* Enterprise never looked as hip" as the room at Stephen Starr's "*Jetsons*-meets–Howard Johnson's" "retro"-"futuristic" Asian Fusion venture on the Penn campus; it's a "fun and illuminating" place to dine, for both the "tasty" "novelty items" on the "glam" sushi conveyor belt and the "funky" do-it-yourself

vote at zagat.com 97

Philadelphia   F | D | S | C |

lighting in the "*Austin Powers*" "party pods", and if service is a bit "robotic", perhaps the staff's just in character.

Pompeii Cucina D'Italia 🆂   — | — | — | E |
1113 Walnut St. (bet. 11th & 12th Sts.), 215-735-8400
At press time, this "dressed-up" Italian was getting ready to relocate from its Avenue of the Arts space into even swankier accommodations across from the Forrest Theatre in Center City; while you could order off chef Frankie Chiavaroli's seafood-centric menu, for a real treat let him design a special meal for you.

Porcini   23 | 12 | 19 | $27 |
2048 Sansom St. (bet. 20th & 21st Sts.), 215-751-1175
■ "Am I related to these guys?" ask diners, because the Sansone brothers "make you feel" "like a long-lost relative every time you walk in the door" of their "tiny joint" in Center City; the Italian "home cooking" is "yummy", but you might not be able to eat too much of it, since the "crammed-in" "table is pressed against your stomach."

Portofino 🆂   18 | 15 | 18 | $33 |
1227 Walnut St. (bet. 12th & 13th Sts.), 215-923-8208
◪ Even if you don't have a lot of dough, "you won't starve" with the "reasonably priced" "big portions" served at this Northern Italian "theater district standby", but the "ok" chow "lacks zing"; despite some reports of a "lousy attitude", supporters insist "they try hard", and it's clear from the ratings that many reviewers missed its recent changeover to "sparkling new decor."

Potcheen ●🆂   14 | 13 | 13 | $25 |
Sheraton Rittenhouse Square Hotel, 227 S. 18th St. (Locust St.), 215-546-9400
◪ "What is this place?" ask patrons "confused" by the no-smoking policy at what otherwise seems like a "sports bar/Irish pub" with "blaring TVs" in the Sheraton Rittenhouse Square; healthy lungs "love" it for the ban on cigs, but as for the Eclectic eats, there's nothing on the menu to "separate it from a million similar places", and maybe that's why you're "guaranteed quick seating" (i.e. it's "always empty").

Primavera Pizza Kitchen 🆂   18 | 20 | 17 | $27 |
Rittenhouse Pl., 7 E. Lancaster Ave. (Cricket Ave.), Ardmore, 610-642-8000
Ashbridge Shopping Ctr., 853 E. Lancaster Ave. (Uwchlan Ave.), Downingtown, 610-873-6333
◪ No doubt the "trompe l'oeil" "murals are lovely" at these "popular" "Tuscan" twins in Ardmore and Downingtown, but the "quality" of the Italian eats is in question; some say you can "get a pretty good plate of pasta" and a "creative pizza", but others say the grub is just "so-so", adding as an aside "train the help."

Philadelphia

| | F | D | S | C |

PRIME RIB ⑤   26 | 26 | 24 | $55
Radisson Plaza Warwick Hotel, 1701 Locust St. (17th St.), 215-772-1701

■ "Melt-in-your-mouth" and "laughably large", the "name is the specialty" at this "glamorous" "carnivore's delight" in the "elegant" Warwick Hotel in Center City; a "class act" all the way, the "grand" chainster is so "'50s"-"opulent", it makes you feel like "dressing for the occasion", which is appropriate, since jackets are required – but don't worry "if you forget yours", because they're so "professional" "they'll loan you one."

Radicchio ⑤   – | – | – | M
314 York Ave. (bet. N. 4th & Wood Sts.), 215-627-6850

Simple is often better, as proved by this consistently satisfying Southern Italian seafood house that draws fans from the Old City neighborhood and beyond into a (alas) too-small room with its straightforward, fresh fish dishes (with some prepared tableside); it's hard to go wrong with any menu selection – just be sure to bring your own bottle, as it's BYO.

Ralph's ⑤   22 | 14 | 19 | $29
Italian Mkt., 760 S. Ninth St. (bet. Catharine & Fitzwater Sts.), 215-627-6011
110 E. Butler Pike (York St.), Ambler, 215-619-4550

■ The centenarian "king of red sauce" is still holding court in South Philly, maintaining its royal "reputation" as an "institution" by bestowing "the real deal" on its loyal subjects – "modestly priced", "old-fashioned" Italian "soul food" and service with plenty of "character"; "bring out-of-towners", "earplugs" and cash; the Ambler offspring was coronated post-*Survey*.

Rangoon ⑤   22 | 13 | 19 | $21
112 N. Ninth St. (bet. Arch & Cherry Sts.), 215-829-8939

◪ "When something different and cheap is in order", aficionados tout this "unassuming" Chinatown Burmese where "you'll be happy" if you "ask for recommendations" from the "charming" staff; the "authentic", "spicy" fare "explodes with flavor" and comes in "huge portions" that make it one of the "best bargains in town", so who cares if the "plain" decor "could use help"?

Ravenna   – | – | – | E
2960 Skippack Pike (Valley Forge Rd.), Lansdale, 610-584-5650

Chef Shawn Sollberger (ex Davio's) named his bright, polished Northern Italian BYO in Central Montco after his hometown in Ohio, but there's no mistaking the tantalizing tastes of Emilia-Romagna that come out of his open kitchen (insiders advise start with the crispy chicken livers and make sure you leave room for the cheese plate); the only

Philadelphia F | D | S | C

drawback: all that noise (blame the tile floor), making sensitive sorts opt for the patio seating.

Ray's Cafe & Tea House S 23 | 14 | 18 | $20
141 N. Ninth St. (bet. Cherry & Race Sts.), 215-922-5122
■ The space may be "small", but enthusiasts say the "food comes up big" at this Chinatown cafe serving "fantastic" dumplings and other "superb", "home-cooked" Taiwanese fare in addition to "awesome" (and "pricey") coffees that are "unlike any others, anywhere"; "friendly" service only adds allure.

Reading Terminal Market 23 | 17 | 16 | $13
51 N. 12th St. (Arch St.), 215-922-2317
■ When "downtown at lunch", this "landmark" farmers' market in the old Reading Terminal is a "must-stop" "for all your indulgences", offering a "melting pot of flavors", including "Mexican, Greek, Amish, Philly cheese steaks" and much more; "sparse" seating doesn't deter "tourists" or locals from partaking of a "unique experience" that can "almost make jury duty fun."

Rembrandt's S 19 | 18 | 20 | $32
741 N. 23rd St. (Aspen St.), 215-763-2228
■ There's a "varied palette" of "great" plates and live entertainment at this "pleasant" "neighborhood" American in Fairmount; locals say it has "a good sense of place and the ability to excel within those bounds", but it's about to burst its mold, as at press time it's slated for additions including a coffee shop/non-smoking bar next door and a 130-seat banquet room upstairs.

Restaurante La Encina – | – | – | M
2 Waterview Rd. (West Chester Pike), West Chester, 610-918-9715
A "wonderful surprise" for West Chester is this "great" Spanish BYO, winning kudos for "very good seafood dishes", a "friendly atmosphere" and service with "personal touches"; foodies fuss that there are "kinks" on the menu, so for now you may want to "skip the entrées and order several tapas" instead.

Restaurant Taquet 24 | 23 | 22 | $49
Wayne Hotel, 139 E. Lancaster Ave. (Wayne Ave.), Wayne, 610-687-5005
■ Jean-Francois Taquet runs the show long-distance from New Zealand, but his "soigné" New French in Wayne remains "very good all around"; "outstanding" chef Larbi Dahrouch mans the burners, turning out "exquisite" plates ferried by a "refined" staff; the chandeliers and Dalí prints courtesy of a mid-*Survey* redo make the dining rooms look "better than ever", but it can still be argued that seating is "best on the porch in the summer."

Philadelphia | F | D | S | C |

RIB CRIB ◐≠ | 24 | 7 | 15 | $16 |
6333 Germantown Ave. (bet. Duval St. & Washington Ln.), 215-438-6793

■ "Bring a bib and don't wear white" when picking up a pile of "fantastic ribs done over the charcoal pit fire" at this Germantown BBQ "take-out joint"; it's "nothing fancy", but "year in, year out", regulars' "addiction" to the "delicious, succulent, cardiac-arresting" grub grows; N.B. open Thursday–Saturday.

Ristorante La Buca | 23 | 19 | 23 | $44 |
711 Locust St. (bet. 7th & 8th Sts.), 215-928-0556

■ Meal takers aren't just masochists when they say this "dungeon" "has its charms"; the "superior" "subterranean" Italian seafooder off Washington Square is "the real thing", with "delicious" dishes, an "excellent wine selection" and "old-world waiters" "who flirt with the ladies."

Ristorante Mediterraneo S | 21 | 20 | 20 | $39 |
Pine Run Corners, 303 Horsham Rd. (Easton Rd.), Horsham, 215-672-5595

■ It's "South Philly meets the suburbs" at this "solid" spot in Horsham, where everything is "very Italian, especially the servers"; they make "recommendations" on "amazing fish", some of the "best gnocchi out there" and other "super food", and they sure do "know their stuff"; some view this trait as "arrogance", though, which matches a menu that's "pricey, pricey."

Ristorante Panorama S | 23 | 22 | 21 | $42 |
Penn's View Hotel, 14 N. Front St. (Market St.), 215-922-7800

■ Oenophiles fancy the "fabulous flights" at this Old City Italian eatery and wine bar; given the "knowledgeable bartenders" pouring 120 selections by the glass, "everybody talks about the wine, but the food is excellent" also, and the setting, graced by a "beautiful wall mural", is appropriately "dark and romantic"; the only problem is that the prices seem to be on their own upward flight.

Ristorante Positano S | 19 | 18 | 19 | $38 |
21 W. Lancaster Ave. (bet. Ardmore & Cricket Aves.), Ardmore, 610-896-8298

■ *Amici* of this "classic" Southern Italian in Ardmore say its "special specials" and "relaxing" airs are "especially good in the summer, when everyone [else] is away"; the disenchanted say "too much fanfare" and too much money for "unspectacular" chow "turns them off."

Ristorante Primavera S | 21 | 18 | 19 | $33 |
148 South St. (2nd St.), 215-925-7832
384 W. Lancaster Ave. (Conestoga Rd.), Wayne, 610-254-0200

■ "Slightly better sisters to Primavera Pizza Kitchen", these "dependable" Italian twins on South Street and in Wayne

vote at zagat.com 101

Philadelphia

F | D | S | C

turn out "tasty" eats at "reasonable prices", even if "bored" surveyors suggest "waking the chefs every 10 years to tell them to change the menu" – though it's a wonder they can sleep at all with such "deafening" acoustics.

Ristorante San Carlo S   23 | 18 | 22 | $34
214 South St. (bet. 2nd & 3rd Sts.), 215-592-9777

■ The "perfect" platters "taste like mom's" "at home in Italy" at this "hidden gem among South Street's tacky baubles", a "benchmark" for "classic" "neighborhood trattorias"; after "waiting a long time" for a table, "family groups" beg "let us linger a while" in the "crowded" "little charmer" where the weekday BYO is a "money saver."

Rock Bottom Restaurant & Brewery ●S   – | – | – | M
Plaza at King of Prussia Mall, 1001 Mall Blvd. (DeKalb Pike), King of Prussia, 610-337-7737

A corporate takeover has brought the space-themed Brew Moon back down to the rock we call Earth with a casual Southwestern menu and brass-and-wood decor; the friendly brewpub is a decent stop for King of Prussia shoppers hankering for stick-to-your-ribs eats and homemade suds.

Roller's S ⌀   22 | 12 | 18 | $30
Top of the Hill Plaza, 8705 Germantown Ave. (Bethlehem Pike), 215-242-1771

■ Depending on your point of view, Paul Roller's "frenzied" fishery in Chestnut Hill is "lively" and "uniquely crowded" or "earsplittingly noisy" and such a "tight squeeze" you may wind up "sitting in your neighbor's lap"; "despite the tempo" and the "cluttered" quarters, diners rolling in for the "always tasty", "pleasantly un-trendy" preparations consider it a "terrific" "local standby."

Roma S   19 | 16 | 17 | $26
2400 Lombard St. (24th St.), 215-731-9711

■ What a "great, unpretentious neighborhood" Italian BYO say some surveyors who "swear" that the "special specials" and "personal service" at their "favorite regular haunt" near Fitler Square are "divine"; the less enthused say that the "food ain't all that" – it's "like a '72 Chevy: dependable but not exciting."

Ron's Schoolhouse Grille S   15 | 13 | 16 | $17
Heritage Ctr., Uwchlan Ave. (Pottstown Pike), Lionville, 610-594-9900

■ "Don't expect miracles" at this "casual" Italian-American "family place" in Chester County, just a "nice" variety of decent hoagies and pizzas that are especially "good for kids"; naysayers scoff that the "chef should go back for classes", and make that ditto for the "young, 'I don't give a damn'" staff.

Philadelphia   F | D | S | C

ROSELENA'S COFFEE BAR S   21 | 24 | 21 | $23
1623 E. Passyunk Ave. (bet. Morris & Tasker Sts.), 215-755-9697

A "little treasure" brimming with "antiques galore", this "warm, inviting, romantic" South Philly Continental lures locals with "great old-world" savories and sweets that are like "heaven on a fork"; while most rate service "excellent to incomparable", a few are put off by management's "prima donna" airs and find it "too quaint for its own good" – kitschy-"kitschy-coo."

ROSE TATTOO CAFE   23 | 22 | 20 | $37
1847 Callowhill St. (19th St.), 215-569-8939

"Still awesome after all these years", this "all-time favorite" New American makes its mark in an otherwise "lackluster neighborhood" near the Free Library with a "New Orleans–style atmosphere that really puts you in the mood" for a "superb" meal "with your sweetie"; the balcony "overlooking the garden" "is the place to be" – it's so "beautiful" "you'll feel like you're eating in a greenhouse."

Rose Tree Inn S   23 | 21 | 21 | $41
1243 N. Providence Rd. (Rte. 1), Media, 610-891-1205

"Thank heaven for this consistently good establishment" crow customers who claim that this American-Continental in Media is "always wonderful", especially when you're looking for a "nice quiet place to meet old friends and talk"; the "interesting menu" is a bit of a "surprise" given the "old-fashioned" "country-club atmosphere", and the "fine service" helps make for a "lovely evening."

ROUGE ●S   23 | 23 | 19 | $40
Rittenhouse Sq., 205 S. 18th St. (bet. Locust & Walnut Sts.), 215-732-6622

A "Parisian experience" on Rittenhouse Square, Neil Stein's "perfect bistro", graced with some of the "best streetside dining", "friendly service" and "fabulous" Continental fare in Philly, is a "swanky place" for "cafe society" "to see and be seen"; "watch the world go by" from an outdoor table or "ogle" from a window seat – either way, it's the "ultimate" people-watchers' "jackpot"; "oh to be hip" sniff a smattering of squares who snipe that a staff of "stuck-up Barbies" matches the "anorexic portions."

Roux 3 S   – | – | – | E
4755 West Chester Pike (Crum Creek Rd.), Newtown Square, 610-356-9500

Main Liners like what they're finding at this smart-looking Asian-tinged New American bistro situated on the edge of a shopping center on 'Roux 3' (that's Route 3, West Chester Pike) in Newtown Square; in the kitchen, Jay Caputo transforms potentially ho-hum ingredients such as chicken breasts into mouthwatering creations that pair well with

vote at zagat.com

Philadelphia   F D S C

the selection of wines by the glass, all served in a pitched-ceiling dining room and out on the lovely patio.

Roy's S   ▽ 25 | 24 | 25 | $42
124-34 S. 15th St. (Sansom St.), 215-988-1814
■ "Aloha!" – it's "about time" that this "super Hawaiian fusion" chain added a "Philadelphia outpost" fawn fans who hope to relive their "fond Maui memories" at Roy Yamaguchi's Center City site; most report "luscious looking and tasting" cuisine served in a "beautiful", "comfortable", smoke-free setting, though a few fret over the "exorbitantly" priced wine list.

Ruby's S   15 | 15 | 14 | $15
Suburban Sq., 5 Coulter Ave. (Anderson Ave.), Ardmore, 610-896-7829
Plaza at King of Prussia Mall, 160 N. Gulph Rd. (DeKalb Pike), King of Prussia, 610-337-7829
◪ The "killer shakes" and "innovative burgers" make these "nifty '50s"-style diners-cum-"romper rooms" in Ardmore and King of Prussia "adolescent favorites" and "treats for the [really] little ones", who "love" to watch the "model train buzzing around the ceiling"; "it's a great place to be seen – if you're 16", but "if you have no children, do not enter."

Ruth's Chris Steak House S   22 | 21 | 21 | $50
260 S. Broad St. (Spruce St.), 215-790-1515 ☽
220 N. Gulph Rd. (DeKalb Pike), King of Prussia, 610-992-1818
◪ For "buttery, sizzling" "steaks to which all others aspire", carnivores canter over to Center City and King of Prussia to visit these meatery chainsters; they're "worth every penny" announce admirers who also adore the "dark, clubby yet cozy atmosphere" and the "prompt" service; detractors say the fare ferried by a "pushy staff" "should be served on gold plates", since it costs a "king's ransom."

Rx S   – | – | – | E
4443 Spruce St. (45th St.), 215-222-9590
In a former drugstore sporting old-time apothecary items, this West Philly American is just what the doctor ordered for excellent breakfasts, lunches, brunches and dinners made with free-range and organic ingredients from local producers; service is helpful and totally without pretense, but it's BYO, so you've got to pack your own poison.

Sabrina's Cafe S   ▽ 22 | 16 | 23 | $27
910-912 Christian St. (8th St.), 215-574-1599
■ The kitchen "takes chances" at this "delightful" Eclectic BYO near the Italian Market in Bella Vista, and the menu brims with "chichi" dishes that "two people could share" at breakfast, lunch or dinner; add in "homemade desserts"

Philadelphia F | D | S | C

and "charming" service and you see why people "would love to keep it a secret."

Saffron House ▽ 17 | 20 | 18 | $32
121 S. 19th St. (Sansom St.), 215-564-6070
☑ "No one would be surprised to see the Addams family at a table" at this "beautiful home" dating from 1848 in Center City, and the "Persian menu" would appeal to Morticia and Victor's flair for the exotic; though "the taste and aroma of saffron permeates" the plates, "disappointed" diners deem the Mediterranean selections "toned down for the American palate" and the service "disorganized."

SALOON 24 | 22 | 22 | $53
750 S. Seventh St. (bet. Catharine & Fitzwater Sts.), 215-627-1811
■ "Big, bold and amazingly consistent" since 1967, this "clubby" "pub" of an Italian steakhouse is "home away from home" for anyone from the "heart of South Philly" who "wants to go back to their roots"; the food is so "absolutely fabulous" that "the chef should teach all chefs how to cook" but the staff swings from "fawning" to "abusive", and you're "paying extra for the possibility of seeing or being seen", though don't try to pay with anything but cash or AmEx, because that's all they take.

Salt – | – | – | E
253 S. 20th St. (Rittenhouse Sq.), 215-545-1990
Even by chic Rittenhouse Square standards, this tiny, sophisticated New American newcomer is a showy standout; the product of photographer David Fields' bold vision, it has quickly become a destination for serious foodies seeking chef Vernon Morales' frequently changing lineup of ambitious (daring, even), eclectic innovations; while the portions are small (and some preparations border on the precious), adventurous appetites proclaim it's worth its salt.

Samosa S ▽ 22 | 12 | 15 | $10
1214 Walnut St. (12th St.), 215-545-7776
■ "Students and spendthrifts hankering for spicy Indian delicacies" can get them on the "cheap", "with a smile" on the side, at this "family-run" Center City joint that satisfies with its Vegetarian buffet; just don't fill up on the main courses, because the "rice pudding is the best anywhere."

Sang Kee Peking Duck House S ⌿ 23 | 10 | 17 | $19
238 N. Ninth St. (Vine St.), 215-925-7532
Reading Terminal Mkt., 51 N. 12th St. (bet. Cuthbert & Filbert Sts.), 215-922-3930
☑ "Loud, busy and crowded", it's "not the place for a leisurely meal", but with such a "moist, perfect" eponymous bird and "exceptional" noodle soups, the "friendly help"

Philadelphia   F | D | S | C

can't get the bowls out "quickly" enough anyway at Michael Chow's "affordable" Chinese eatery in Chinatown; a "renovation" a couple of years ago has made it only "slightly less dumpy", but "everyone goes" anyway, and no one's there for the ambiance; N.B. there's a take-out branch at the Reading Terminal.

Sansom Street Oyster House S   20 | 16 | 18 | $30
1516 Sansom St. (bet. 15th & 16th Sts.), 215-567-7683
■ "Sit at the counter and have chowder with a judge", or "bump elbows" with a barrister in the "old-timey" dining room at this "quintessential" Center City seafood house serving "robust, straightforward, good fish" and "quite a selection of fresh oysters"; it's "nothing fancy", just "simple, quick and reliable" for a "power lunch at a reasonable price" – in other words, it's "a joy."

Sassafras International Cafe ● S   17 | 17 | 16 | $23
48 S. Second St. (bet. Chestnut & Market Sts.), 215-925-2317
◪ "Good burger, 'nuff said" – well, maybe you could add "interesting sandwiches" and "super dumplings" at this "cute", "casual" Eclectic "standby" "for before or after the nearby movies"; it's been a "favorite" for an "easy dinner" since its bicentennial year opening, though the "cheapest Chopin martini in Old City" may make the "drinking better than the eating."

Savannah S   – | – | – | M
1836 Callowhill St. (19th St.), 215-557-9533
Insiders hope this "sophisticated" dinner-only soul food addition near the Free Library "stays a secret"; the "help is superb" and dishes like meatloaf are "consistently" "tasty", though trencherpeople posit that "authentic" homestyle grub "shouldn't come in such skimpy portions."

SAVONA S   26 | 26 | 24 | $59
100 Old Gulph Rd. (Matsonford Rd.), Gulph Mills, 610-520-1200
■ "Two more payments and the meal is mine!" say those who save up for a "vacation" at this "big leaguer" on the Main Line, a "class act" that's "worth the train date" from the city; it might be "ostentatious", but there's no quibbling with Dominique Filoni's "superb" Riviera-inspired food, an "awesome" wine cellar, "Italian country" decor and "pampering" service from a staff led by wife Sabine.

Sawan's Mediterranean Bistro S   19 | 14 | 19 | $25
116 S. 18th St. (bet. Chestnut & Sansom Sts.), 215-568-3050
◪ The "unusual menu" "mixes" Moroccan, Lebanese, Greek, Israeli, French and Italian flavors, "but it works" and it's a "bargain" at this "reliable" Mediterranean near Rittenhouse Square, "great" for a "fresh and delicious

Philadelphia

F | D | S | C

lunch" or "casual dinner"; the surroundings are "a little shady", but the "accommodating" owners treat you right.

Seafood Unlimited 🆂 — | — | — | M
270 S. 20th St. (Spruce St.), 215-732-3663
A "terrific makeover" has transformed a "former dump" in Center City into this "bright" beauty with a "nice bar" to "match" the quality of "fresh", "simple" seafood dishes such as signature jumbo shrimp stuffed with crab imperial; but it's "still a good value" for "generous portions", so the "small dining room" remains "busy."

Serrano 🆂 21 | 19 | 19 | $31
20 S. Second St. (bet. Chestnut & Market Sts.), 215-928-0770
◪ "Jude [Erwin] and Rich [Machlin] keep it clicking" with a "warm hippie" vibe and "creative" cuisine including "a wealth of vegetarian options" at their "intimate" Eclectic "bistro" in Old City; despite "service as slow as molasses", it's "a happy place", particularly when most of the crowd is "going to the Tin Angel" music venue upstairs.

Seven Stars Inn 🆂 21 | 16 | 19 | $37
Hoffecker Rd. & Rte. 23, Phoenixville, 610-495-5205
■ The "gargantuan" "prime rib is kick-ass", and the "huge" "lobster melts in your mouth" at this Continental settled into a 1736 farmhouse; the "decor is very plain", but ambiance isn't the point – big eaters make the "long ride" to Chester County just so they can groan "I finished mine", while less-ambitious appetites "leave with a doggy bag."

Shank's & Evelyn's Luncheonette ⌀ 23 | 9 | 16 | $14
932 S. 10th St. (Carpenter St.), 215-629-1093
■ "Hungry" "insiders" "make friends with Evelyn" and order an "unbelievable" meatball or roast beef or chicken parmigiana sandwich with "gossip" and a lotta "attitude" on the side at her "classic" Italian luncheonette; the "joint's" "great culture" encompasses "pork, politics" and an "homage to Mussolini", but "don't be afraid", 'cause once in a while "ya gotta have" "a South Philly experience."

Shiao Lan Kung ●🆂 ▽ 28 | 9 | 23 | $21
930 Race St. (bet. 9th & 10th Sts.), 215-928-0282
■ It's a "far cry from chicken chow mein" at this "authentic", bare-bones bastion of "excellent salt-baked" dishes and "fabulous" hot pots in Chinatown; "more Chinese regulars per capita" chow here than at the other joints, but the "helpful" staff steers non-Asians as well to "down-home" delicacies "done right."

Shiroi Hana 🆂 22 | 16 | 20 | $28
222 S. 15th St. (bet. Locust & Walnut Sts.), 215-735-4444
■ "When you're in a zen mood", this "quiet", "earthy" Center City Japanese has "all the elements" to "satisfy":

vote at zagat.com

Philadelphia

F | **D** | **S** | **C**

"sparse decor", "peaceful, efficient" service and a "creative, extensive" menu featuring "fresh and tasty" sushi, "lunch-box specials" and "lots of veggie options"; if, on the other hand, you're looking to unbalance, try the sake bar upstairs.

Shivnanda S
▽ 20 | 16 | 21 | $26

114 Chestnut St. (bet. Front & 2nd Sts.), 215-925-1444

■ "They don't drown the food in sauce, and they use a good blend of spices", so the dishes at this Old City Indian are a "delicious" "step above" those at some others of its ilk; plus, they're so "nice" and "friendly" that they want to see you all the time, so they've added a second-floor lounge.

Shula's Steak House S
▽ 15 | 17 | 18 | $43

Wyndham Philadelphia at Franklin Plaza, 17th St. (Race St.), 215-448-2700

◪ The "manly" "portions are big enough for the Jolly Green Giant", or at least a "Dolphins" linebacker, at former coach Don Shula's pigskin-themed cow palace in the Wyndham at Franklin Plaza; the "typical chain"-quality steaks don't score with everyone though, particularly "at those prices", and the little green sprouts who work here could use some more "polish."

Siam Cuisine S
21 | 16 | 19 | $26

925 Arch St. (bet. 9th & 10th Sts.), 215-922-7135
Buckingham Green Shopping Ctr., 4950 York Rd. (Rte. 202), Buckingham, 215-794-7209
80 W. State St. (bet. Clinton & Hamilton Sts.), Doylestown, 215-348-0708
Village at Newtown, 2124 S. Eagle Rd. (Richboro Rd.), Newtown, 215-579-9399

■ Invite your "taste buds" to "a party for your mouth", and order up some "rockin'" signature crispy duck or shrimp curry for entertainment at these "modest" Thai siblings; there's "extraordinary flavor" to be had here, and the "accommodating" staff "welcomes" you and makes you feel "relaxed"; N.B. Newtown is BYO, while the new Doylestown branch (the site of the former Black Walnut Cafe) displays a certain French flair.

Silk City ●S⊄
17 | 13 | 15 | $15

435 Spring Garden St. (bet. 4th & 5th Sts.), 215-592-8838

◪ "Hungover" "hipsters" "hang" "post-clubbing" at this "ultimate" 24/7 (on weekends) diner in Northern Liberties, where yet another Bloody Mary is a must"; the "trendy crowd" might make you feel you've been "transported to a Gap ad", but the "old-fashioned" eats are not mass-produced – "amazing chocolate bread pudding", cheese fries with gravy and a veggie burger (not necessarily in that order) almost excuse the "inconsistent service" and "smoky", "tight space."

subscribe to zagat.com

Philadelphia | F | D | S | C |

Silk Cuisine ⑤ — 21 | 15 | 19 | $23
656 W. Lancaster Ave. (Old Lancaster Rd.), Bryn Mawr, 610-527-0590

☑ The "great, fresh" Thai flavors are "consistent" "from one visit to the next" at this bare-bones Bryn Mawr BYO, but though you may "never have a bad meal here", you'd better "dress like you belong on the Main Line or you might get seated in the basement."

Simon Pearce on the Brandywine ⑤ — 18 | 22 | 19 | $40
1333 Lenape Rd. (Pocopson Rd.), West Chester, 610-793-0948

☑ It's "glass-blowing", not "mind-blowing" cuisine that lures folks to this Traditional American "on the premises of a factory" to "watch the artisans work" and purchase their "beautiful" hand-blown creations; in "lovely" surroundings "overlooking the Brandywine Creek", the "fancy joint" "sparkles" at "sunset", but "overpriced", "overdone" dishes lead some to deem it "a great place for a drink" only.

Singapore Kosher Vegetarian ⑤ — 20 | 14 | 20 | $20
1006 Race St. (bet. 10th & 11th Sts.), 215-922-3288

■ "The name speaks for itself" at these "reliable" BYO twins in Chinatown and Cherry Hill, where the attitude is "no meat, no problem"; ask the "knowledgeable" staff to make recommendations from the "huge" menu of "unique" and "exciting" dishes, and remember "they do an excellent job with tofu."

Sitar India ⑤ — ∇ 17 | 11 | 15 | $14
60 S. 38th St. (bet. Chestnut & Market Sts.), 215-662-0818

☑ Poor "Penn grad students who want inexpensive Indian" can get it at this "basic" "buffet joint"; "less crowded" than neighboring spots, it's "enjoyable" for a "bargain" lunch or dinner, but there's really "nothing special" about it.

Smith & Wollensky ⑤ — 19 | 19 | 19 | $49
Rittenhouse Hotel, 210 W. Rittenhouse Sq. (bet. Locust & Walnut Sts.), 215-545-1700

☑ "Stiff drinks, big steaks" and "non-threatening sides" are "great for a guys' night out" at this "masculine" meat palace chainster in the Rittenhouse Hotel; spend "a ton of money" and you get "a ton of food", but you can also opt for "solid pub fare" at more modest prices; naysayers don't bother, simply snorting "send it back to New York."

Snockey's Oyster & Crab House ⑤ — 17 | 12 | 16 | $28
1020 S. Second St. (Washington Ave.), 215-339-9578

☑ Aw, shucks, say afishionados, "all that's missing is sawdust" at this "old-time" "neighborhood" seafood "shack" near the Mummers Museum in South Philly, where for 90 years pearl-diving patrons have shellfishly gobbled

vote at zagat.com

Philadelphia

F | D | S | C

up "a large variety of oysters and clams" and "great", "no-frills" fin fare; citing "abysmal atmosphere", modernists say this is one local "tradition" that's "past its prime."

Society Hill Hotel ●S   14 | 14 | 14 | $20
Society Hill Hotel, 301 Chestnut St. (3rd St.), 215-925-1919
◪ "If you're not wearing black and want to escape from the trendy Old City hot spots", this "quaint", "convivial bar" is your place for decent American grub and "a few drinks"; though it may be somewhat "cramped and smoky", just "eat the burger and shrug it off."

Solaris Grille S   18 | 18 | 18 | $28
8201 Germantown Ave. (Highland Ave.), 215-242-3400
◪ The "good" chopped salad makes for a "memorable" Chestnut Hill "shopping" break at this "attractive" American seafooder with a "pleasant patio" where "people-watchers" focus on the "great-looking" staff; the "rest of the menu is so-so" say those "yawning" over "unrealized potential."

Sonoma S   18 | 17 | 17 | $32
4411 Main St. (bet. Gay & Levering Sts.), 215-483-9400
◪ When "sexy" Manayunk "singles" "loudly" suggest "stick to the basics", they might mean vodka, since the "cool bar" at Derek Davis' "jumping", "multilevel" "hangout" sports 300 brands of the white lightning to make "old-timers feel young again" as they "sit outside and sample the quirky menu" of "well-prepared" Italian-Californian cuisine; "blah, blah, blah" drone dissenters, "lose the image and the attitude" or "pull the plug."

Sotto Varalli S   19 | 21 | 19 | $38
231 S. Broad St. (Locust St.), 215-546-6800
◪ The "ultramodern", squid-centric surrounds are "cool as ice" and "calming" at this "interesting" Italian seafooder "convenient" to the theaters on the Avenue of the Arts; there are some "fine fish dishes" here, but culinary Captain Nemos say the "overreaching" "undersea" spot is "not in the same league" as its sibling upstairs, Upstares at Varalli.

South St. Souvlaki S   21 | 13 | 18 | $21
509 South St. (bet. 5th & 6th Sts.), 215-925-3026
■ "You can see what they're cooking from the street", and it's "huge portions" of "consistently" "delicious" "renditions of Greek taverna classics" at this "old", "comfy" "favorite", still "cheap" and "great after all these years"; "plate-licking" patrons proclaim "come down to earth" and come down to South Street for a "simple", "yummy" meal.

Spaghetti Warehouse S   11 | 13 | 14 | $19
1026 Spring Garden St. (bet. 10th & 11th Sts.), 215-787-0784
◪ "Watch out for screaming children" at this "cheap", "no-frills pasta" emporium on the northern edge of Center

Philadelphia F | D | S | C

City, where all those "noisy" "kids" crammed into a "literal warehouse" chowing down "spaghetti that tastes like we had in school" take parents back to their parochial days; the "decor is far out", and there's a certain thrill to "eating in a trolley car or brass bed", but foodies just say "eeew."

Spasso S — 21 | 18 | 20 | $32
34 S. Front St. (bet. Chestnut & Market Sts.), 215-592-7661

■ "You don't have to take out a second mortgage to have a really good meal" at this "very authentic" Italian grill "near Penn's Landing", where "terrific service makes you feel like you're at home", that is if you're used to having someone fillet an "awesome" whole fish at your dining room table; it's a "good date place", particularly "if you sit in the booth that overlooks Front Street."

Spence Cafe S — 21 | 17 | 20 | $31
29-31 E. Gay St. (bet. High & Walnut Sts.), West Chester, 610-738-8844

■ "Early" in the evening the "older set eats" a "nice", "quiet dinner" of "very good seafood" at this New American fish house in West Chester; the "college kids take over after 9 PM" to bang heads to local bands, guzzle the nightly drink specials and hopefully score some digits, inspired as they are by "dark", "lovely" digs that "look like a brothel."

Spezia S — ▽ 20 | 17 | 20 | $39
614 W. Lancaster Ave. (bet. Old Lancaster & Pennswood Rds.), Bryn Mawr, 610-526-0123

◪ The "young, talented crew" at the helm of this "lovely addition to the local scene" in Bryn Mawr worked previously at Le Mas and Toscana Cucina Rustica, so you can be sure the Italian-influenced New American fare is "inspired" and the "ingredients excellent"; but down-to-earth coin counters crab that it's "pretentious and overpriced" – "it's BYO, but if you want special wineglasses" made of Riedel crystal, "it's $7" extra per table.

Spotted Hog S — 15 | 16 | 15 | $25
Peddler's Village, Rte. 263 & Street Rd., Lahaska, 215-794-4040

◪ "They're lucky to have a great location" at this "easy" Traditional American in Peddler's Village, a "tourist destination" for "casual dining after a day of shopping"; though the "family atmosphere" is "fun for kids", even hogs say the bites are "bland", but you can take a stool at the bar and "thank God for peanuts."

Sprigs S — – | – | – | M
3749 Midvale Ave. (Ridge Ave.), 215-849-9248

East Falls has fallen hard for this funky, family-run bistro and it's easy to see why – Howard Greene's honest French-inflected New American cooking comes from the heart

Philadelphia   F | D | S | C

(don't miss his short ribs or chocolate soufflé) and it's delivered by unfailingly friendly and helpful folks; it also doesn't hurt that every bottle of wine on the predominately Californian list is priced at only $10 over cost.

Spring Mill Café S   22 | 20 | 20 | $38
164 Barren Hill Rd. (bet. Ridge Pike & River Rd.), Conshohocken, 610-828-2550

■ "Quirky doesn't begin to describe" this "charming" French BYO in an 18th-century "country" store in Conshy; the "junky decor", Michèle Haines' "wonderful" "nouvelle-eccentric" use of North African and Thai influences and her "weird" "temperament" all add "funky" "charm" to a "romantic" experience literally and figuratively "off the beaten track."

Standard Tap ● S   21 | 17 | 17 | $20
901 N. Second St. (Poplar St.), 215-238-0630

■ "Hands-down the best addition to the pub scene in years" according to sudsheads is this "real neighborhood spot" "in hip and happening Northern Liberties"; "not your standard" grub, the American fare "is really quite excellent and amazingly low-cost"; that, plus a "great beer selection" and "first-rate jukebox", makes it a "neat place to take a date", but it's a bar, mind you, so you both "have to like smoke and noise as your side dishes."

State Street Grill S   – | – | – | M
115 W. State St. (Union St.), Kennett Square, 610-925-4984

Fayette Street Grille's upscale American bistro sibling "satisfies" downtown Kennett Square with "outstanding" prix fixe "gourmet" dinners at a "great" BYO value; it's light, airy and lively inside, with an open kitchen to add to the energy, and to the "noise."

Stefano's S   20 | 20 | 18 | $37
2519 Huntingdon Pike (Red Lion Rd.), Huntingdon Valley, 215-914-1224

◪ "Mom and dad's food is great" at this "affordable" BYO in Huntingdon Valley offering a "limited menu" of "pleasant" pastas and other "tasty" Italian treats; however, diners discern that it "can't decide" what to be, as "inconsistent" "help that yells" as if the joint is a "family" restaurant undermines its "classy" aspirations.

Stella Notte S   – | – | – | E
Chestnut Hill Hotel, 8229 Germantown Ave. (Southampton Ave.), 215-247-2100

Local culinary legend Aliza Green has surfaced in the kitchen at this trattoria in the Chestnut Hill Hotel; while the "pretty" interior with its twinkling ceiling is enough to make "grown-up" romantics starry-eyed, it's the menu that really

Philadelphia

F | D | S | C

shines with "delicious" "wood-fired" specialties and old-time Italian favorites.

STRIPED BASS ●S 26 | 28 | 25 | $59
1500 Walnut St. (15th St.), 215-732-4444

■ Neil Stein's "absolutely posh" big-ticket "treat" on Restaurant Row remains one of Philly's most popular power trips, with Terence Feury's "bite-by-bite succulent" seafood supplied by a "staff that knocks itself out to please you" in digs so "hip" and "glamorous" that the "atmosphere is worth the price" in itself; you "feel like a star", and at Sunday brunch or prix fixe lunch, that "beautiful" illusion is ticketed as a relative "deal."

Sugar Mom's
Church Street Lounge ●S 14 | 17 | 13 | $16
Sugar Refinery, 225 Church St. (bet. 2nd & 3rd Sts.), 215-925-8219

☑ When you've got a "craving" for a "greasy burger" and "Pabst on tap", go "underground" for your "fix" at this Old City backstreet joint; "smoky", "dark" and filled with "young" folk, it "looks like a Viennese rathskeller, just funkier", with "lots of toys to play with" and a "great" "heavy metal" jukebox; plus, at prices this "decent", you can afford to play sugar mom to your crew.

Sukhothai S 20 | 18 | 19 | $29
225 S. 12th St. (Locust St.), 215-627-2215

■ Wash West "welcomes" this "promising" addition to the "gayborhood" for "sweet food" served by "sweet people"; "extremely delicious" Thai-Continental dishes, including "standout curries", are "prepared with finesse" to be enjoyed in a "cool, dark yellow" room, and while dinner comes at fairly steep "Center City prices", lunch (served only in the summer) is "economical."

Sullivan's Steakhouse S 23 | 21 | 21 | $44
King of Prussia Mall, 700 W. DeKalb Pike (Mall Blvd.), King of Prussia, 610-878-9025

See review in the Wilmington/Nearby Delaware Directory.

Summer Kitchen S ▽ 25 | 16 | 21 | $31
2310 Second Street Pike (Penns Park Rd.), Penns Park, 215-598-9210

■ "The patio is best on a nice evening" in the namesake season at this Cuban-Eclectic off a country road in Bucks; "small but charming", it's a beneath-the-radar "treat" for "talented" Mario Korenstein's "fabulous multicultural menu items" and David Van Ess's "down-to-earth" service.

SUSANNA FOO S 26 | 25 | 25 | $55
1512 Walnut St. (bet. 15th & 16th Sts.), 215-545-2666

☑ Chef-owner Susanna Foo's "justly famous" and "high-rent" Restaurant Row "landmark" "tingles the palate" with

vote at zagat.com

Philadelphia

"light but complex" Chinese-French "originals" "perfectly paced" by "impeccable but not snooty" servers in an atmosphere of "understated" "elegance"; it's an "exquisite" experience "fit for an emperor", but commoners who come to celebrate "those super-special life events" implore "can't we make the portions just a bit bigger?"

Swanky Bubbles ●S | 19 | 20 | 16 | $33

10 S. Front St. (Market St.), 215-928-1200

■ "Let the bubbly flow" cry cork poppers at this "retro" "hangout" in Old City, a vision in "velvet, velour" and Veuve, with Pan-Asian "taste treats" for "sharing"; though it's "hoppin'" with young "trendies" bouncing to that "techno beat", at least they're not "shot-hammering"; snobs still sniff "swanky it isn't."

SWANN LOUNGE ●S | 27 | 27 | 27 | $48

Four Seasons Philadelphia, 1 Logan Sq. (B.F. Pkwy. & 18th St.), 215-963-1500

■ The "poor man's Fountain" is a "classy joint" in its own right; down the hall from that "other place" at the Four Seasons, this Franco-American's "casually elegant" digs and "waiters who cater to your every need" place it among the city's tops, and – "ooh-la-la" – that "bargain brunch" buffet is "scrumptious", the "dessert buffet is chocolate heaven" and "for tea, it's perfect."

Syrenka ⇍ | ▽ 21 | 11 | 16 | $15

3173 Richmond St. (Allegheny Ave.), 215-634-3954

■ Second-generation sorts say it's "like eating in your grandmother's 1940s kitchen" at this "traditional Polish" BYO in Port Richmond, where pierogiphiles pig out on the "best" "comfort foods" "west of Warsaw", including "fantastic potato pancakes and stuffed cabbage", at prices "so cheap it's almost free."

TACCONELLI'S PIZZERIA S⇍ | 25 | 8 | 15 | $16

2604 E. Somerset St. (bet. Almond & Thompson Sts.), 215-425-4983

■ "Who ever heard of reserving pizza dough?" – apparently, a whole lot of pieheads who "schlep" to this "forsaken" Port Richmond location to pick up their goods made from ingredients "ordered ahead"; "what's the excitement about?" – simply the "best pizza in Philadelphia", no, scratch that, "in America", oh ok, make that "on planet Earth."

Taco House ⇍ | 17 | 8 | 13 | $11

1218 Pine St. (bet. 12th & 13th Sts.), 215-735-1880

■ "Another one of those holes-in-the-wall that, unless someone tells ya about it, you wouldn't go" is this "little" Mexican place "tucked away on Pine Street", where a "rather avant-garde" "quick fix" "with the local Gen X" "art students" is "decent" enough and almost "cheaper than

Philadelphia

F | D | S | C

McDonald's"; *queso* lovers "dream about" the "unbelievable cheese crisps", though south-of-the-border experts "don't think of it as authentic."

Tai Lake ●S
▽ 21 | 10 | 17 | $24
134 N. 10th St. (bet. Cherry & Race Sts.), 215-922-0698
You "choose your entrée from the tanks" at the door, so there's "no doubt about the vitality" of your vittles at this Cantonese-Mandarin seafooder in Chinatown; even "late at night", the fin fare's "fresh" and flipping for an "authentic" "family-style banquet", so "no wonder Asians eat here", despite "annoying smoke" and sometimes "slow" service.

Taj Mahal S
▽ 17 | 12 | 16 | $19
1903 Chestnut St. (19th St.), 215-575-1199
It's not as "fancy" as its namesake, but that doesn't stop gorgers from lining up for the "decent" "all-you-can-eat" weekday buffet at this "big, dark cave" of an Indian BYO in Center City; "they should lose the shrill music" say quiet types, but keep the "cheap" prices.

Tamarindo's S
21 | 15 | 20 | $27
Homemaker's Shopping Plaza, 36 W. Skippack Pike (Butler Pike), Broad Axe, 215-619-2390
Montco mealsters "didn't know" "gourmet Mexican" wasn't "an oxymoron" until this "authentic" Broad Axe BYO came along; they might have driven by the "strip maller" and "thought it was a Taco Bell", but then they ventured in and found "beautifully presented", "upscale" dishes "seasoned just right" and served by a "staff that bends over backward"; "it's very surprising", they said to themselves, "we will come back", even though it's "overpriced."

Tandoor India S
21 | 11 | 16 | $16
106 S. 40th St. (bet. Chestnut & Walnut Sts.), 215-222-7122
"What can we say but 'love that buffet'?" boast Penn students on a budget at this University City Indian where the steam table's filled with the "food of the gods", and if you order off the menu, "they will make a dish any way you like"; it's "dark and dingy" and the "service is usually apathetic", but it's "cheap and fast if you're on the go" between classes.

TANGERINE S
24 | 26 | 23 | $48
232 Market St. (bet. 2nd & 3rd Sts.), 215-627-5116
Stephen Starr is rockin' the "casbah" at his "sexy" "dream" in Old City, where the Mediterranean "fun"-fare is a "fez-tival of fantastic flavors" served "family-style"; the "exotic" interior "draped in red and gold brocade" "transports you to another world", and you'll want to take a "date" along for the ride because "see-and-be-seen" takes on a "wildly" "romantic" meaning in the "candlelight"; in other words, "wow."

vote at zagat.com

Tango S | 18 | 19 | 17 | $36

39 Morris Ave. (Bryn Mawr RR Station), Bryn Mawr, 610-526-9500

◪ Surveyors can't keep in step over this "fashionable" New American "meeting place for young professionals" in the Bryn Mawr train station; one set of partners calls it an "attractive" "keeper" with "tasty, interesting dishes" and a "wonderful by-the-glass wine list", while the other side of the dance card dismisses "hit-or-miss" "small portions" and servers who have two "disorganized" left feet.

Taqueria Moroleon S | ▽ 24 | 8 | 14 | $17

15 New Garden Shopping Ctr. (Scarlet Rd.), Kennett Square, 610-444-1210

■ "The authentic Mexican" cuisine at this BYO "favorite" in a Kennett Square "strip mall" is so "simple, down-home, cheap and good", it "would be famous if it were closer to Philly"; the "casual" room, on the other hand, might be infamous – "it's like a poorly refinished basement"; but "locals" say "you can't beat" the eats, so just "bring your bottle of red and enjoy."

Tartine S⊭ | – | – | – | M

701 S. Fourth St. (Bainbridge St.), 215-592-4720

After putting in 50 years in the restaurant business, Yves Longhi finally decided to retire, but now he's back behind the stove at this quirky (for example, it has both a liquor license and a BYO policy) little French bistro in Queen Village; the menu, written nightly on index cards, leans toward the classics (think quiche, cassoulet, fish meunière), while the service veers between hospitable and gallingly Gallic.

Taste of Thai Garden S | ▽ 21 | 19 | 20 | $27

101 N. 11th St. (bet. Appletree & Arch Sts.), 215-629-9939

■ "Big fans" of spice "put their mouths on fire with the Thai salad" and other flaming fare on the "diverse menu" at this Siamese "well located" across from the Pennsylvania Convention Center; for tamer palates, the signature steamed "dumplings are the best" choice.

Tavern S | – | – | – | M

261 Montgomery Ave. (Old Lancaster Rd.), Bala Cynwyd, 610-667-9100

Old-school restaurateur Nick Zaravalas has returned to this Bala Cynwyd landmark after taking a five-year hiatus; neighbors who grew up with his Traditional American fare (shrimp cocktail, snapper soup, steaks) and no-nonsense attitude are welcoming him back with open arms, proving that you can go home again.

Tavern on Green S | 15 | 14 | 15 | $24

2047 Green St. (21st St.), 215-235-6767

◪ No, it's not that fabled romantic New York spot, but this "favorite neighborhood bistro" with "sidewalk tables" near

Philadelphia | F | D | S | C |

the Art Museum might still be the place to "fall in love", if you can do it over a "quick burger", some beers and "rocking live music"; otherwise, the Eclectic vittles are "nothing to rave about", and the servers can be as "snotty" as if they worked at its near-namesake.

Teikoku S | – | – | – | E |
5492 West Chester Pike (bet. Delchester & Garrett Mill Rds.), Newton Square, 610-644-8270
Win and Sutida Somboonsong (Thai Pepper) are garnering applause for their new Japanese-Thai combo in Newtown Square; the surroundings, which include a waterfall at the entrance and accents of bamboo and mahogany, are nothing short of gorgeous, as are the artistic presentations of the sophisticated dishes.

Tenth St. Pour House S ∌ | ▽ 19 | 11 | 15 | $13 |
262 S. 10th St. (Spruce St.), 215-922-5626
◪ "Jefferson University" med students "nurse hangovers" with "amazing" cinnamon rolls, "awesome pancakes" and signature Cajun eggs Benedict at the "excellent, low-key weekend brunch" at this N'Awlins-style American near the hospital; "service can be so slow", though, that "it's lunch by the time you're served breakfast", and remember to stuff those scrubs with cash because they don't take cards.

Teresa's Cafe of Wayne S | 21 | 14 | 19 | $26 |
124 N. Wayne Ave. (Lancaster Ave.), Wayne, 610-293-9909
◼ Even with a "no-reservations" policy, "it's hard not to like" this Italian "in the center of Wayne"; it's the "place to have a great casual meal, see friends and meet neighbors", but if you can't stand "incredible noise", "take the kids at 5:30" to "get there before the crowds" "pack in like sardines"; that "no-no", the corkage fee, has been done away with, but it's still BYO, so "have drinks down the street while you're waiting for your table."

Tex Mex Connection S | 17 | 14 | 16 | $25 |
201 E. Walnut St. (Sumneytown Pike), North Wales, 215-699-9552
◪ It's "no frills, but who eats frills?" ask amigos of this North Wales Tex-Mex; it's a good question, but a better one might be asked by those who "can't understand its popularity" for "so-so" fare, a "bored" staff and decor as "worn as old blue jeans"; maybe the "fun" lies in its "killer margaritas" and karaoke.

Thai Orchid S | 23 | 17 | 20 | $26 |
1748 DeKalb Pike (Township Line Rd.), Blue Bell, 610-277-9376
◼ Sam-I-Ams "love lamb of Siam", but do they love it in a "strip mall"?; really, there's nothing *Seussical* about the "huge selection" of "yummy curries" and other "exquisite"

vote at zagat.com

Philadelphia

F | D | S | C

eats at this BYO Thai "jewel" in Blue Bell, where the "unassuming" environs are "quiet and relaxed" enough for "people who avoid the city"; N.B. there's a new offshoot in Marlton, NJ.

Thai Pepper ⑤ | 19 | 16 | 18 | $23
64 E. Lancaster Ave. (Argyle Rd.), Ardmore, 610-642-5951
372 W. Lancaster Ave. (Conestoga Rd.), Wayne, 610-688-5853
◪ Buddies boast of a "light-touch" "treat for the taste buds" at these "affordable" Siamese twins dishing out "big servings" of "solid, affordable" "staples", while diners who've 'been there and eaten that' find it all "slightly boring"; N.B. Ardmore offers wine and beer, but Wayne is BYO.

Thai Singha House ⑤ | 21 | 16 | 19 | $23
3939 Chestnut St. (39th St.), 215-382-8001
■ "Thai one on" with a "funky" martini at this Penn-area Siamese where "delicate, flavorful" dishes, both "exotic" and "standard", get "high marks"; "time in and time out", the "witty staff" serves it all up at "scary-cheap prices."

Thomas' ⑤ | 18 | 16 | 19 | $36
4201 Main St. (Pensdale St.), 215-483-9075
◪ "On a snowy day", some Manayunk barflies "go to drink" at this "old favorite that continues to be worth revisiting" for its "inviting" vibe; as for the New American–New French–Asian Fusion eats, they're "pricey" but "not bad", though some who knew it when are "disappointed" nowadays.

Three Little Pigs ⌿ | ▽ 21 | 14 | 15 | $14
131 N. High St. (Chestnut St.), West Chester, 610-918-1272
■ Wolf down a "great sandwich" named for a West Chester thoroughfare at this "chichi" "little" "lunch spot" in a "quaint" storefront on North High Street; it's such a "fun place to eat" that locals who "don't mind a short wait" to get in swear by the hair on their chinny-chin-chins that "they should name a table after us"; if you can't stick around, huff and puff your way back home with takeout.

333 Belrose ⑤ | 22 | 19 | 20 | $38
333 Belrose Ln. (King of Prussia Rd.), Radnor, 610-293-1000
■ "The fare is delicious, and so is the crowd" at Carlo deMarco's "bright, sunny" New American in Radnor, where "inventive cooking" "keeps the foodies in the suburbs" and the "cool bar scene" brings out "middle-aged singles" "looking for a good time"; it can be "painfully loud", but maybe that's just all the "moans induced" by the desserts.

Tierra Colombiana ⑤ | 22 | 16 | 19 | $23
4535-39 N. Fifth St. (3 blocks south of Roosevelt Blvd.), 215-324-6086
■ "Don't let the neighborhood scare you away" from this "authentic" Cuban-Colombian near Roosevelt Boulevard;

Philadelphia   F | D | S | C

while the decor is "plainly not elegant", the "spectacular" fare will "transport" you, though when you literally want to take off, "pray your car's still there."

Time Out Falafel S   ▽ 19 | 8 | 13 | $15
Presidential Plaza, 9846 Bustleton Ave. (south of Haldeman Ave.), 215-969-7545

◪ "Garlic lovers" take time out and "drive out of their way" to this glatt kosher Middle Eastern in Northeast Philly for "cheap", "authentic" falafel, "good schwarma" and "solid" Israeli salad; service is lacking at times, and there's "no atmosphere" unless you count the "kids running around."

Tira Misu Ristorante   22 | 19 | 19 | $39
528 S. Fifth St. (bet. Lombard & South Sts.), 215-925-3335

◪ The "best of [Alberto] Delbello's enterprises" is "nice for a change" from red-sauce Italians; his Roman Jewish flagship off South Street still serves some "heavenly" "tastes" "with a different touch", from "homemade matzo" to "excellent artichokes", but yentas gossip that it's "always empty", perhaps because the service varies is so variable.

Tir Na Nog S   – | – | – | M
1600 Arch St. (N. 16th St.), 267-514-1700

Named after the Celtic phrase for "land of eternal youth" (which also sizes up much of the clientele), this inviting pub next to Suburban Station is straight out of Dublin, literally (craftsmen from Ireland put in all the dark woods, inlaid glass and stone fireplaces), and for the most part, so are the servers (just listen to their brogues); expect the traditional pub grub – shepherd's pie, fish 'n' chips, etc. – along with some more ambitious dishes.

Tony Luke Jr.'s   23 | 8 | 14 | $11
Old Philly Style Sandwiches S
118 S. 18th St. (Sansom St.), 215-568-4630
Tony Luke's
Old Philly Style Sandwiches ◐≠
39 E. Oregon Ave. (Front St.), 215-551-5725

◪ "Get in line with truckers and lawyers" at this "classic" deli duo where devotees swear "all the fancy food in the world can't hold a candle" to the "belly-bustin'" "pork sammiches", though sitting down to one in Rittenhouse Square or having them deliver it ain't quite "the same as eating on the street" at the South Philly "original"; the staff can be "rude, rude, rude", "so order quickly", youse guys.

Toscana Cucina Rustica S   22 | 20 | 20 | $43
24 N. Merion Ave. (bet. Lancaster & Montgomery Aves.), Bryn Mawr, 610-527-7700

◪ "Smartly dressed" Main Liners are "sure they'll see someone they know" at this "sophisticated" Italian in Bryn Mawr, noted for "wonderful" veal chops and "awesome"

vote at zagat.com   119

Philadelphia

F | D | S | C

wines capped off with a "sinful" soufflé; *amici* who can't get enough of all that "luscious food" are "sorry they stopped serving lunch", even though "intimate" can be "too close for comfort" and the staff verges on "chilly."

Totaro's
24 | 14 | 21 | $46

729 E. Hector St. (bet. Righter & Walnut Sts.), Conshohocken, 610-828-9341

◪ "This is Conshohocken?" is the question most asked about this "top-of-the-line" Italian-heavy Eclectic in an "unlikely" location at the "back of a neighborhood bar"; "large tables of men discussing business" as they dig into "exotic meats" lend it a "relaxed" "private club" feel, though the interior designers among them say the "prices are absurd" for seating amid the "early '50s"-style digs.

Toto
20 | 23 | 20 | $46

1407 Locust St. (bet. Broad & 15th Sts.), 215-546-2000

◪ Academy of Music mavens make the "perfect light meal" of the "enjoyable small plates" "pre- or post-concert" at this "Milan-chic" "mural"-and-"mirror"–filled Italian across the street; but in answer to fans who "don't know why it isn't more popular", critics complain that the "overpriced" eats "aren't as good as in the past", when the spot was DiLullo's, and the service is sometimes "snooty."

Trattoria Alberto
∇ 23 | 20 | 21 | $36

116 E. Gay St. (bet. High & Matlack Sts.), West Chester, 610-430-0203

■ "Alberto's done it again" – the owner of the eponymous steakhouse in Newtown Square brought his millennial Northern Italian to downtown West Chester, and it's "ranking among the best" in the area for "memorable" fare ferried, or "filleted tableside", by "outstanding" servers in a "nice, relaxing" atmosphere with a "beautiful bar" and "tables in the wine cellar" where they store the "nice list" of bottles, including the man's own label of Super Tuscans.

Trattoria San Nicola
24 | 18 | 21 | $33

668 Lancaster Ave. (Main Ave.), Berwyn, 610-296-3141

■ "What more could you ask for" Berwyn "locals" wonder than "well-spiced" Italian that "borders on gourmet" and a "bill that's never high"?; you could ask for "friendly service" and a "cozy, romantic ambiance" too, and when a "place is mobbed on a Tuesday, you know" you're getting it all, so call this "charming" spot for a "res" and hope for the best.

TRE SCALINI S
25 | 14 | 22 | $33

1533 S. 11th St. (Tasker St.), 215-551-3870

■ "Mother hen" Franca DiRenzo "delivers more than you expect" at this "unpretentious" BYO Italian in a "converted row house" in South Philly: "intense flavors, the best ingredients and prompt service", all at "affordable" prices;

Philadelphia   F | D | S | C

"in a city of expense-account eateries where half your bill goes toward paying for decor", her "dumpy" joint dishes up the "real deal", and boy, is it "scrumptious."

Trinacria   22 | 19 | 21 | $40
1016 DeKalb Pike (Skippack Pike), Center Square, 610-275-0505

◪ Serving "excellent Sicilian", including signature veal and "great grilled fish", this Southern Italian "outside of Philly" in Center Square "looks good, but it really caters to its regulars" say surveyors less familiar to the house; it's also considered "pricey for the neighborhood" and the "size of the portions."

Trolley Car Diner S   14 | 16 | 14 | $15
7619 Germantown Ave. (Cresheim Valley Dr.), 215-753-1500

◪ "Standard" American grub, "plus a liquor license"? – "hey, life is good" say "down-home" diners who think it's "nice to have" a "wonderfully preserved 1952 stainless-steel diner" transported to Mount Airy; critics pout "the neon draws you in, but the servers keep you waiting" and the eats are "unremarkable" for the trouble.

Trust S   – | – | – | E
121-127 S. 13th St. (Sansom St.), 215-629-1300

Matthew Spector (ex N. 3rd, Novelty) is cooking up creative Med-inspired fare at this sleek, chic, retro-modern addition housed in a former bank in an emerging section of Center City; the line is that the new chef has come into his own with excellent meals dished out of the open kitchen; the circular fieldstone bar is still the place to be, and after a few 'electronic cocktails' with light-up ice cubes, you'll have to check out the aquarium-like lower-level rest rooms.

Twenty Manning S   21 | 21 | 19 | $39
261 S. 20th St. (bet. Locust & Spruce Sts.), 215-731-0900

◪ "Where the beautiful people go" you'll find "another Audrey Claire hit"; this "sleek", "cosmopolitan" Asian-American off Rittenhouse Square, where chef Kiong Banh "proudly" puts out "creative", "tasty" treats like barbecued ahi tuna and foie gras meatloaf, is ravaged by a "noise storm" so severe that "conversation is impossible", but if you're "curious" as to what's "trendy", the joint sure is "in."

Twenty21   – | – | – | E
2005 Market St. (bet. 20th & 21st Sts.), 215-851-6262

Amid the towering skyscrapers of Center City, this sleek, upscale establishment is a suitable place for a business lunch given the extremely comfortable quarters (the space is cavernous, but it's smartly warmed up with amber tones and fabric-draped columns), attentive service and a refined New American menu; it may prove to be a worthwhile dinner destination too, as it features an award-winning

vote at zagat.com

Philadelphia F | D | S | C

wine selection, as well as alfresco dining in the courtyard with Commerce Square's lighted fountain serving as a lovely backdrop.

211 York 21 | 18 | 20 | $39
211 Old York Rd. (bet. Greenwood & Summit Aves.), Jenkintown, 215-517-5117

■ "Le Bec-Fin alum" Tim Papa "learned his lessons well"; his "jewel" of a New American is Jenkintown's "hidden treasure", bringing "Center City style" to "the northern suburbs" with a "fantastic", "imaginative menu", "friendly", "attentive service" and "sophisticated" decor, all "much needed in the area."

2 Goodfellas ▽ 18 | 15 | 18 | $16
4101 Walnut St. (41st St.), 215-382-3600

◪ The "friendly" fellas behind this "pleasant addition" to West Philly serve up their "moms' Italian food" to hungry Penn patrons, some of whom think it's "melt-in-your-mouth" "great"; but foodies fuss that, despite its name, the grub is "not that good", and design divas dismiss "decor that could only have been chosen by straight men", not that there's anything wrong with that.

UMBRIA ⊄ 24 | 18 | 22 | $37
7131 Germantown Ave. (bet. Mt. Airy & Mt. Pleasant Aves.), 215-242-6470

■ "Don't let the storefront look keep you away" from this Eclectic BYO "gem" "out of the way" in "unlikely" Mount Airy; inside you'll find "cozy" environs for a "low-priced" meal that's "exquisite if chosen right"; "thank God it's not downtown or we'd never get in" say locals; N.B. open Wednesday–Saturday.

Upstares at Varalli ⑤ 20 | 18 | 19 | $35
1345 Locust St. (Broad St.), 215-546-4200

◪ Friendly audiences consider "the perfect overture to a concert" at the Academy to be a meal at this "handy" Northern Italian, "reliable" for "reasonably priced" pasta and seafood dishes; harsher critics comment that despite "attitude problems" and "mediocre" fare, it's "a nice place for dinner" because of its "fabulous" location overlooking the Avenue of the Arts.

U.S. Hotel Bar & Grill ⑤ ▽ 20 | 18 | 18 | $26
4439 Main St. (Green Ln.), 215-483-9222

■ "Really tasty fries", mac 'n' cheese "just like mom's" and a "wide variety" of other "fantastic" New American eats are responsible for a rise in food ratings for this "beautifully restored" "pub" in Manayunk; "an excellent selection of beers" draws "unmanageable crowds" "on weekends", but visit on a weeknight for a "comfortable" and "classy" meal.

Philadelphia F | D | S | C

Valanni ●S 22 | 19 | 19 | $37
1229 Spruce St. (bet. 12th & 13th Sts.), 215-790-9494
☛ "Latin-Mediterranean fusion? – honest, it works" at this "chic" Wash West boîte where the "health-conscious cuisine" is as "yummy" as the "super" late-night "scene", and "you don't have to take out a loan to pay" for either; one of the "hottest spots in the gayborhood", it's where the "hip" sip and the staff slips, delivering "incompetent" service that only a few "clever mixed drinks" can allay.

Valley Forge Brewing Company S 14 | 13 | 14 | $21
Gateway Shopping Ctr., 267 E. Swedesford Rd. (DeKalb Pike), Wayne, 610-687-8700
☛ "Gimme the chicken pot pie" cluck "colonial" "comfort food" fans at Wayne's Traditional American brewpub paean to the winter of 1777–78; however, revolutionaries holler "have a beer and get out to cut your losses" rather than spend your George Washingtons on "truly unspectacular" vittles served in a "family restaurant" with "all the charm and atmosphere of a bowling alley."

Vesuvio S – | – | – | M
736-38 S. Eighth St. (Fitzwater St.), 215-922-8380
In the red-gravy neighborhood of Bella Vista, this family-run, white-tablecloth newcomer has erupted on the scene by tossing out all the tired, preconceived notions about what a South Philly Italian *should* serve; not only does the kitchen offer contemporary takes on familiar ingredients, but a late-night bar menu is served till 1:30 AM.

VETRI 28 | 23 | 26 | $62
1312 Spruce St. (bet. Broad & 13th Sts.), 215-732-3478
■ "There are not enough superlatives" to describe this "most excellent" of Philly's Italians housed in a "charmingly designed townhouse" where a "flawless" staff serves "culinary genius" Marc Vetri's "lovingly prepared and beautifully presented treasures", including a "spinach gnocchi unlike anything else in the world"; diners lucky to score an "almost impossible-to-get reservation" at this Center City "jewel" exclaim "may it always thrive."

Vickers Tavern 22 | 22 | 20 | $43
E. Welsh Pool Rd. & Gordon Dr., Exton, 610-363-7998
■ "The owners have done a remarkable job" with this "country-quaint" Continental in an 1820s Exton farmhouse, "modernizing it without losing its charm"; it's a "pleasurable experience" to dine on "excellent" fare amid "rustic" decor that "brings history to life."

Victor Café ●S 18 | 21 | 21 | $36
1303 Dickinson St. (bet. Broad & 13th Sts.), 215-468-3040
☛ It's "all about the opera" at this South Philly Italian "institution" where the "singing waiters and waitresses"

vote at zagat.com

Philadelphia F | D | S | C

are such "a hoot" they "make you want to go home and croon in the shower"; while most think the "food's not bad either", no one's belting out "arias" about it.

Victory Brewing Co. S ▽ 18 | 14 | 18 | $19
420 Acorn Ln. (Chestnut St.), Downingtown, 610-873-0881
■ Sure, it's a "neighborhood favorite", but it's also one of the "best microbreweries in the tri-state area" according to guzzling groupies who gather for "a game of pool or darts", a "noisy party" and "delicious homemade" suds on tap on "really hopping nights and weekends" in Downington; oh yeah, and the "typical" American pub grub is "ok" too.

Vientiane Café ⌽ – | – | – | I
4728 Baltimore Ave. (bet. 47th & 48th Sts.), 215-726-1095
Popular with college students and local denizens, this humble BYO Laotian cafe in West Philly is run by a friendly, eager-to-please family that started out cooking for folks in their home backyard, perfumed by a fragrant kaffir lime tree; now installed in a tiny storefront, the Phanthavongs continue to turn out such dishes as green papaya salad, rice-noodle dumplings and chicken laab.

VIETNAM S 24 | 19 | 20 | $21
221 N. 11th St. (bet. Race & Vine Sts.), 215-592-1163
■ "Spring rolls, spring rolls and more spring rolls", "I can't stop eating the spring rolls" moan "addicts" who "get their fix" of "fresh", "complex" fare at "super-cheap" prices at this "excellent" Vietnamese on the east side of Chinatown's 11th Street; it's "fabulously" decorated in "chic" "French colonial" fashion, the staff is "fast" and "attentive" and – lest it wasn't clear – "oh, those spring rolls!"

Vietnam Palace S 23 | 14 | 21 | $20
222 N. 11th St. (bet. Race & Vine Sts.), 215-592-9596
■ The "hard-core following" of this "less commercial" Vietnamese on the west side of Chinatown's 11th insist the "plentiful", "authentic", "consistent food wins the contest against the guys across the street", with "wonderful soups" and "good happy pancakes" making diners, well, happy at "shockingly low prices"; the "waiters are cute" too, even if the "spartan decor" is "not as pretty" as the competition's.

Viggiano's S 18 | 19 | 19 | $28
16 E. First Ave. (Fayette St.), Conshohocken, 610-825-3151
◪ Who knew a "funeral home" could be "fun, fun, fun"?; this "hospitable" Southern Italian in former morticians' digs in Conshohocken "often has a musician strolling" for "family-friendly" entertainment, and – "great idea" – there's a wine store on the premises for BYO made easy; it's "crowded", "noisy" and "tacky", and the eats are "nothing great", but with "portions fit for the Klumps", you can

Philadelphia F | D | S | C

"take the kids", and the "next day", fill their lunch pails with the leftovers.

Villa di Roma S ⌿ 21 | 10 | 17 | $26
Italian Mkt., 932-36 S. Ninth St. (bet. Carpenter & Christian Sts.), 215-592-1295

■ Rome is called the Eternal City, and true to its name, this "old South Philly standby" "never changes"; with "down-home", "delicious" "red gravy" fare and "waitresses with great smiles and attitudes" straight outta the "WWF", it's "like visiting an old friend"; "soak up that Italian Market mood", order the eponymous salad and "wait for Rocky to come in" "at any moment."

Village Porch Bistro S 17 | 13 | 17 | $22
Olde Sproul Shopping Village, 1178 Baltimore Pike (Sproul Rd.), Springfield, 610-544-3220

◪ "If you were at Woodstock, you'll love this" New American BYO that opened in Delco a few years after you danced in the mud at Yasgur's farm; surveyors who "used to go here in high school" say "pretty much everything is the same" as back then: "excellent soups and salads" and "tasty sandwiches" still make a "great little sit-down place" out of what's basically a "glorified ice cream parlor", even if squares say the joint is "just a little bit strange."

Villa Strafford 21 | 20 | 22 | $43
115 Strafford Ave. (Lancaster Ave.), Wayne, 610-964-1116

◪ "Little ladies with blue hair do lunch" at this "clubby" Continental "institution on the Main Line", and once you know that you'll have "no surprises"; expect a "very good (and predictable) menu" of "standbys" like sautéed calf's liver and Dover sole, a "great jazz singer" in the bar on weekends and a "classic" setting "filled with smoke" from all the grandmas who are unreconstructed nicotine fiends.

Vincent's S ▽ 20 | 18 | 21 | $32
10 E. Gay St. (bet. High & Walnut Sts.), West Chester, 610-696-4262

■ The "courthouse crowd" rules in favor of "tasty", pricey lunches at this "comfortable" West Chester Mediterranean, and the dinner crowd gets "great joy" too from the meals served in the downstairs dining room, while "live jazz and blues" are played upstairs Thursday–Saturday.

Vinny T's of Boston S 14 | 16 | 17 | $25
Wynnewood Square Shopping Ctr., 260 E. Lancaster Ave. (bet. Chatham & Old Wynnewood Rds.), Wynnewood, 610-645-5400

◪ When it's "consume-mass-quantities day", "bring the kids" to this "loud, loud, louder" ("what did you say?") Wynnewood Italian paean to "overindulgence" bordering on the "grotesque"; it sure "doesn't equal mama's cooking",

vote at zagat.com

Philadelphia

F | **D** | **S** | **C**

but if you find its "popularity inexplicable", just count the doggy bags exiting the place.

Vivo Enoteca S   – | – | – | E

110 N. Wayne Ave. (Lancaster Ave.), Wayne, 610-964-8486
The crew from Christopher's has opened this darkly chic, oh-so-hip, oh-so-LOUD enoteca in Wayne that instantly became a magnet for Main Line trendies, who congregate downstairs in a bar that screens black-and-white Fellini films; upstairs, above most of the din, gourmands tuck into small plates of modern Italian dishes courtesy of chef James Burke (ex Vetri).

Warmdaddy's ◐S   17 | 18 | 16 | $31

4 S. Front St. (Market St.), 215-627-8400
☑ The "music is why you go" to this "jammin'" Old City Southerner serving up "decent fried chicken" and other appropriately "heavy", "down-home" treats that go "best with the blues"; hushed souls warn, however, that when the band gets cooking even "street drilling is quieter."

Warsaw Cafe   19 | 16 | 20 | $33

306 S. 16th St. (Spruce St.), 215-546-0204
■ "Cornering the market on Middle European cooking" in Center City, this "cozy" cafe offers up "cholesterol in each bite" with "consistent" "old-world" "comfort food" "faves" like beef stroganoff, veal roulades and stuffed cabbage; it's "quiet" enough for "conversation", and there's a certain "understated romance" to a room so small "you feel like you're eating in a dollhouse."

Washington Crossing Inn S   19 | 21 | 20 | $38

Rtes. 32 & 532, Washington Crossing, 215-493-3634
☑ By George, "they have it all" say troops loyal to this "lovely" late-"colonial" Continental near Washington Crossing State Park: "good meat and potatoes" ferried by a "pleasant staff", a patio overlooking "beautiful grounds" and, of course, "history"; dissenters are Whigged out by the "outdated" "workmanlike" fare.

Washington House S   ▽ 22 | 20 | 20 | $31

136 N. Main St. (Temple Ave.), Sellersville, 215-257-3000
■ For "classic, comfortable PA inn dining", "history" buffs drive to "the middle of nowhere" for a meal at this "quaint" New American situated in a "very well-maintained" 1742 building in Sellersville; "good food well prepared and served" amid "nice Victorian decor" makes for "one of Upper Bucks' best" meals "on a special occasion."

WHITE DOG CAFE S   23 | 21 | 20 | $36

3420 Sansom St. (34th St.), 215-386-9224
■ "Pioneer" Judy Wicks' "politically correct" "University City landmark" is as "reliable as man's [um, person's] best

Philadelphia F D S C

friend", "serving your social conscience" and your "tummy" with an "amazing combo of community [spirit] and cuisine"; chef Kevin von Klause's "delicious" Eclectic eats made from "fabulous" "organic and free-range" ingredients can be had "with or without" "activist" "films and lectures" in the "tchotchke-filled" quarters.

White Elephant S — | — | — | M
759 Huntingdon Pike (bet. Berkley & San Diego Aves.), Huntington Valley, 215-663-1495
Pack your trunk and march to this stylish Thai in Huntingdon Valley, where the pleasing decor is positively populated by pachyderms; the playful menu applies unforgettable names (Evil Jungle Princess, Royal Bath) to the well-seasoned dishes, and upon request the accommodating staff will tone down the spice; while it's a casual, BYO experience, know that the tab is not quite peanuts.

WILLIAM PENN INN S | 21 | 24 | 22 | $37
William Penn Inn, DeKalb & Sumneytown Pikes, Gwynedd, 215-699-9272
■ "Grandma's fave" for a "fantasy" "holiday" meal might be this "old-fashioned" 18th-century Montco Continental-American that's been around longer than she has; "classic" dishes, "unobtrusive service" and "lovely" decor set the "gold standard" for "mature dining", particularly during "early-bird" hours, when "blue-haired" gourmands garner the "best buy in town"; youngsters say the "adequate but unadventurous" "institution" is "stodgy."

Willistown Grille | 22 | 20 | 21 | $35
4 Manor Rd. (Lancaster Ave.), Paoli, 610-695-8990
■ "Upscale" yet "unpretentious", this Continental in Paoli "impresses the boss" as well as Main Line "locals" with "consistently good" food and "attentive" service, "even for a large party"; a few feel the setting "needs windows", but others appreciate the "privacy."

Winberie's S | 15 | 16 | 16 | $24
1164 Valley Forge Rd. (bet. Anthony Wayne Dr. & Walker Rd.), Wayne, 610-293-9333
■ It "might as well be a chain" whine Wayners, and so it is; this "run-of-the-mill Bennigan's-esque" French bistro link will do "in a pinch" for a "casual" lunch with "grandma or a 5-year-old", especially on the "wonderful patio" in "nice weather" before a visit to the Valley Forge National Historical Park nearby.

Wooden Iron S — | — | — | VE
118 N. Wayne Ave. (Lancaster Ave.), Wayne, 610-964-7888
The Main Line blue-blazer set favors this golf-themed American in Wayne, where the menu of steaks, crab cakes and the like is par for the course and the "great martini"

Philadelphia

F D S C

and scotch selections can fill a scorecard, though the panel is out on whether it's worth the drive.

World Fusion ▁ ▁ ▁ E
123 Chestnut St. (bet. Front & 2nd Sts.), 215-629-1100
It may be hard to tell just where you are at this Old City site, because while the lofty setting (sky-blue ceiling, enormous columns) suggests you're still at Rococo (the previous occupant), the Eclectic menu – billed as Polynesian-French, Mediterranean and Spanish inspired – is all over the map; though most of chef Mark Muszynski's tapas-style small plates are excellent, the service can be lackluster.

YANGMING S 24 21 22 $35
1051 Conestoga Rd. (Haverford Rd.), Bryn Mawr, 610-527-3200
■ Main Liners "fall in love with the food" "again and again" at this "classy-to-the-core" "institution" in Bryn Mawr; the "innovative" Chinese-Continental specials "melt in your mouth", the service is "stellar", the "bartenders know what they're doing" and it always "feels like a party", making it among the "suburbs' best" for a "beautiful" Sino supper.

Yardley Inn S ▁ ▁ ▁ E
82 E. Afton Ave. (Delaware Ave.), Yardley, 215-493-3800
Perched along the Delaware River in scenic Bucks County, this elegant country destination recently got a major boost with the arrival of chef David Cunningham, who did a *Green Acres* escape from Manhattan with his family; he has redesigned the dining room and tavern menus, which now feature seasonal New American cuisine and pair well with the fairly extensive wine list (which commendably includes a selection of 30 bottles for only $30 apiece).

Yellow Springs Inn S 21 22 21 $44
1701 Art School Rd. (Yellow Springs Rd.), Chester Springs, 610-827-7477
◪ Yellow with "candlelight", this classic French "out of the way" in the Chester County "countryside" plans to move even farther down the road in the near future, but until then, loyalists can "look forward" to a "lovely evening" in an "antique-filled" setting, dining on "delicious" dishes; hope springs eternal that the new quarters will quell contemporary stylists' complaints of a "tired" interior.

Ye Olde Concordville Inn S ∇ 20 18 19 $31
Best Western Concordville Hotel, 780 Baltimore Pike (Rte. 322), Concordville, 610-459-2230
◪ An olde "standby" for 20 or so years, ye family-run American-Continental in the Concordville Best Western provides a "reliable" dining experience with "good food" at "reasonable" prices; the inn crowd, however, claims it's a "stuffy" "throwback" with an "uninspired, traditional" menu.

Philadelphia | F | D | S | C |

ZanzibarBlue ●◐ S | 20 | 22 | 20 | $40 |
The Bellevue, 200 S. Broad St. (Walnut St.), 215-732-4500
■ "The food and jazz never miss a beat" at the Bynum brothers' "sophisticated" "lair" on the lower level of The Bellevue on the Avenue of the Arts; the "creative" Eclectic fare is much "better than you'd expect" from a club, the music is "amazing" and if you mix it with the "exciting" decor, you've got a rhapsody in blue that the tongue-tied consider "too cool for words"; N.B. there's a new offshoot in Wilmington, DE.

Zesty's S | 18 | 15 | 18 | $32 |
4382 Main St. (Levering St.), 215-483-6226
◪ Dionysians delight in this "casual" Greek-Italian "favorite" in Manayunk that's "as lively as its name implies", with "cheerful" service and "decent" fare at non-ex-Zorba-tant prices "that won't break the bank"; party-poopers point out it gets "crowded" and "noisy", but more maintain that's the by-product of the "friendly atmosphere."

Zocalo | 21 | 19 | 19 | $31 |
3600 Lancaster Ave. (36th St.), 215-895-0139
■ Several "steps above taco-and-beans" cuisine is this "mini-vacation to Mexico" "tucked away" on the edge of University City; chef Jackie Pestka's "superior", "creative" dishes pair up perfectly with "fantastic" sangria and margaritas, and there's "nice", "heads-up" service to help keep this "sunny little place" "going strong."

vote at zagat.com

Lancaster/ Berks Counties

Top Food
- **26** Green Hills Inn
- **25** Gracie's
- **24** Log Cabin
- **23** Restaurant at Doneckers
- **22** Lemon Grass Thai

Top Decor
- **24** Gracie's
- Log Cabin
- **22** Green Hills Inn
- **21** Restaurant at Doneckers
- **20** Groff's Farm Restaurant

Top Service
- **24** Green Hills Inn
- Log Cabin
- **23** Gracie's
- **22** Restaurant at Doneckers
- **21** Groff's Farm Restaurant

Best Buys
1. Isaac's Restaurant & Deli
2. Windmill
3. Zinn's Diner
4. Good 'N Plenty
5. Bird-in-Hand

	F	D	S	C

Bird-in-Hand Family Restaurant   17 | 14 | 18 | $19
2760 Old Philadelphia Pike (Ronks Rd.), Bird-in-Hand, 717-768-8266

■ "Amish folks actually eat" at this "above-average" Lancaster County PA Dutchery where the buffet groans under the weight of enough "home-calling fare" to "feed a farmer", some "tourists" and a whole lotta "blue-haired" folks; who says there's "nothing innovative or inspiring" here? – "how about those ham balls?"

Cafe Unicorn   – | – | – | E
116 Lafayette St. (Pennsylvania Ave.), Reading, 610-929-9992

If you're looking for a "great place to eat" in Hyde Park, try this "quaint" New American where hearty fare like oyster stew and rack of lamb goes well with a "good wine list"; it's "hard to find", but once you get there, you'll see how the "incredibly attentive" service helps make it a "favorite."

Carr's S   – | – | – | M
50 W. Grant St. (Market St.), Lancaster, 717-299-7090

"The best thing to happen to dining in years" is the return of this New American–Asian in Market Fare's former digs say Lancaster locals; for that hot "downtown action" PA Dutch Country–style, ascend from the "basement" room to the "upstairs sushi and martini bar" and groove on some jazz.

Damon's Grill ●S   ▽ 17 | 15 | 14 | $23
680 Park City Ctr. (Harrisburg Pike), Lancaster, 717-481-9800

■ "If you can get in" to this American "sports bar" in Lancaster, you can gnaw on "great ribs" while rooting for

Lancaster/Berks Counties | F | D | S | C |

your team on the giant screens; with some house BBQ sauce to go, you can pour on the "good family" fun at home.

Doc Holliday's S | ▽ 17 | 13 | 14 | $20 |
931 Harrisburg Pike (College Ave.), Lancaster, 717-397-3811

■ The Franklin & Marshall gang "hangs" at this casual Traditional American joint across from their Lancaster corral; "good hamburgers" are "kid-pleasing" during the day, while live bands and drink specials are "great for college students" by night.

Good 'N Plenty | 19 | 14 | 19 | $20 |
Eastbrook Rd. (1 mi. north of Rte. 30), Smoketown, 717-394-7111

■ In a converted 1871 farmhouse in Lancaster County, this behemoth Pennsylvania Dutchery "caters to the buses" that tour the area, boasting capacity for 600 bellies; "eat, eat, eat" all you can and meet, meet, "meet your neighbors" – as "delicious, homestyle meals are served" "fast and friendly" "on long tables", it's "plenty good" for "making new pals."

Gracie's 21st Century Cafe | 25 | 24 | 23 | $49 |
1534 Manatawny Dr. (north of Rte. 422), Pine Forge, 610-323-4004

■ "Once you find it, you'll find it a find" – this "cool" Eclectic is "exceptional in all categories", but file it under "remote but worth the drive", since Lancaster/Berks' No. 1 Decor, the "eccentric" "character" and "delicious food" are "out of this world", and if the location isn't so far afield, it's still near Pottstown; "expect the unexpected", but so you're not too surprised, note it's dinner-only, Wednesday–Saturday.

Green Hills Inn | 26 | 22 | 24 | $53 |
2444 Morgantown Rd. (9 mi. north of Pennsylvania Tpke., exit 22), Reading, 610-777-9611

■ For "big-city dining in a country farmhouse" setting, this Franco-American housed in a "charming" 1805 Reading inn is "consistently marvelous"; "you can tell the chef has a great eye for detail", since his "intensely flavored" fare garners the No. 1 Food rating in Lancaster/Berks, and the "cordial", "caring" staff follows suit with the area's No. 1 Service, so you "can't go wrong for special occasions" here.

Groff's Farm Restaurant | 20 | 20 | 21 | $30 |
650 Pinkerton Rd. (south of Mount Joy Pike), Mount Joy, 717-653-2048

◪ "Delightful" dish refers to both the "real American" eats and "the stories told by Mrs. Groff" at this long-standing family-run Pennsylvania Dutch attached to a Lancaster County golf course; fill up on such esoteric creations as signature chicken *stoltzfus* served à la carte or family-style in the 1756 farmhouse, and afterward lumber back to

Lancaster/Berks Counties F | D | S | C |

your room in the B&B beside the first tee; N.B. open only on Friday and Saturday nights.

Haydn Zug's ▽ 22 | 23 | 21 | $36 |
1987 State St. (Rte. 72), East Petersburg, 717-569-5746
■ "Out in Lancaster County", this Traditional American serves up "must-have cheese chowder", "super crab cakes" and other delectables to be savored with a bottle from the "good wine list" amid "beautiful decor" in an 1852 building; those who don't relish the drive to East Petersburg "wish they had one in Philly."

Historic Revere Tavern S ▽ 17 | 15 | 19 | $27 |
Best Western Revere Inn & Suites, 3063 Lincoln Hwy. E. (west of Belmont Rd.), Paradise, 717-687-8601
■ Oh Susanna, now don't you cry for me, 'cause I'm getting "consistently good food" and "attentive but not hovering" service sing surveyors about this "great, historic" Traditional American where Stephen Foster first hummed some of his most famous tunes, smack "in the heart" of the Lancaster County "tourist area"; the signature turtle soup is as "far above typical" as the tavern's colorful past.

Hoss's Family Steak & Sea House S 14 | 12 | 12 | $17 |
100 W. Airport Rd. (Lititz Pike), Lititz, 717-519-6853
☑ "So much quantity!" gasp "travelers" pit-stopping at these "family steakhouse" chainsters in Lititz and Exton, where "well-supplied" is an understated description for the soup and salad bar accompanying entrées; gastronomes may groan that it's "the height of mediocrity", but it's a "good place for a quick, filling meal before retiring to your room at the Microtel", or before retiring altogether, since seniors eat at a discount.

Isaac's Restaurant & Deli S 17 | 13 | 16 | $13 |
Cloister Shopping Ctr., 120 N. Reading Rd. (Martin Ave.), Ephrata, 717-733-7777
Granite Run Sq., 1559 Manheim Pike (Rte. 283), Lancaster, 717-560-7774
25 N. Queen St. (Orange St.), Lancaster, 717-394-5544
Shoppes at Greenfield, 565 Greenfield Rd. (Rte. 30), Lancaster, 717-393-6067
Sycamore Ct., 245 Centerville Rd. (Rte. 30), Lancaster, 717-393-1199
4 Trolley Run Rd. (Owl Hill Rd.), Lititz, 717-625-1181
Shops at Traintown, Rte. 741 E. (Rte. 896), Strasburg, 717-687-7699
94 Commerce Dr. (Broadcasting & State Hill Rds.), Wyomissing, 610-376-1717
☑ Those pretzel rolls sure are "clever", plus they're the main attraction at the area's No. 1 Bang for the Buck, so for a "really" "different sandwich creation" at a really reasonable

Lancaster/Berks Counties   F | D | S | C

rate, try one of these "consistent" deli chain links in Lancaster and beyond; the "nifty pickle bowl served with every meal" is as "fun" as the buns, but critics are soured on "slow service."

Kegel's Seafood S   – | – | – | M
551 W. King St. (Pine St.), Lancaster, 717-397-2832
A "stable" staple since 1941, this downtown Lancaster seafooder serves "she-crab soup to die for" and fin fare that's the "freshest around" in "nice, quiet" surroundings that haven't "changed a bit in years" – yep, "granddad came here", and his offspring "can see why."

Lemon Grass Thai S   22 | 16 | 18 | $24
2481 Lincoln Hwy. E. (Eastbrook Rd.), Lancaster, 717-295-1621
See review in the Philadelphia Directory.

Lily's on Main S   ▽ 27 | 21 | 22 | $35
Brossman Business Complex, 124 E. Main St. (Lake St.), Ephrata, 717-738-2711
■ "You'll think you're in NYC", which is quite a "surprise" when you're actually in the "quaint", "small town" of Ephrata; signature raspberry chicken, triple-layer chocolate cake and other "great tastes" off the "wonderful" New American menu set the stage for "gracious" dining in a "lovely setting" with an art deco flair.

Log Cabin S   24 | 24 | 24 | $43
11 Lehoy Forest Dr. (Rte. 272), Lancaster, 717-626-1181
■ "As one would expect of a former speakeasy", "directions are necessary to find" this "well-hidden" steakhouse over the "covered bridge" and through the woods of Lancaster; "art-filled surroundings" provide a "wonderful" backdrop for "hearty" meals off a "circa-1970" menu, and the "friendly, efficient staff" helps make it "memorable" for both you and "your sweetheart."

Miller's Smorgasbord S   18 | 15 | 17 | $26
2811 Lincoln Hwy. E. (1 mi. east of Rte. 896), Ronks, 717-687-6621
■ To naysayers who claim "nothing exciting happens here", one surveyor offers up a "son who has a record of 13 different desserts at one sitting" at this "all-you-can-eat" "hog trough of solid Pennsylvania Dutch fare" in Ronks; after such a "huge variety" of "good-value" eats, "you'll need a U-Haul to get you out" the door.

Olde Greenfield Inn S   20 | 20 | 18 | $32
595 Greenfield Rd. (William Penn Way), Lancaster, 717-393-0668
◪ "Be sure to ask for a table downstairs in the romantic (but chilly) wine cellar" at this "comfortable" Traditional

vote at zagat.com

Lancaster/Berks Counties | F | D | S | C |

American in a "lovely" 1780 farmhouse; with "great Bloody Marys" at brunch and a "very good selection of salads" and entrées, fans say it's among "the best Lancaster has to offer", but passé patrons are "bored top to bottom."

Outback Steakhouse S | 17 | 14 | 16 | $27 |
Oregon Pike & Rte. 30, Lancaster, 717-569-4500
See review in the Philadelphia Directory.

Plain & Fancy Farm S | 18 | 15 | 16 | $22 |
3121 Old Philadelphia Pike (1 mi. east of Ronks Rd.), Bird-in-Hand, 717-768-4400

◪ A trip to Bird-in-Hand is worth two in your belly when you gobble from the "homestyle" platters at this PA Dutch "mob scene"; it's "nothing more" than a "touristy starch-fest", but you sure "get your money's worth", and "besides, you meet people from all over at your communal table."

Red Caboose S | ▽ 13 | 18 | 17 | $15 |
312 Paradise Ln. (Rte. 741), Strasburg, 717-687-5001

◪ For a slice of the "best shoofly pie" and other traditional PA Dutch fare, hop onboard the Strasburg steam train that loops around this kitschy outpost and disembark at the Victorian-style dining car near the same-named motel; it's "fun for the kids", but as for the type of heavy eats that put padding on your caboose, ratings suggest adults might want something on a different track.

Restaurant at Doneckers | 23 | 21 | 22 | $39 |
The Doneckers Community, 333 N. State St. (Walnut St.), Ephrata, 717-738-9501

■ When you're "out in the country" in Ephrata, "shop till you drop" at Doneckers Community store, then "refresh yourself" at this New French "surprise"; chef Greg Gable, an alum of Le Bec-Fin, raises the fare to a "gourmet level" in a "lovely", "pleasant room" with "quality service" to boot; a few nitpickers pout that the "price is high", but most are willing to pay for an experience this "charming."

Stoltzfus Farm | ▽ 19 | 13 | 21 | $22 |
3716A E. Newport Rd. (Old Philadelphia Pike), Intercourse, 717-768-8156

◪ Motorists tooling through Intercourse pit-stop at this "true Pennsylvania Dutch" spot for "hearty" grub that "captures the Amish [country] family dining experience" to a tee; though they "appreciate the absence of a gift shop", fussy foodies ask "did they lose grandma's recipes?"

Stoudt's Black Angus S | 20 | 18 | 20 | $32 |
Rte. 272 & Stoudtburg Rd. (Pennsylvania Tpke., exit 21/286), Adamstown, 717-484-4386

■ Stout supporters insist that you "absolutely cannot beat Carol's beer and Ed's bread" at the couple's "antiquey"

Lancaster/Berks Counties   F | D | S | C

cow palace where you can "order from the steakhouse or brewpub menu" for an "excellent" slab of beef or "good German" grub; it's a "reason to visit Lancaster County besides the outlets."

Sweet Bay Cafe ⊭   – | – | – | M
1131 Muhlenberg St. (bet. 11th & 12th Sts.), Reading, 610-376-0100
A sweet bay of "surprisingly gourmet" cuisine in the "blue-collar" sea of East Reading, this bare-bones Eclectic BYO serves dishes like signature oyster bisque, veal chops and fresh fish "exquisitely prepared for each table", so "ignore the surroundings" and dig into a "great" meal.

Tony Wang's S   – | – | – | M
2217 Lincoln Hwy. E. (Harvest Rd.), Lancaster, 717-399-1915
Lincoln Highway's patrolling patrons proclaim that the eponymous chef-owner's BYO is just "what a local Chinese joint should be", with "delicious gourmet" dishes in sauces so good you'll "buy some to go"; he's a "hands-on" guy who "remembers the regulars", so though you might "wish he would franchise", do you really want to spread him too thin?

Willow Valley Family Restaurant S   ▽ 19 | 16 | 18 | $19
Willow Valley Resort, 2416 Willow Street Pike (Rte. 222S), Lancaster, 717-464-2711
◪ "Take your appetite" on the "tourist bus" to this "large" smorgasbord in Lancaster, where "you'll find all the PA Dutch staples solidly prepared" and dished up in "overwhelming quantities" at "great prices"; gourmands grouse "if you like fresh vegetables boiled into submission, this is your place."

Windmill S   13 | 10 | 15 | $14
2838 Main St. (Rte. 10), Morgantown, 610-286-5980
◪ Hightailers have a "hefty" hog-out "in a hurry" at this "typical PA Dutch" stop on the turnpike in Morgantown; however, where one diner's "quaint" is another's "scary", style mavens scream "spare me" from an "interior decorator who relied a little too heavily on a Cracker Barrel gift shop."

Zinn's Diner S   15 | 11 | 17 | $16
2270 N. Reading Rd. (Pennsylvania Tpke., exit 21/286), Denver, 717-336-2210
■ "People need stretch pants" after "loading up on the calories" in the "massive quantities" of "old-fashioned" "Amish cookin'" at this Denver diner on the PA Turnpike; think "starch, starch and more starch" "heaped in butter or lard" – "who needs sex" ask fans of the joint, and who can possibly do it after all this anyway?

vote at zagat.com

New Jersey Suburbs

Top Food
29 Siri's
26 Sagami
   Fuji
   La Campagne
25 Little Café

Top Decor
29 Rat's
24 Beau Rivage
   La Campagne
23 Braddock's Tavern
   Siri's

Top Service
26 Siri's
23 Beau Rivage
   Rat's
   La Campagne
22 Little Café

Best Buys
1. El Azteca
2. Singapore Kosher Veg.
3. Norma's Middle Eastern
4. Authentic Turkish Cuis.
5. Ponzio's

| F | D | S | C |

Andreotti's Viennese Cafe S   19 | 16 | 19 | $33
Pine Tree Plaza, 1442 Rte. 70 E. (bet. I-295 & Kings Hwy.), Cherry Hill, 856-795-0172

☑ BYA ("bring your appetite") to this "convenient" "old" Franco-Italian "hiding" in a Cherry Hill "strip mall", where the trencher-"ladies who lunch" lap up enough "flavorful" "extras" and "great dessert" selections "for three meals"; a bored contingent of refined palates, however, yawn "ho-hum", having grown "tired" of the prix fixe cafe's "tacky" "delusions of grandeur."

Authentic Turkish Cuisine S   21 | 18 | 22 | $25
8011 Centennial Blvd. (Evesham Rd.), Voorhees, 856-489-1212

■ This Voorhees "treat" is so "reminiscent of Istanbul" you feel as if you've been "invited into a family's home" in that city; surveyors suggest that you "give Turkish food a try" and in the process "get an education" in "exotic, sincere" savoriness "served with pride" at this "popular" BYO with a "bargain" lunch buffet.

Barnacle Ben's S   19 | – | 17 | $27
Moorestown Commons, 300 Young Ave. (Marter Ave.), Moorestown, 856-235-5808

☑ Afishionados agree "the crab cakes are a must" at this "steady" BYO seafooder, which recently relocated to larger, spiffier quarters in the Moorestown Commons; gone (to the relief of some design divas) is the "blue aquarium" interior, replaced by an airy California-y look indoors and a garden-like dining area outside; in addition to "good fish" "for the money", the menu now offers more items in the landlubber category.

New Jersey Suburbs | F | D | S | C |

Barone Trattoria S | 21 | 15 | 18 | $28 |
Barclay Farms Shopping Ctr., 210 Rte. 70 E. (I-295), Cherry Hill, 856-354-1888

Villa Barone S
753 Haddon Ave. (bet. Frazer & Washington Aves.), Collingswood, 856-858-2999

◪ "Great gravy" gasp groupies, and they mean it in the Italian sense at these "nice joints" in South Jersey; if you can stomach the "very long wait" amid the "big crowds" clamoring for "reasonable prices", once you score that hard-to-get table, "keep the ordering simple" and you're sure to have an "awesome" meal, but "bring a book to read between courses" 'cause "service is slooow."

Beau Rivage S | 23 | 24 | 23 | $54 |
128 Taunton Blvd. (Tuckerton Rd.), Medford, 856-983-1999

◪ "Why bother with Philadelphia" when you can be "queen for a day" right here in Medford at this "romantic" "fine" French eatery in the woods; the "elegant" "ambiance promises" what the kitchen "delivers in cuisine", so "take your honey" for a "wonderful dining experience" and "you won't regret it", despite the "expense."

Black Swan S | 22 | 19 | 20 | $37 |
Larchmont Commons Shopping Ctr., 127 Ark Rd. (Rte. 38), Mount Laurel, 856-866-0019

◪ Francis Hannan earns his Mount Laurels with "beautifully presented" New American dishes at his "tastefully" done BYO; though music lovers chime that the player piano "adds a nice touch" to an "enjoyable meal", critics strike a sour note, complaining that the "pretentious" place is "not as sophisticated as it would like to be" – "it's in a shopping center, for goodness sake."

Braddock's Tavern S | 22 | 23 | 21 | $43 |
39 S. Main St. (Coates St.), Medford, 609-654-1604

◪ It's "like a Charles Dickens novel" with Tiny Tim and the whole Cratchit clan at the themed holiday meal at this "cozy", "colonial" Traditional American in "quaint" Medford, where regulars know to "get an upstairs table" on the "attractive" porch; the "home-cooked" fare is "dependably" "delicious", even if the "menu has changed very little" over the years.

Buca di Beppo S | 15 | 17 | 17 | $24 |
2301 Kaighn Ave. (Church Circle Rd.), Cherry Hill, 856-779-3288
See review in the Philadelphia Directory.

Café Gallery S | 19 | 22 | 21 | $36 |
219 High St. (bet. Broad St. & Delaware River), Burlington, 609-386-6150

◪ For "a summer's eve delight", "sit outside, have a drink by the river" and enjoy a "spectacular view" at this "gussied

vote at zagat.com

New Jersey Suburbs

F | D | S | C

up" Continental in Burlington; the "longtime" "fave" is still quite "popular" for its "nice" Sunday buffet brunch, though modernists find it "past its prime."

Cafe M S
–|–|–|E

141 Kings Hwy. E. (Haddon Ave.), Haddonfield, 856-795-7232

Catering to yuppie Haddonfield, this sleek new storefront appeals with Jay Jones' (ex Susanna Foo) sophisticated Continental dishes and a BYO policy that encourages oenophiles to raid their cellars for their best bottles; it doesn't hurt either that its prime location on the main drag make for some of the area's best people-watching from the sidewalk tables.

Caffe Aldo Lamberti S
21 | 20 | 20 | $38

2011 Rte. 70 W. (Haddonfield Rd.), Cherry Hill, 856-663-1747

◪ Fans fawn "mama mia!" – even your "91-year-old mother-in-law" will be pleased when she's "catered to" by "servers who elevate the customer to the god or goddess level" at this "showy" Cherry Hill Italian with a "modern look" and "delicious" dishes; foes disagree, "hissing" over "snotty" servers and "just-above-average, overpriced food."

Catelli S
24 | 23 | 21 | $46

Plaza 1000 Main St. (Evesham & Kresson Rds.), Voorhees, 856-751-6069

■ The Voorhees "chic" set "goes to be seen" while sampling Louis Imbesi's "exquisite" fare at this "wonderful" Italian; "ask to sit in the conservatory", where the "religious experience" might include your impulse to "bless the waiters who repeat" elaborate recitations of "unusual" specials "over and over" above the "noise."

Chez Elena Wu S
23 | 20 | 21 | $33

910 Haddonfield-Berlin Rd. (east of I-295), Voorhees, 856-566-3222

◪ "The Susanna Foo of South Jersey", this "classy" BYO near the Ritz in Voorhees "elevates Chinese to a new level", with "light" "French touches", "elegant" decor and waiters who "baby you"; however, down-to-earth dollar-counters dis the "pricey" "pretensions" of "microscopic portions."

Creole Café S
∇ 25 | 18 | 21 | $35

1333 Black Horse Pike (Corkery Ln.), Williamstown, 856-262-2334

■ It may be the only serious thing going in South Jersey's "restaurant no-man's land", which explains why locals "love the place", so "call a week or two in advance for weekend reservations" at this "small" Cajun-Creole BYO; "save room for dinner" after sampling the "huge appetizers" because the "food is so outstanding" that even "Emeril would be happy, happy, happy."

New Jersey Suburbs | F | D | S | C |

East Side Mario's S | 12 | 15 | 14 | $20 |
1370 Blackwood-Clementon Rd. (Rte. 42), Clementon, 856-782-1969
See review in the Philadelphia Directory.

El Azteca S | 18 | 11 | 17 | $17 |
Ramblewood Shopping Ctr., 1155 Rte. 73N (Church Rd.), Mount Laurel, 856-914-9302
See review in the Philadelphia Directory.

Elements Café | – | – | – | M |
517 Station Ave. (White Horse Pike), Haddon Heights, 856-546-8840
Chef-owner Fred Kellermann (ex Philly's White Dog Cafe) has already developed a cult following at his spare new BYO cafe in Haddon Heights; at lunchtime, he turns out an array of salads and sandwiches, while his New American dinner menu (with elements of French, Asian and Latin flavors) is composed of a variety of small and large plates that allow patrons to make up their own tasting menus.

Elephant & Castle S | 11 | 13 | 13 | $21 |
Clarion Hotel & Conference Ctr., 1450 Rte. 70 E. (I-295), Cherry Hill, 856-427-0427
See review in the Philadelphia Directory.

Emerald Fish S | 21 | 15 | 20 | $33 |
Barclay Farms Shopping Ctr., Rte. 70 E. (bet. I-295 & Kings Hwy.), Cherry Hill, 856-616-9192
◪ From an "open kitchen" come "fresh" fish "interestingly prepared" with Asian and Latin flair at this "reasonably priced" BYO seafooder in Cherry Hill; architecturally inclined diners bemoan the "hectic strip-mall rectangle's" "awful layout", and though the waiters "know their stuff", at times they're so "thoughtful" that their minds seem elsewhere, resulting in "lackluster" service.

Filomena Cucina Italiana S | 21 | 16 | 19 | $32 |
Commerce Plaza I, 1245 Blackwood-Clementon Rd. (Laurel Rd.), Clementon, 856-784-6166
Filomena Lakeview S
1738 Cooper St. (Rte. 41), Deptford, 856-228-4235
■ "If your nana in heaven were sending down gnocchi", "lots and lots" of them would land on your plate at this "very fine", "no-nonsense" Southern Italian in a Clementon strip mall; "real" food at "reasonable" prices has fans filling the "favorite", so beware of "long waits on weekends"; N.B. there's an offshoot in Deptford.

Filomena Cucina Rustica S | 21 | 19 | 19 | $35 |
13 Cross Keys Rd. (White Horse Pike), Berlin, 856-753-3540
■ "You forget you're in South Jersey" at this "lovely" Italian off the Berlin Circle sporting "attractive rooms" and a "chef's

vote at zagat.com

New Jersey Suburbs | F | D | S | C |

table that makes you feel like royalty"; "wonderful mussels" and other "delicious" dishes "never disappoint", so it's a given you "won't walk away hungry", and you can even dance to the strains of the DJ and live bands.

Food for Thought S | 24 | 23 | 21 | $41 |
Marlton Crossing Shopping Ctr., 129 Rte. 73 S. (Rte. 70), Marlton, 856-797-1126
■ Marlton's "ladies who lunch" think warm thoughts about this "fancy" New American BYO where "everything is delicious" and the "rooms are beautifully appointed" with "decor they'd like to have in their homes"; it's "pricey for suburbia", but South Jersey cheers in unison "I'm worth it."

Fuji S | 26 | 13 | 21 | $38 |
404 Rte. 130 (N. Cinnaminson Ave.), Cinnaminson, 856-829-5211
◪ Those who've traveled to "genius" chef-owner Masaharu Ito's Japanese BYO in Cinnaminson are wowed by this "world-class" culinary peak, whether they order "fantastic" sushi, "imaginative" entrées or relish the "real thing": the big-ticket (much bigger than the cost estimate reflects) kaiseki tasting menu, a "complete surprise" every time; even its "shoebox" building and "plain" interior don't deter disciples, so be sure to "make reservations."

Giumarello's | ▽ 29 | 27 | 27 | $51 |
329 Haddon Ave. (bet. Cuthbert Blvd. & Kings Hwy.), Westmont, 856-858-9400
■ "From the time you make your reservation to tipping the valet for your car", this "upscale" Northern Italian is a "super experience"; its "fine" environs in Westmont are "wonderful for special-occasion" dining on "elegant", "nontraditional" "dishes that leave the kitchen in perfect condition", though after a few hits off the "fabulous martini list", you might not be in such great shape yourself.

Italian Bistro S | 16 | 16 | 17 | $24 |
1509 Rte. 38 (Chapel Ave.), Cherry Hill, 856-665-6900
590 Delsea Dr. (Holly Dr.), Sewell, 856-589-8883
See review in the Philadelphia Directory.

La Campagne S | 26 | 24 | 23 | $52 |
312 Kresson Rd. (bet. Brace & Marlkress Rds.), Cherry Hill, 856-429-7647
■ City slickers are surprised to stumble on this "elegant" bit of "Provence in the suburbs" of Cherry Hill, where chef Eric Hall's "truly upscale" New French fare gives gourmands a "sensual experience", from "imaginative" starters to "superior" desserts; the "lovely country home" setting and "attentive" service make for a "relaxing" atmosphere, and though it's admittedly "pricey", the BYO policy "adds to the value."

subscribe to zagat.com

New Jersey Suburbs | F | D | S | C |

Lamberti's Cucina S | 18 | 16 | 18 | $27 |
*1491 Brace Rd. (bet. Haddonfield-Berlin & Kresson Rds.),
Cherry Hill, 856-354-1157*
*Village of Taunton Forge Shopping Ctr., 200 Tuckerton Rd.
(Taunton Blvd.), Medford, 856-985-2975*
1643 Rte. 38 (Lumberton Rd.), Mount Holly, 609-261-2345
3210 Rte. 42 (Black Horse Pike), Turnersville, 856-728-4505
See review in the Philadelphia Directory.

Lambertville Station S | 19 | 20 | 19 | $33 |
*11 Bridge St. (Delaware River), Lambertville,
609-397-8300*
◼ Set in a "beautifully restored" 19th-century train station graced with antiques, polished oak, brass and etched glass, this "cutesy" New American in historic Lambertville offers an "interesting" menu featuring "exotic" game in season (including caribou, kangaroo and zebra); it makes for a "quaint getaway" "well located for a jaunt from New Hope", even though local foes find it merely a "tourist attraction" with fare that "tastes mass-produced."

Le Mê Toujours S | 24 | 22 | 20 | $41 |
*515 Rte. 73 S. (bet. Brick & Evesham Rds.), Marlton,
856-810-2000*
◼ Run by a "smart, sweet young couple", this "beautiful", "sophisticated" New French–Vietnamese BYO in Marlton promises an "adventure" with "outstanding" "gourmet" fusion fare priced at perhaps "half" of what an "equivalent" "meal in Philly or NYC" would cost; it's a "welcome change" from the ordinary, bringing "unexpected class to a Jersey shopping strip", but dissenters note that the "kitchen can be challenged by big crowds" and the servers need to lose their "be-a-regular-or-be-forgotten" attitude.

Little Café, A | 25 | 17 | 22 | $37 |
*Plaza Shoppes, 118 White Horse Rd. E. (Burnt Mill Rd.),
Voorhees, 856-784-3344*
◼ "Yahoo for Jersey!" – like the state itself, this Voorhees Eclectic BYO is "small but mighty", favored for "delicious" "bargain early dinners" that are "creative without being gimmicky"; while some find the strip maller's "intimate" interior "charming", others dub it A Little "Claustrophobic", especially when weekend crowds descend.

Little Tuna S | – | – | – | M |
*403 Haddon Ave. (Hawthorne Ave.), Haddonfield,
856-795-0888*
Amiable chef-owner Marcus Severs' (ex Pelican Fish Company) new shoebox-size BYO seafood house has found a welcoming home in Haddonfield, as evidenced by the nightly crowds that line up for his creamy bisques, honey-jalapeño glazed tuna and homemade desserts, all served at affordable prices by sweet folks in understated environs.

New Jersey Suburbs | F | D | S | C |

Max's S | – | – | – | E |
602 Burlington Pike N. (bet. Highland Ave. & Riverton Rd.), Cinnaminson, 856-663-6297
Alex Capasso, an alum of Center City's Brasserie Perrier, is winning raves at this contemporary Italian set in a lovingly restored Friends meetinghouse along a honky-tonk stretch of Route 130 in Cinnaminson; fans return again and again for his crispy black bass, osso buco and gnocchi with porcini cream, served amid a polished hardwood interior with a pair of working fireplaces; it's BYO, but there's a climate-controlled wine locker where regulars can store their own.

Mélange Café S | 23 | 15 | 21 | $35 |
1601 Chapel Ave. (Rte. 38), Cherry Hill, 856-663-7339
◪ Chef-owner Joe Brown's "exciting" mélange of Louisiana and Italian cuisines is much more than ok "bayou", as adherents in a "party mood" pack into his "unassuming" Cherry Hill BYO for "terrific" "inspirations" like a savory signature crabmeat cheesecake; some say he "could upgrade the decor" and slow down the "rushed" service.

Mexican Food Factory S | 20 | 18 | 18 | $24 |
601 Rte. 70 W. (Rte. 73), Marlton, 856-983-9222
■ Despite its moniker, this "old reliable staple" in Marlton offers "more than chain Mexican fare"; "authentic" "salsas make you weep with joy", the "margaritas are yummy" and "delicious, creative" dishes like mango-Brie quesadillas come in "generous portions" "for your buck" – no wonder there's "always a wait list" in the "good-vibe" *casa*.

Mikado ◐S | ▽ 22 | 17 | 21 | $30 |
2320 Rte. 70 W. (Cuthbert Blvd.), Cherry Hill, 856-665-4411
■ It's "well worth the drive" from Philly for the "super" Japanese offerings at this "diamond in the rough" in Cherry Hill; hyperbolic fans rave that the chefs slice the "best sushi in three states and two continents", claiming the "gem" "rivals Nobu" in New York – "really", it "rules."

Norma's Middle Eastern S | 22 | 13 | 19 | $22 |
Barclay Farms Shopping Ctr., Rte. 70 E. (bet. I-295 & Kings Hwy.), Cherry Hill, 856-795-1373
■ Expect "generous portions" of "simple, unadorned" Middle Eastern cooking at this "low-key" strip-mall BYO in Cherry Hill, which offers "impressively fresh and flavorful" fare at a "great value"; it "could use a face-lift", since there's "no decor to speak of", unless you count the belly dancers, who are always an "interesting" experience.

Olga's Diner ◐S | 12 | 10 | 14 | $18 |
Marlton Circle, 100 Rte. 70 E. (Rte. 73), Marlton, 856-596-1700
◪ "At a crossroads" both literally and figuratively, this "greasy spoon" on the Marlton Circle is "convenient" for "typical" "old-fashioned" "comfort food" – where else in

New Jersey Suburbs

the area can you get a "throw-back dieter's delight of cottage cheese and a hamburger patty" till 1 AM?

Olive S | 16 | 19 | 16 | $34
Short Hills Farm, 482 Evesham Rd. (west of Springdale Rd.), Cherry Hill, 856-428-4999

Olive it, olive it not – surveyors are split on this "very popular" Ameri-Med in a "chic" "converted farmhouse" in Cherry Hill; fans praise "astonishingly good" grub like sesame-crusted tuna while foes pick at a "posh atmosphere with no culinary substance" and a staff that's barely "out of diapers"; in sum, it may be "trying too hard to be trendy."

Outback Steakhouse S | 17 | 14 | 16 | $27
230 Lake Dr. E. (Rte. 38), Cherry Hill, 856-482-1350
4600 Rte. 42 (off of Atlantic City Expwy.), Turnersville, 856-728-3700
See review in the Philadelphia Directory.

Pelican Fish Company S | ▽ 25 | 18 | 23 | $34
508 Hurffville Crosskeys Rd. (Ganttown Rd.), Sewell, 856-589-6969

"Finally, decent fish in the suburbs" say Sewell seafood lovers of this "surprisingly elegant" and "excellent" BYO "find"; after lapping up "so-good drunken bisque", signature wasabi-crusted tuna and "great crab cakes", you'll "leave wanting to come back" for "more."

Ponzio's ●S | 18 | 13 | 17 | $21
7 Rte. 70 W. (Kings Hwy.), Cherry Hill, 856-428-4808

"Suburban power lunchers", "families" and "seniors" alike pack this "darn good" Cherry Hill "diner" for "comfort food" done up with "flair", even though it's "more expensive" than less "popular" joints; it's such an "institution" that, basically, "if you don't eat here, you don't live in Jersey."

Pub, The S | 18 | 13 | 17 | $29
Airport Circle, 7600 Kaighn Ave. (Crescent Blvd.), Pennsauken, 856-665-6440

It "seems like the '60s again" at this South Jersey meat palace, an "open-pit" "throwback" where "families feast" on "consistently" "good plain steaks" after bellying up to the "incredible salad bar"; the "warehouse" quarters show their age, but if you need somewhere to "take the in-laws" "at a reasonable price", this is it.

Rat's S | 24 | 29 | 23 | $55
16 Fairgrounds Rd. (Sculptor's Way), Hamilton, 609-584-7800

"Skip the mortgage" and splurge at this "outstanding" New French château "in the middle of nowhere" (actually, just outside of Trenton) on "gorgeous grounds" inspired by Claude Monet's home; garnering Jersey's No. 1 Decor rating, it's a "complete experience of beauty, supreme service" and "superb food" that must be capped off with a stroll through J. Seward Johnson Jr.'s "incredible" sculpture garden.

vote at zagat.com

New Jersey Suburbs | F | D | S | C |

Ritz Seafood S | 24 | 17 | 21 | $34 |
910 Haddonfield-Berlin Rd. (White Horse Rd.), Voorhees, 856-566-6650

"Nirvana in a strip mall" is attainable at this Pan-Asian seafooder near the Ritz cinema in Voorhees; it "draws a crowd (and it should)" for "knock-'em-dead" dishes served in a "peaceful" environment that includes a koi pond, waterfalls and a well-stocked tea bar, but it's "a little slow in the service department", so figure on a "long wait."

Sagami S | 26 | 15 | 21 | $33 |
37 W. Crescent Blvd. (Haddon Ave.), Collingswood, 856-854-9773

New Jersey "love, love, loves" this "special" BYO Japanese joint where some of "the best sushi in the tri-state area" make it a fin fan's "dream come true" (i.e. the fish is "so fresh it may still be breathing"); the "crowded", "low-ceilinged" room is "no-frills" and service is "rushed", but "tuna like buttah", "heavenly" hamachi and other "sublime" slices will take even the most queasy landlubbers and "turn them into believers."

Sage Diner ●S | 14 | 12 | 15 | $19 |
1170 Rte. 73 (Church Rd.), Mount Laurel, 856-727-0770

"When everything else is closed", this "mirror"-bedecked diner is "ok" for your "standard" greasy-spoon eats, i.e. a "large breakfast" at the crack of dawn or the stewed beef and a cuppa; plus, if you slouch in your booth long enough, "in another decade or so, it will become a nostalgic retro '80s" hangout and you'll be on the cutting edge.

Singapore Kosher Vegetarian S | 20 | 14 | 20 | $20 |
219 Berlin Rd. (Kresson Rd.), Cherry Hill, 856-795-0188
See review in the Philadelphia Directory.

Siri's Thai French Cuisine S | 29 | 23 | 26 | $38 |
2117 Rte. 70 W. (Haddonfield Rd.), Cherry Hill, 856-663-6781

"Don't be fooled by the storefront" – behind the "strip-mall" facade looms "paradise", New Jersey's No. 1 for Food and Service; devotees drive "from the suburbs of Philly" "across the bridge" to Cherry Hill to partake of Thai-French "fusion" meals that are "exquisite from beginning to end", with "superb" appetizers, "incredibly sauced" entrées and "unfailingly fabulous" desserts served in a "lovely setting"; the entirety leaves some tasters tongue-tied, as in "oh my God, what can I say? – no words can do it justice."

Thai Orchid S | 23 | 17 | 20 | $26 |
Crossing Plaza, 147-49 Rte. 73 S. (south of Rte. 70), Marlton, 856-985-5300
See review in the Philadelphia Directory.

Wilmington/ Nearby Delaware

Top Food
26 Green Room
   Restaurant 821
   Eclipse
   Brandywine Room
   Deep Blue

Top Decor
28 Green Room
27 Brandywine Room
26 Krazy Kat's
24 Restaurant 821
23 Eclipse

Top Service
26 Green Room
   Brandywine Room
24 Restaurant 821
23 Krazy Kat's
   Eclipse

Best Buys
1. Charcoal Pit
2. Brew HaHa!
3. La Tolteca
4. Mrs. Robino's
5. China Royal

F	D	S	C

Back Burner — 23 | 18 | 19 | $35
425 Hockessin Corner (Old Lancaster Pike), Hockessin, 302-239-2314
◪ "The kitchen's hard work shows" in the "delicious pumpkin-mushroom soup", "excellent steak" and other "wonderful" New American dishes at this "country-chic" spot in Hockessin; it "feels like an English tearoom" where "mostly ladies" of the "senior" variety fill their bellies before descending upon the nearby "neat shops to browse."

Brandywine Brewing Co. ●S — 15 | 15 | 15 | $23
Greenville Ctr., 3801 Kennett Pike (Buck Rd.), Greenville, 302-655-8000
◪ "The best part is the beer" at this Greenville brewpub, especially during the "good happy hour" or on "packed Friday nights" when eight housemade selections are tapped for a "noisy crowd"; food snobs say it's "a great place to meet people", if you're looking to hook up with "yuppies who like to be ripped off" on "overpriced", "average" eats.

Brandywine Room S — 26 | 27 | 26 | $49
Hotel du Pont, 11th & Market Sts., Wilmington, 302-594-3156
■ The "old-fashioned elegance" and "flawless" service of the Hotel du Pont's "clubby" Traditional American "makes you feel grown up", and "top-drawer" fare and "flawless" service live up to the sense of sophistication; "don't expect anything funky", but definitely expect a Wilmington dining experience that's "excellent in every way"; N.B. open to the public on Sunday and Monday nights only.

vote at zagat.com   145

Wilmington/Nearby Delaware F | D | S | C

Brew HaHa! ⊅ 16 | 14 | 15 | $11
3842 Kennett Pike (Buck Rd.), Greenville, 302-658-6336 S
Branmar Plaza, 1812 Marsh Rd. (Silverside Rd.), N. Wilmington, 302-529-1125 S
3636 Concord Pike (Silverside Rd.), Wilmington, 302-478-7227 S
Hotel du Pont, 1007 N. Market St. (10th St.), Wilmington, 302-656-1171
5329 Limestone Rd. (west of Stoney Batter Rd.), Wilmington, 302-234-9600 S
835 N. Market St. (bet. 8th & 9th Sts.), Wilmington, 302-777-4499
Rockford Shops, 1420 N. du Pont St. (Delaware Ave.), Wilmington, 302-778-2656 S

☒ Javaheads judge this "endearing" local coffeehouse chain with Wilmington, Bucks and Montco outlets "not as annoying" as its Seattle-based national competitor; the "comfortable" joints offer "every magazine to read over a decent cappuccino", "tasty sandwich" or "good salad", though caffeine fiends who find them "dull" question the moniker, wondering "what's so funny?"

Buckley's Tavern S 18 | 18 | 18 | $28
5812 Kennett Pike (south of Rte. 1), Centerville, 302-656-9776

■ You'll see "more du Ponts per square foot" at this New American that draws the "diamonds-and-denims" denizens to "colonial" quarters near the Winterthur Museum; the "fireplace is nice" for a "cozy" "Christmas vacation lunch", and the "upstairs deck in summer is wonderful" when chock-full of "fun, young" things sipping on the "best wine selection anywhere", courtesy of the adjacent vintner, and nibbling on "adequate" eats.

Caffè Bellissimo S 18 | 15 | 19 | $23
Depot Shopping Ctr., 3421 Kirkwood Hwy. (west of Rte. 141), Wilmington, 302-994-9200

☒ Sportive appetites scale "mountains o' pasta" at these "generic Italians" "busy" with bargain eaters in Wilmington and Springfield, PA; they're "great" for a "casual" pig-out and "guaranteed" leftovers, but "excessive quantity doesn't make up for" "skimping on quality" say noodle aficionados.

Charcoal Pit ◐S 19 | 12 | 17 | $12
240 Fox Hunt Dr. (off Wrangle Hill Rd.), Bear, 302-834-8000
2600 Concord Pike (Woodrow Ave.), Wilmington, 302-478-2165 ⊅
714 Greenbank Rd. (Kirkwood Hwy.), Wilmington, 302-998-8853
5200 Pike Creek Blvd. (Limestone Rd.), Wilmington, 302-999-7483 ⊅

■ Locals "all remember the Pit, puberty" and, it's implied, pimples because these "old-fashioned", "kid-friendly" "institutions" are "great places to get greasy burgers and fries" to wash down with "very good" "extra-thick black-and-white shakes"; dishing out "big servings" at "cheap"

Wilmington/Nearby Delaware F | D | S | C

prices straight "from the past", the area's No. 1 Bang for the Buck "hasn't kept up with the times – thank God!"

China Royal S 20 | 16 | 18 | $23
1845 Marsh Rd. (Silverside Rd.), Wilmington, 302-475-3686
☑ Residents of Wilmington count on this "cute" spot for "competent", "fast service" and "delicious", if somewhat "Americanized", Chinese standards, including "good soups and seafood preparations"; skeptics craving more variety say "it feels like they serve about three dishes and rename them to sound like 30."

Columbus Inn S 22 | 22 | 21 | $38
2216 Pennsylvania Ave. (Woodlawn Ave.), Wilmington, 302-571-1492
☑ "Power" trippers "who need to be seen" "always count on" this "stately" "old favorite" in a "historic setting" on Pennsylvania Avenue; both the "hearty" American fare and the entertainment feature a "wide range of choices", and the patio's perfect for "lethargy" after a "fabulous Sunday brunch buffet"; perhaps it's Republicans who say it's "tired", since word is this is "where the Democrats go."

Culinaria 23 | 18 | 19 | $27
Branmar Plaza, 1812 Marsh Rd. (Silverside Rd.), Wilmington, 302-475-4860
■ "Wilmington's stab at a modern restaurant" – "what a clever concept" crack sarcastic surveyors; but it seems to be working at this "hip" "gem of a place in a strip mall" on Marsh Road, where "straight-ahead" New American fare and a "good choice of wines by the glass" can be had in an "attractive" room at "reasonable prices"; it's "popular", of course, so "no reservations" means expect "a wait."

Deep Blue 26 | 22 | 23 | $42
111 W. 11th St. (bet. Orange & Tatnall Sts.), Wilmington, 302-777-2040
■ The "yuppie feeding fest" at Dan Butler's "stylish" seafood house is as "lively" as a school of barracuda on a bender; "have a drink and soak up" the "show-offy" vibe at the "great bar" before diving into "unbelievably fresh, exotic goodies from the ocean" at this "hopping" spot that's roiling the Wilmington backwaters; "friendly" waiters "work" to make everyone feel at home, though aging Mr. Limpets sigh "I think I'm too old for this place."

Eclipse S 26 | 23 | 23 | $42
1020 N. Union St. (10th St.), Wilmington, 302-658-1588
■ "The young and hip crowd" flocks to this "first-class" "restaurant-for-the-millennium" where a "trendy" but "comfortable" tile-heavy interior creates just the right setting for "reliable" yet "innovative" New American fare, including the chocolate-tower dessert; "comparable to

vote at zagat.com

Wilmington/Nearby Delaware   F | D | S | C

good Philadelphia" spots, it's "one of Wilmington's best for lunch or dinner."

Feby's Fishery S 21 | 12 | 18 | $27
3701 Lancaster Pike (bet. Centre & du Pont Rds.), Wilmington, 302-998-9501
■ "Especially during Lent", this "family-style" fish house on Lancaster Pike is "a bit crowded" with Wilmingtonians who "keep going back for the steamers" and "fine" "fried and broiled" seafood, even though afishionados claim it "not the greatest in town", while the "dive" decor "detracts from the pleasure" of the evening.

Green Room S 26 | 28 | 26 | $52
Hotel du Pont, 11th & Market Sts., Wilmington, 302-594-3154
■ "Old-money" "movers and shakers" mingle with folks just "pretending they made a million on Wall Street" at the Hotel du Pont's "dress-up" French, an "oasis of civility" that's Wilmington's No. 1 for Food, Decor and Service; needless to say, you'll be "pampered" as you dine on "heavenly", "sophisticated" cuisine to "soft live music" in an "outstandingly beautiful and relaxing" setting; all that's required of you in return is a hefty "expense account."

Harry's Savoy Grill ●S 23 | 20 | 21 | $37
2020 Naamans Rd. (Foulk Rd.), Wilmington, 302-475-3000
■ Wilmington's "big beef eaters" "never turn down an invitation" to Xavier Teixido's New American since "if you love great slabs o' meat, this place is it"; the "prime rib is wonderful" for a "corporate" "treat" or an "upscale" "Sunday dinner with the kids" in a "private clubhouse" setting, but if you're dining without the boss or the babies, "leave time for the great bar after dinner."

Hibachi S 19 | 17 | 19 | $26
5607 Concord Pike (north of Naamans Rd.), Wilmington, 302-477-0194
See review in the Philadelphia Directory.

Iron Hill
Brewery & Restaurant ●S 17 | 17 | 18 | $24
Traders Alley, 147 E. Main St. (bet. Chapel & Haines Sts.), Newark, 302-266-9000
■ "The beer's drinkable, the food's edible" – "not bad for a chain" slur guzzlers at these "competent" American brewpubs in PA and DE serving both burgers and "fancier" fare; "good" homemade suds and live music help make them "hot spots for informal dining" among "fun", "friendly" "young" "locals", so beware "long waits."

Italian Bistro S 16 | 16 | 17 | $24
4301 Kirkwood Hwy. (Farrand Dr.), Wilmington, 302-996-0700
See review in the Philadelphia Directory.

Wilmington/Nearby Delaware F | D | S | C

John Harvard's Brew House ●S 14 | 15 | 16 | $21
303 Rocky Run Pkwy. (Concord Pike), Wilmington, 302-477-6965
See review in the Philadelphia Directory.

Krazy Kat's S 25 | 26 | 23 | $47
Inn at Montchanin Village, Kirk Rd. & Rte. 100, Montchanin, 302-888-4200

■ It might be "tricky to find", but this "classy" Franco-Asian in a "historic inn" in Delaware's "château country" is "well worth the search"; "exquisite crab cakes" and other "krazy-good" dishes, potent drinks and "terrific service" are all the cat's meow, but it's the "gorgeous setting" with "whimsical" portraits of felines in "formal dress" that makes it a truly "magical" place purr patrons.

Lamberti's Cucina S 18 | 16 | 18 | $27
514 Philadelphia Pike (Marsh Rd.), Wilmington, 302-762-9094
Prices Corner Shopping Ctr., 1300 Centerville Rd. (Kirkwood Hwy.), Wilmington, 302-995-6955
See review in the Philadelphia Directory.

La Tolteca S 18 | 12 | 17 | $18
2209 Concord Pike (Rte. 141), Wilmington, 302-778-4646
4015 Concord Pike (bet. Brandywine Blvd. & Silverside Rd.), Wilmington, 302-478-9477

▲ "Always packed", these Wilmington joints are "family favorites for Mexican comfort food", pleasing with south-of-the-border specialties, as well as the "best margaritas in the known universe" according to besodden and sated surveyors; granted, the decor's "not too exciting", but the "authentic" food is "cheap and filling", the atmosphere "lively" and the service "kind and attentive."

L'Osteria Cucina Italiana 24 | 17 | 22 | $35
407 Marsh Rd. (Philadelphia Pike), Wilmington, 302-764-5071

■ "You'll quickly feel at home" in the "comfort" of Anthony Stella's "distinctive" Italian in northern Wilmington, a spot so "super-friendly" that the chef-owner himself might "come to your table" to "make recommendations" and "share a glass as well as his grandmother's wonderful recipes"; "gnocchi are the stars" here, and the "spectacular rice pudding is better than your mother's", but whatever you order, it's "never a bad meal."

Luigi Vitrone's Pastabilities S 22 | 18 | 19 | $29
415 N. Lincoln St. (5th St.), Wilmington, 302-656-9822

▲ "Now this is real Italian food" say *amici* of this "upscale" "gem" in Wilmington, where "everything is made to order", "nicely portioned" and "tasty"; "entry through the kitchen" is "entertainment in itself", though the "dark", "quaint"

vote at zagat.com

Wilmington/Nearby Delaware F D S C

dining room is "a little short on space", so of course it's barely pastable to get a table without a reservation.

Mikimotos S 23 | 22 | 21 | $32
1212 N. Washington St. (12th St.), Wilmington, 302-656-8638
■ It's "sushi gone disco" at this "in spot" where a "multi-ethnic crowd" gets its fill of Japanese "authenticity"; though the "splashy" setting may be "a bit pretentious and cool for its own good", the "wonderful" hot plates and "excellent" raw fish are "gifts" to Wilmingtonians seeking "lively" eats.

Mona Lisa ▽ 22 | 15 | 16 | $28
607 N. Lincoln St. (6th St.), Wilmington, 302-888-2201
◪ The "jury's still out" on this Wilmington addition, though numbers suggest that Italian dishes like signature chicken in white wine sauce are "good" enough to keep customers smiling like you-know-who; the decor is only "fair", however, and the room can get "noisy" when it's "crowded."

Moro – | – | – | E
1307 N. Scott St. (bet. 13th & 14th Sts.), Wilmington, 302-777-1800
Clang, clang, clang went sleepy Wilmington's Trolley Square, which is now wide awake as CIA grad Michael DiBianca (ex Restaurant 821) is taking bold risks nightly in the New American kitchen at his theatrically dramatic, dressy-casual row house; add on a 250-bottle international wine list and the result is one of the most auspicious debuts in town in years; for an even bigger treat, book ahead and the chef will design a special tasting dinner for your table.

Mrs. Robino's S 17 | 10 | 16 | $18
520 N. Union St. (bet. 5th & 6th Sts.), Wilmington, 302-652-9223
■ For more than 60 years, this "old-fashioned" Italian "mainstay" in Wilmington has been feeding "generations" of neighbors "simple" "red-gravy" pasta like "grandmother fixed", plus the "absolute best cannolis in the galaxy"; though critics say it's "nothing too special", it's a "solid spaghetti house" with "very affordable prices."

Outback Steakhouse S 17 | 14 | 16 | $27
27 Possum Park Plaza (Kirkwood Hwy.), Newark, 302-366-8012
See review in the Philadelphia Directory.

Restaurant 821 26 | 24 | 24 | $48
821 N. Market St. (bet. 8th & 9th Sts.), Wilmington, 302-652-8821
■ For a "magical night that's as close to heaven as you'll get in Delaware", conjure up a table at this "*très* chic" Med "gourmet treat" across the street from the Grand Opera House in Wilmington, where the "excellent food",

Wilmington/Nearby Delaware F | D | S | C

"exquisite" decor and "attentive service" come together for a "standout" meal; if you're up for an "unusually" "elegant" evening, splurge on the chef's tasting menu offered in the wine cellar.

Stoney's ●S ▽ 18 | 14 | 15 | $22
3007 Concord Pike (Cleveland Ave.), Wilmington, 302-477-9740

🖃 Owner Michael Stone, aka "Stoney", "makes everyone feel welcome" at his "London-like" British pub on Concord Pike, where the lads and lasses lap up "great fish 'n' chips and beer"; even if the "pricing adds up" after a few too many pints and nibbles, regulars can't stop returning because the publican "is irresistible even if the food isn't."

Sullivan's Steakhouse S 23 | 21 | 21 | $44
Market Sq., 5525 Concord Pike (Naamans Rd.), Wilmington, 302-479-7970

🖃 "Take your sister" "for the food, and for the men" "in their 20s", at one of these "macho" meat chainsters in King of Prussia and Wilmington, where the "juicy" beef is "better than at many more expensive" places, but if she's a vegetarian, she can "skip the steak and feast on the sides", which are just as "mouthwatering"; amid the "high energy" and "live jazz", brace yourself for all the "noise."

Terrace at Greenhill S 15 | 16 | 16 | $24
800 N. du Pont Rd. (bet. Lancaster & Pennsylvania Aves.), Wilmington, 302-575-1990

🖃 A "good hamburger" at a "window table" with a "nice view of the course and the city" fits Wilmington "summer golfers" to a tee at this Traditional American "overlooking" the du Pont Road duffers; it's a "good date place" if you like the sport and you sit on the "nice patio", but the interior could use some work.

Toscana Kitchen & Bar S 24 | 21 | 22 | $36
Rockford Shops, 1412 N. du Pont St. (Delaware Ave.), Wilmington, 302-654-8001

■ Dan Butler has "nicely revamped" his Northern Italian kitchen in the Rockford Shops, and the "minimalist decor" and "superb regional cuisine" garners applause from the "thirtysomething crowd"; though an "older clientele" might "think the former menu was superior", today's "more reasonable prices" and the same "knowledgeable and enthusiastic" service as ever make it "a very hip place" to hang, despite the fact that it's no-reserve.

Vincente's 20 | 15 | 20 | $45
Independence Mall, 1601 Concord Pike (Rte. 202), Wilmington, 302-652-5142

🖃 Thrill to the "great cheese-tossing display", behold the wonder of the "walking menu", marvel at the "overpricing"

vote at zagat.com

Wilmington/Nearby Delaware F D S C

at resident ham/owner Vincent Mancari's Italian "for the old at heart" in Independence Mall; his shtick is "worth the trip", but foodies feel the fare "isn't."

Walter's Steakhouse S | 19 | 16 | 19 | $38
802 N. Union St. (8th St.), Wilmington, 302-652-6780

Not sure what age your mother is, but probably the "waitresses are older" than she is at this "dark", "homey" "blue-collar" steakhouse in downtown Wilmington; "long-term customers" claim it's a "great place to take a date" for a "cholesterol fix", plus a raw bar is thrown in gratis on Sunday, Monday and Thursday, even if non-"traditionalists" deem the joint "worn out."

Washington St. Ale House ●S | 16 | 15 | 15 | $22
1206 N. Washington St. (12th St.), Wilmington, 302-658-2537

The "*Animal House*" of Wilmington is "popular" with "post-collegiates" pining "loudly" for their toga days "over drinks" "on the patio in summer" and, come to think of it, in "wintertime" too, since it's "equipped with heaters"; of course there's a "large beer selection", but the Traditional American eats are "surprisingly good" as well.

ZanzibarBlue S | 20 | 22 | 20 | $40
1000 West St. (Delaware Ave.), Wilmington, 302-472-7000
See review in the Philadelphia Directory.

Indexes

**CUISINES
LOCATIONS
SPECIAL FEATURES**

Indexes list the best of many within each category.

All restaurants are in the Philadelphia metropolitan area unless otherwise noted (LB=Lancaster/Berks Counties; NJ=New Jersey Suburbs; DE=Wilmington/Nearby Delaware).

vote at zagat.com 153

Cuisine Index

CUISINES

Afghan
Ariana
Kabul

African
Fatou & Fama

American (New)
Alison/Blue Bell
America B&G
Ardmore Station
Astral Plane
Back Burner/DE
Basil Bistro
Bella
Black Bass Hotel
Black Swan/NJ
Bravo Bistro
Bridget Foy's
Buckley's Tav./DE
Cafe Unicorn/LB
Carambola
Carr's/LB
Chlöe
Christopher's
circa
Cresheim Cottage
Culinaria/DE
Denim Lounge
Dilworthtown Inn
Drafting Room
Eclipse/DE
Elements Café/NJ
Epicurean
Esca
EverMay/Delaware
Fayette St. Grille
Food for Thought/NJ
Fork
Fountain Rest.
Four Dogs Tav.
Gables/Chadds Ford
Goat Hollow
Grill
Grill Rest.
Gullifty's
Gypsy Rose
Hadley's Bistro
Harry's Savoy Grill/DE
Havana
Inn on Blue. Hill
Inn Philadelphia

Jake's
Jenny's Bistro
John Harvard's
Joseph Ambler
Knight House
Lambertville Stat./NJ
Landing
Latest Dish
Liberties
Lily's on Main/LB
London Grill
Mainland Inn
Marathon Grill
Marathon/Square
Mendenhall Inn
More Than/Ice Cream
Moro/DE
Moshulu
New Wave
Novelty
Olive/NJ
Opus 251
Passerelle
Rose Tattoo Cafe
Roux 3
Salt
Spence Cafe
Spezia
Sprigs
State St. Grill
Swann Lounge
Tango
Thomas'
333 Belrose
Twenty Manning
Twenty21
211 York
U.S. Hotel B&G
Village Porch
Washington Hse.
Yardley Inn

American (Regional)
Azalea
Bird-in-Hand/LB
bluezette
Carversville Inn
Good 'N Plenty/LB
Groff's Farm/LB
Jack's Firehse.
Kimberton Inn
Miller's Smorg./LB
Plain & Fancy/LB

Cuisine Index

Red Caboose/LB
Stoltzfus Farm/LB
Vickers Tavern
Willow Valley/LB
Windmill/LB
Zinn's Diner/LB

American (Traditional)
Avalon
Azalea
Bay Pony Inn
Blue Bell Inn
Blue in Green
Braddock's Tav./NJ
Brandywine Brew./DE
Brandywine Rm./DE
Brick Hotel
Century House
Chadds Ford Inn
Cheesecake Fact.
Chestnut Grill
City Tavern
Cock 'n Bull
Columbus Inn/DE
Copabanana
Copa Too
Cuttalossa Inn
Damon's Grill/LB
Dave & Buster's
Day by Day
D'Ignazio's
Doc Holliday's/LB
Duling-Kurtz Hse.
Fountain Side
Friday Sat. Sun.
General Lafayette
General Warren
Goose Creek Grill
Green Hills Inn/LB
Hank's Place
Hard Rock Cafe
Haydn Zug's/LB
Historic Revere/LB
Independence Brew
Iron Hill Brewery
Jones
Judy's Cafe
Keating's
Kimberton Inn
King George II
Le Bus
L2
Magazine
Manayunk Brew.
McFadden's
McGillin's
Mothers'
Nifty Fifty's
Nodding Head
North by NW
N. 3rd
Olde Greenfield/LB
Old Guard Hse.
Olga's Diner/NJ
Pace One
Pantheon
Paradigm
Peacock/Parkway
Plate
Plumsteadville Inn
Rembrandt's
Ron's Schoolhouse
Rose Tree Inn
Rx
Simon Pearce
Society Hill Hotel
Solaris Grille
Spotted Hog
Standard Tap
Sugar Mom's
Tavern
Tenth St. Pour Hse.
Terrace/Greenhill/DE
Trolley Car Diner
Valley Forge Brew.
Victory Brew.
Washington St. Ale/DE
William Penn Inn
Wooden Iron
Ye Olde Concordville

Asian
August Moon
Blue Pacific
Buddakan
Bunha Faun
Carr's/LB
FuziOn
Joseph Poon
Krazy Kat's/DE
Marg. Kuo's
Pod
Thomas'
Twenty Manning

Bakeries
Main-ly Café

Barbecue
August Moon
Bomb Bomb BBQ

Cuisine Index

Damon's Grill/LB
Kim's
Korea Garden
Rib Crib

Belgian
Abbaye
Eulogy Belgian
Monk's Cafe

Brasseries
Cadence
Loie
Pigalle

Brazilian
Brasil's

Burmese
Rangoon

Cajun/Creole
Bourbon Blue
Carmine's Cafe
Creole Café/NJ
High St. Caffe
Mélange Café/NJ
New Orleans Cafe
Ortlieb's
Tenth St. Pour Hse.

Californian
California Cafe
Sonoma

Caribbean
bluezette
Havana

Cheese Steaks/Hoagies
Campo's Deli
Dalessandro's
Geno's Steaks
Jim's Steaks
Pat's King/Steaks
Ron's Schoolhouse
Tony Luke Jr.'s

Chinese
Abacus
Beijing
Billy Wong's
Charles Plaza
Cherry St. Veg.
Chez Elena Wu/NJ
China Royal/DE
Chun Hing
CinCin
Garnian Wa
Harmony Veg.
H.K. Gold. Phoenix
House of Jin
Hunan
Imperial Inn
Joe's Peking
Joy Tsin Lau
Kimono Sushi
Kingdom of Veg.
Lai Lai Garden
Lakeside Chinese
Lee How Fook
Long's Gourmet
Mandarin Garden
Marg. Kuo's Mand.
Mustard Greens
Noodle Heaven
North Sea
Ocean Harbor
Peking
Ray's Café
Sang Kee
Shiao Lan Kung
Singapore Kosher
Susanna Foo
Tai Lake
Tony Wang's/LB
Yangming

Coffeehouses/Dessert
Beau Monde
Brew HaHa!
Capriccio's
Cassatt Lounge
Cosi
La Colombe Panini
Main-ly Café
More Than/Ice Cream
Pink Rose Pastry
Ray's Café
Roselena's Coffee

Coffee Shops/Diners
Blue in Green
Capriccio's
Country Club
Down Home Din.
Little Pete's
Mayfair Diner
Melrose Diner
Morning Glory
Nifty Fifty's

Cuisine Index

Olga's Diner/NJ
Ponzio's/NJ
Ruby's
Sage Diner/NJ
Silk City
Trolley Car Diner
Zinn's Diner/LB

Colombian
Mixto
Tierra Colombiana

Continental
Avalon
Barrymore Rm.
Bay Pony Inn
Brick Hotel
Café Gallery/NJ
Cafe M/NJ
Centre Bridge Inn
Chef Charin
Cuisines
Duling-Kurtz Hse.
Friday Sat. Sun.
General Warren
Kennedy-Supplee
King George II
Lucy's Hat Shop
Main-ly Café
Marker
Odette's
Old Guard Hse.
Paradigm
Plough & Stars
Roselena's Coffee
Rose Tree Inn
Rouge
Seven Stars Inn
Sukhothai
Vickers Tavern
Villa Strafford
Washington Cross.
William Penn Inn
Willistown Grille
Yangming
Ye Olde Concordville

Cuban
Alma de Cuba
Café Habana
Cuba Libre
Mixto
Summer Kit.
Tierra Colombiana

Delis/Sandwich Shops
Ben & Irv
Campo's Deli
Famous 4th St.
Hymie's Merion
Isaac's Rest.
Izzy & Zoe's
Koch's Deli
Le Bus
Marathon Grill
Marathon/Square
Murray's Deli
Shank's & Evelyn's
Three Little Pigs
Tony Luke Jr.'s

Dim Sum
H.K. Gold. Phoenix
Imperial Inn
Joy Tsin Lau
Kingdom of Veg.
Lakeside Chinese
Ocean Harbor
Ray's Café

Eclectic
Abilene
Black Sheep Pub
Bridgid's
Cafe Preeya
Cafette
Carman's Country
Continental
Django
Gracie's/LB
Half Moon
Knave of Hearts
Latest Dish
Little Café/NJ
Marigold Din. Rm.
Mirna's Cafe
Moody Monkey
Places! Bistro
Potcheen
Reading Terminal
Sabrina's Cafe
Sassafras
Serrano
Summer Kit.
Sweet Bay Cafe/LB
Tavern on Green
Totaro's
Umbria
White Dog Cafe
World Fusion
ZanzibarBlue

English
Dark Horse Pub
Elephant & Castle
Stoney's/DE

vote at zagat.com

Cuisine Index

Eritrean
Dahlak

Ethiopian
Abyssinia
Dahlak

European
Django
Pigalle
Warsaw Cafe

Filipino
Manila Bay B&G

Fondue
Melting Pot

French (Bistro)
Abbaye
Bistro St. Tropez
Bleu
Cafe Arielle
Caribou Cafe
Inn at Phillips Mill
Le Bar Lyonnais
Pif
Tartine
Winberie's

French (Classic)
Alisa Cafe
Andreotti's/NJ
Beau Monde
Beau Rivage/NJ
Birchrunville Store
Deux Cheminées
Gilmore's
Golden Pheasant
Green Hills Inn/LB
Green Room/DE
Hotel Du Village
La Bonne Aub.
Lacroix/Rittenhse.
La Terrasse
Le Bec-Fin
Le Mas
Le Petit Café
Overtures
Pigalle
Spring Mill Café
Yellow Springs

French (New)
Brasserie Perrier
Bunha Faun
Chez Colette
CinCin
Crier/Country
Founders
Fountain Rest.
Gourmet
Grasshopper
Happy Rooster
Krazy Kat's/DE
La Boheme
La Campagne/NJ
Le Mê Toujours/NJ
Nais Cuisine
Nan
Paloma
Passerelle
Rat's/NJ
Rest. at Doneckers/LB
Rest. Taquet
Siri's Thai French/NJ
Susanna Foo
Swann Lounge
Thomas'

Fusion
Buddakan
FuziOn
Joseph Poon
Pod
Roy's
Thomas'
Valanni

German
Blüe Ox
Ludwig's Garten
Otto's
Stoudt's/LB

Greek
Athena
Effie's
Lourdas Greek
Mokas
South St. Souvlaki
Zesty's

Hamburgers
Charcoal Pit/DE
Copabanana
Copa Too
Doc Holliday's/LB
Hadley's Bistro
Iron Hill Brewery
John Harvard's

Cuisine Index

Jolly's
Moriarty's
Nifty Fifty's
Nodding Head
Ruby's
Society Hill Hotel
Sugar Mom's

Hawaiian
Roy's

Health Food
Charles Plaza
Horizons Cafe
White Dog Cafe

Indian
Cafe Spice
Darbar Grill
Fatou & Fama
Khajuraho
Minar Palace
New Delhi
Palace of Asia
Passage/India
Samosa
Shivnanda
Sitar India
Taj Mahal
Tandoor India

Indonesian
Indonesia

Irish
Bards
Fadó Irish Pub
Fergie's Pub
Finnigan's Wake
McFadden's
Plough & Stars
Tir Na Nog

Italian
(N=Northern; S=Southern)
Alberto's
Andreotti's/NJ
Barone Tratt./NJ
Bella Luna
Bella Trattoria
Bertolini's
Birchrunville Store
Bistro La Baia
Bistro La Viola
Bistro Romano
Bomb Bomb BBQ
Buca di Beppo
Butcher's Cafe
Caffe Aldo Lam./NJ
Caffè Bellissimo
Caffe Casta Diva
Carambola
Carmella's (S)
Catelli/NJ
Cucina Forte
D'Angelo's Rist.
Dante & Luigi's
Davio's (N)
D'Ignazio's
DiPalma (N)
East Side Mario's
Ernesto's 1521
Felicia's
Fellini Café
Filomena Cuc. Ital./NJ (S)
Filomena Cuc. Rust./NJ
Fountain Side
Franco & Luigi's
Frederick's
Girasole Rist.
Giumarello's/NJ (N)
Gnocchi (S)
Hosteria Da Elio
Il Cantuccio
Illuminare
Il Portico (N)
Il Sol D'Italia (S)
Il Tartufo (N)
Io E Tu Rist.
Italian Bistro
Kristian's Rist.
La Collina (N)
La Famiglia
La Locanda (N)
Lamberti's (S)
L'Angolo
Langostino
La Padella
Lauletta's Grille
La Veranda
La Vigna (N)
Le Castagne (N)
L'Osteria Cuc. Ital./DE
Luigi Vitrone's/DE
Maggiano's
Mama Palma's (S)
Ma Ma Yolanda's
Mamma Maria
Marabella's

vote at zagat.com   159

Cuisine Index

Marco Polo
Marra's (S)
Max's/NJ (N)
Mélange Café/NJ
Mezza Luna
Michael's
Mona Lisa/DE
Monte Carlo
Moonstruck (N)
Mr. Martino's
Mrs. Robino's/DE
Paganini Pizza
Paganini Tratt.
Penne
Pepper's Cafe
Pizzicato
Pompeii Cucina
Porcini
Portofino (N)
Primavera Pizza (N)
Radicchio (S)
Ralph's (S)
Ravenna (N)
Rist. La Buca
Rist. Mediterraneo
Rist. Panorama
Rist. Positano (S)
Rist. Primavera
Rist. San Carlo
Roma
Ron's Schoolhouse
Saloon
Savona (N)
Shank's & Evelyn's
Sonoma
Sotto Varalli
Spaghetti Warehse.
Spasso
Spezia
Stefano's
Stella Notte
Teresa's Café
Tira Misu Rist.
Toscana Cuc. Rust.
Toscana Kitchen/DE (N)
Totaro's
Toto
Tratt. Alberto (N)
Tratt. San Nicola
Tre Scalini
Trinacria (S)
2 Goodfellas
Upstares/Varalli (N)
Vesuvio
Vetri
Victor Café
Viggiano's (S)
Villa di Roma
Vincente's/DE
Vinny T's
Vivo Enoteca
Zesty's

Jamaican
Jamaican Jerk

Japanese
Aoi
August Moon
Fuji/NJ
Genji
Hibachi
Hikaru
House of Jin
Kawabata
Kimono Sushi
Kisso Sushi
Kobe
Lai Lai Garden
Mikado
Mikado/NJ
Mikimotos/DE
Morimoto
Oasis
Ooka Jap.
Peking
Sagami/NJ
Shiroi Hana
Teikoku

Jewish
Ben & Irv
Country Club
Famous 4th St.
Hymie's Merion
Il Tartufo
Izzy & Zoe's
La Pergola
Murray's Deli
Tira Misu Rist.

Korean
August Moon
Kim's
Korea Garden

Kosher
Cherry St. Veg.
Kingdom of Veg.

Cuisine Index

Maccabeam
Singapore Kosher
Time Out Falafel

Laotian
Vientiane Café

Latin American
Valanni

Malaysian
Penang

Mediterranean
Aden
Adriatica
Al Dar Bistro
Arpeggio
Audrey Claire
Bitar's
Cafe San Pietro
Cedars
Citron Bistro
Dmitri's
Figs
La Pergola
Lauletta's Grille
Mirna's Cafe
Mokas
Olive/NJ
Overtures
Peacock/Parkway
Rest. 821/DE
Saffron House
Sawan's Med.
Tangerine
Trust
Valanni
Vincent's

Mexican/Tex-Mex
Copabanana
Copa Too
Coyote Crossing
El Azteca
El Sombrero
Johnny Mañana's
La Lupe
Las Cazuelas
La Tolteca/DE
Los Catrines/Teq.
Mad 4 Mex
Mexican Food/NJ
Mexican Post
Paloma

Taco House
Tamarindo's
Taq. Moroleon
Tex Mex Conn.
Zocalo

Middle Eastern
Al Dar Bistro
Alyan's
Maccabeam
Norma's/NJ
Persian Grill
Time Out Falafel

Moroccan
Casablanca
Fez Moroccan
Figs
Little Marakesh
Marrakesh

Noodle Shops
Noodle Heaven
Penang
Pho 75
Sang Kee

Nuevo Latino
Cibucán
¡Pasión!

Pacific Rim
Bamboo Club

Pan-Asian
Ritz Seafood/NJ
Swanky Bubbles

Persian
Saffron House

Pizza
Arpeggio
Bella Trattoria
California Piz. Kit.
Celebre's Pizz.
Franco & Luigi's
Girasole Rist.
Goose Creek Grill
Illuminare
Lombardi's
Mama Palma's
Marra's
Paganini Pizza
Pietro's
Pizzicato

vote at zagat.com

Cuisine Index

Primavera Pizza
Ron's Schoolhouse
Tacconelli's Pizz.

Polish
Syrenka

Portuguese
Mallorca

Pub Food
Black Sheep Pub
Brandywine Brew./DE
Damon's Grill/LB
Dark Horse Pub
Dave & Buster's
Fadó Irish Pub
Fergie's Pub
Finnigan's Wake
Half Moon
Independence Brew
Iron Hill Brewery
John Harvard's
Manayunk Brew.
McFadden's
McGillin's
Moriarty's
Nodding Head
Stoney's/DE
Stoudt's/LB
Sugar Mom's
Tir Na Nog
Victory Brew.

Seafood
Adriatica
Barnacle Ben's/NJ
Bistro La Baia
Bookbinders
Chart House
Chickie's & Pete's
Citrus
Creed's Seafood
Deep Blue/DE
Devon Seafood
DiNardo's
Dmitri's
Emerald Fish/NJ
Feby's Fishery/DE
Gables/Chadds Ford
Hoss's Family
Kegel's Seafood/LB
Little Fish
Little Tuna/NJ
Marco Polo

McCorm./Schmick's
Ocean Harbor
Pelican Fish Co./NJ
Philadelphia Fish
Philly Crab
Radicchio
Rist. La Buca
Ritz Seafood/NJ
Roller's
Sansom St. Oyster
Seafood Unlimited
Snockey's Oyster
Solaris Grille
Sotto Varalli
Spence Cafe
Striped Bass
Tai Lake
Walter's Steak./DE

South American
Azafran

Southern/Soul
Big George's
bluezette
Carversville Inn
Down Home Din.
Fatou & Fama
Jack's Firehse.
Savannah
Warmdaddy's

Southwestern
Adobe Cafe
Rock Bottom

Spanish
Citron Bistro
Mallorca
Rest. La Encina

Steakhouses
Capital Grille
Chops
Creed's Seafood
Davio's
Delmonico's
Engine 46
Hibachi
Hoss's Family
Jolly's
Kansas City Prime
Kobe
Log Cabin/LB
Marmont

Cuisine Index

Morton's/Chicago
Outback Steak.
Palm
Philly Crab
Prime Rib
Pub/NJ
Ruth's Chris
Saloon
Shula's Steak
Smith & Wollensky
Stoudt's/LB
Sullivan's Steak.
Walter's Steak./DE

Tapas
Continental
Rest. La Encina

Tearooms
Cassatt Lounge
Pink Rose Pastry

Thai
Alisa Cafe
Amara Cafe
East of Amara
Jasmine Thai
Lemon Grass
My Thai
Nan
Pattaya Grill
Pho Xe Lua
Siam Cuisine
Silk Cuisine
Siri's Thai French/NJ
Sukhothai
Taste of Thai
Teikoku
Thai Orchid
Thai Pepper
Thai Singha
White Elephant

Turkish
Authentic Turkish/NJ

Vegetarian
Blue Sage Veg.
Charles Plaza
Cherry St. Veg.
Citrus
Harmony Veg.
Horizons Cafe
Kingdom of Veg.
Lemon Grass
Samosa
Serrano
Singapore Kosher

Vietnamese
Le Mê Toujours/NJ
Pho 75
Pho Xe Lua
Vietnam
Vietnam Palace

Location Index

LOCATIONS

PHILADELPHIA

Art Museum
Bridgid's
Figs
Illuminare
Jack's Firehse.
Little Pete's
London Grill
Long's Gourmet
Rembrandt's
Rose Tattoo Cafe
Savannah
Tavern on Green

Avenue of the Arts
Barrymore Rm.
Cadence
Capital Grille
Founders
Grill
Italian Bistro
McCorm./Schmick's
Noodle Heaven
Palm
Pantheon
Sotto Varalli
Toto
Upstares/Varalli
ZanzibarBlue

Center City
(east of Broad St.)
Aoi
Blue in Green
Caribou Cafe
Cosi
Deux Cheminées
Down Home Din.
Effie's
El Azteca
Fergie's Pub
Girasole Rist.
Hard Rock Cafe
Independence Brew
Inn Philadelphia
Jones
La Boheme
Ludwig's Garten
Maccabeam
Maggiano's
Marathon Grill
McGillin's
Mixto
More Than/Ice Cream
Moriarty's
Morimoto
Passage/India
Pompeii Cucina
Portofino
Reading Terminal
Rist. La Buca
Samosa
Sang Kee
Spaghetti Warehse.
Taco House
Tenth St. Pour Hse.
Trust
Valanni
Vetri

Center City
(west of Broad St.)
Alma de Cuba
Amara Cafe
Astral Plane
Audrey Claire
Bards
Bella
Bistro La Baia
Bistro La Viola
Bistro St. Tropez
Black Sheep Pub
Bleu
Bookbinders
Brasserie Perrier
Buca di Beppo
Café Habana
Caffe Casta Diva
Capriccio's
Cassatt Lounge
Chez Colette
Cibucán
circa
Copa Too
Cosi
D'Angelo's Rist.
Davio's
Day by Day
Denim Lounge
Devon Seafood
Dmitri's

Location Index

Elephant & Castle
Ernesto's 1521
Fadó Irish Pub
Fountain Rest.
Friday Sat. Sun.
Genji
Grill Rest.
Happy Rooster
Il Portico
Jolly's
La Colombe Panini
Lacroix/Rittenhse.
Le Bar Lyonnais
Le Bec-Fin
Le Bus
Le Castagne
Little Pete's
Loie
Lombardi's
Los Catrines/Teq.
L2
Magazine
Mama Palma's
Marathon Grill
Marathon/Square
Minar Palace
Monk's Cafe
Morton's/Chicago
Nodding Head
Oasis
Opus 251
¡Pasión!
Peacock/Parkway
Pietro's
Porcini
Potcheen
Prime Rib
Roma
Rouge
Roy's
Ruth's Chris
Saffron House
Salt
Sansom St. Oyster
Sawan's Med.
Seafood Unlimited
Shiroi Hana
Shula's Steak
Smith & Wollensky
Striped Bass
Sukhothai
Susanna Foo
Swann Lounge
Taj Mahal

Tir Na Nog
Twenty Manning
Twenty21
Warsaw Cafe

Chinatown

Charles Plaza
Cherry St. Veg.
Harmony Veg.
H.K. Gold. Phoenix
Imperial Inn
Indonesia
Joe's Peking
Joseph Poon
Joy Tsin Lau
Kingdom of Veg.
Lakeside Chinese
Lee How Fook
North Sea
Ocean Harbor
Penang
Pho Xe Lua
Rangoon
Ray's Café
Sang Kee
Shiao Lan Kung
Siam Cuisine
Singapore Kosher
Tai Lake
Taste of Thai
Vietnam
Vietnam Palace

Delaware Riverfront

Chart House
Dave & Buster's
Hibachi
Keating's
La Veranda
Moshulu

Manayunk/ Roxborough/ East Falls

Adobe Cafe
Bella Trattoria
Bourbon Blue
Carmella's
Dalessandro's
Grasshopper
Hikaru
Il Tartufo
Jake's
Johnny Mañana's
Kansas City Prime

vote at zagat.com

Location Index

La Colombe Panini
Le Bus
Main-ly Café
Manayunk Brew.
Sonoma
Sprigs
Thomas'
U.S. Hotel B&G
Zesty's

Northeast Philly

Blüe Ox
Chickie's & Pete's
Country Club
El Azteca
Gourmet
Italian Bistro
Jim's Steaks
Kawabata
La Padella
Manila Bay B&G
Mayfair Diner
Moonstruck
Nifty Fifty's
Paloma
Philly Crab
Pho 75
Time Out Falafel
Tony Luke Jr.'s

Northern Liberties/Port Richmond

Abbaye
Aden
Finnigan's Wake
Il Cantuccio
Las Cazuelas
Liberties
McFadden's
N. 3rd
Ortlieb's
Pigalle
Silk City
Standard Tap
Syrenka
Tacconelli's Pizz.

North Philly

Kim's
Tierra Colombiana

Northwest Philly (Chestnut Hill/Germantown/Mt. Airy)

Buca di Beppo
Cafette
Chestnut Grill
CinCin
Citrus
Cosi
Cresheim Cottage
Dahlak
Goat Hollow
House of Jin
Melting Pot
North by NW
Rib Crib
Roller's
Solaris Grille
Stella Notte
Trolley Car Diner
Umbria

Old City

Adriatica
Ariana
Azalea
Billy Wong's
Bitar's
Blue in Green
bluezette
Brasil's
Buddakan
Cafe Spice
Campo's Deli
Chlöe
City Tavern
Continental
Cosi
Cuba Libre
Darbar Grill
DiNardo's
DiPalma
Eulogy Belgian
Fork
Hadley's Bistro
Kabul
Kisso Sushi
La Famiglia
La Locanda
Lamberti's
Lucy's Hat Shop
Marmont
Mexican Post
Novelty
Paradigm
Philadelphia Fish
Pizzicato
Plough & Stars
Radicchio

Location Index

Rist. Panorama
Sassafras
Serrano
Shivnanda
Society Hill Hotel
Spasso
Sugar Mom's
Swanky Bubbles
Tangerine
Warmdaddy's
World Fusion

South Philly
Bitar's
Bomb Bomb BBQ
Butcher's Cafe
Carman's Country
Celebre's Pizz.
Cucina Forte
Dante & Luigi's
Engine 46
Felicia's
Franco & Luigi's
Geno's Steaks
Io E Tu Rist.
Kristian's Rist.
La Lupe
L'Angolo
Langostino
Lauletta's Grille
La Vigna
Little Fish
Ma Ma Yolanda's
Mamma Maria
Marra's
Melrose Diner
Mezza Luna
Michael's
Morning Glory
Mr. Martino's
Pat's King/Steaks
Pho 75
Pif
Ralph's
Roselena's Coffee
Sabrina's Cafe
Saloon
Shank's & Evelyn's
Snockey's Oyster
Tony Luke Jr.'s
Tre Scalini
Vesuvio
Victor Café
Villa di Roma

South St./Society Hill/Queen Village
Abilene
Alyan's
Azafran
Beau Monde
Bistro Romano
Bridget Foy's
Cedars
Copabanana
Cosi
Dark Horse Pub
Django
Dmitri's
East of Amara
Famous 4th St.
Fez Moroccan
Frederick's
Gnocchi
Hosteria Da Elio
Jamaican Jerk
Jim's Steaks
Judy's Cafe
Knave of Hearts
Latest Dish
Mallorca
Marrakesh
Monte Carlo
Mustard Greens
My Thai
New Wave
Overtures
Pietro's
Pink Rose Pastry
Rist. Primavera
Rist. San Carlo
South St. Souvlaki
Tartine
Tira Misu Rist.

West Philly/University City
Abyssinia
Beijing
Big George's
Bitar's
Dahlak
Fatou & Fama
Izzy & Zoe's
Jim's Steaks
Koch's Deli
La Terrasse
Lemon Grass
Mad 4 Mex

vote at zagat.com

Location Index

Marigold Din. Rm.
Mokas
Nan
New Delhi
Pattaya Grill
Penne
Pod
Rx

Sitar India
Tandoor India
Thai Singha
2 Goodfellas
Vientiane Café
White Dog Cafe
Zocalo

PHILADELPHIA SUBURBS

Bucks County
Black Bass Hotel
Blue Sage Veg.
Brew HaHa!
Brick Hotel
Cafe Arielle
Carversville Inn
Casablanca
Centre Bridge Inn
Cock 'n Bull
Cuttalossa Inn
El Sombrero
Esca
EverMay/Delaware
Golden Pheasant
Havana
Hotel Du Village
Il Sol D'Italia
Inn at Phillips Mill
Inn on Blue. Hill
Jenny's Bistro
King George II
Knight House
La Bonne Aub.
Lamberti's
Landing
La Pergola
Mothers'
Nifty Fifty's
Odette's
Outback Steak.
Paganini Pizza
Paganini Tratt.
Philly Crab
Plumsteadville Inn
Siam Cuisine
Spotted Hog
Summer Kit.
Washington Cross.
Washington Hse.
Yardley Inn

Chester County
America B&G
Avalon

Birchrunville Store
Brew HaHa!
Buca di Beppo
Dilworthtown Inn
Drafting Room
Duling-Kurtz Hse.
East Side Mario's
Epicurean
Four Dogs Tav.
Gables/Chadds Ford
Gilmore's
Goose Creek Grill
Half Moon
High St. Caffe
Hoss's Family
Iron Hill Brewery
Isaac's Rest.
Kimberton Inn
Marg. Kuo's Mand.
Mendenhall Inn
Outback Steak.
Rest. La Encina
Ron's Schoolhouse
Seven Stars Inn
Simon Pearce
Spence Cafe
State St. Grill
Taq. Moroleon
Three Little Pigs
Tratt. Alberto
Vickers Tavern
Vincent's
Yellow Springs

City Line Ave.
Casablanca
Chun Hing
Delmonico's
Marker

Delaware County
Alberto's
Alisa Cafe
Caffè Bellissimo
Carmine's Cafe

subscribe to zagat.com

Location Index

Chadds Ford Inn
Crier/Country
Cuisines
D'Ignazio's
Fellini Café
Hank's Place
Hibachi
Iron Hill Brewery
Jim's Steaks
John Harvard's
Le Petit Café
Nais Cuisine
New Orleans Cafe
Nifty Fifty's
Outback Steak.
Pace One
Peking
Rose Tree Inn
Village Porch
Ye Olde Concordville

King of Prussia
Bertolini's
California Cafe
California Piz. Kit.
Cheesecake Fact.
Creed's Seafood
Jasmine Thai
Kennedy-Supplee
Kobe
Maggiano's
Morton's/Chicago
Rock Bottom
Ruby's
Ruth's Chris
Sullivan's Steak.

Main Line
Al Dar Bistro
Ardmore Station
August Moon
Basil Bistro
Bella Luna
Bravo Bistro
Brew HaHa!
Bunha Faun
Cafe San Pietro
Chef Charin
Chops
Christopher's
Citron Bistro
Cosi
Fellini Café
Garnian Wa
General Warren
Gullifty's
Hunan
Hymie's Merion
John Harvard's
Khajuraho
La Collina
Le Mas
Lourdas Greek
Marg. Kuo's
Mikado
Murray's Deli
Old Guard Hse.
Passerelle
Pepper's Cafe
Places! Bistro
Plate
Primavera Pizza
Rest. Taquet
Rist. Positano
Rist. Primavera
Roux 3
Ruby's
Savona
Silk Cuisine
Spezia
Tango
Tavern
Teikoku
Teresa's Café
Thai Pepper
333 Belrose
Toscana Cuc. Rust.
Tratt. San Nicola
Valley Forge Brew.
Victory Brew.
Villa Strafford
Vinny T's
Vivo Enoteca
Willistown Grille
Winberie's
Wooden Iron
Yangming

Montgomery County
Abacus
Alison/Blue Bell
Arpeggio
Athena
Bamboo Club
Bay Pony Inn
Ben & Irv
Blue Bell Inn
Blue Pacific
Brew HaHa!

vote at zagat.com　　　　　　　169

Location Index

Buca di Beppo
Cafe Preeya
Carambola
Century House
Coyote Crossing
Drafting Room
Fayette St. Grille
Fountain Side
FuziOn
General Lafayette
Gypsy Rose
Hibachi
Horizons Cafe
Joseph Ambler
Kimono Sushi
Korea Garden
Lai Lai Garden
La Pergola
Little Marakesh
Mainland Inn
Mandarin Garden
Marabella's
Marco Polo
Mirna's Cafe
Moody Monkey
Ooka Jap.
Otto's
Outback Steak.
Palace of Asia
Persian Grill
Ralph's
Ravenna
Rist. Mediterraneo
Spring Mill Café
Stefano's
Tamarindo's
Tex Mex Conn.
Thai Orchid
Totaro's
Trinacria
211 York
Viggiano's
White Elephant
William Penn Inn

OUTLYING AREAS

Lancaster/Berks Counties
Bird-in-Hand
Cafe Unicorn
Carr's
Damon's Grill
Doc Holliday's
Good 'N Plenty
Gracie's
Green Hills Inn
Groff's Farm
Haydn Zug's
Historic Revere
Hoss's Family
Isaac's Rest.
Kegel's Seafood
Lemon Grass
Lily's on Main
Log Cabin
Miller's Smorg.
Olde Greenfield
Outback Steak.
Plain & Fancy
Red Caboose
Rest. at Doneckers
Stoltzfus Farm
Stoudt's
Sweet Bay Cafe
Tony Wang's
Willow Valley
Windmill
Zinn's Diner

New Jersey Suburbs
Andreotti's
Authentic Turkish
Barnacle Ben's
Barone Tratt.
Beau Rivage
Black Swan
Braddock's Tav.
Buca di Beppo
Café Gallery
Cafe M
Caffe Aldo Lam.
Catelli
Chez Elena Wu
Creole Café
East Side Mario's
El Azteca
Elements Café
Elephant & Castle
Emerald Fish
Filomena Cuc. Ital.
Filomena Cuc. Rust.
Food for Thought
Fuji
Giumarello's
Italian Bistro

Location Index

La Campagne
Lamberti's
Lambertville Stat.
Le Mê Toujours
Little Café
Little Tuna
Max's
Mélange Café
Mexican Food
Mikado
Norma's
Olga's Diner
Olive
Outback Steak.
Pelican Fish Co.
Ponzio's
Pub
Rat's
Ritz Seafood
Sagami
Sage Diner
Singapore Kosher
Siri's Thai French
Thai Orchid

Wilmington/Nearby Delaware

Back Burner
Brandywine Brew.
Brandywine Rm.
Brew HaHa!
Buckley's Tav.
Caffè Bellissimo
Charcoal Pit
China Royal
Columbus Inn
Culinaria
Deep Blue
Eclipse
Feby's Fishery
Green Room
Harry's Savoy Grill
Hibachi
Iron Hill Brewery
Italian Bistro
John Harvard's
Krazy Kat's
Lamberti's
La Tolteca
L'Osteria Cuc. Ital.
Luigi Vitrone's
Mikimotos
Mona Lisa
Moro
Mrs. Robino's
Outback Steak.
Rest. 821
Stoney's
Sullivan's Steak.
Terrace/Greenhill
Toscana Kitchen
Vincente's
Walter's Steak.
Washington St. Ale
ZanzibarBlue

Special Feature Index

SPECIAL FEATURES

(Restaurants followed by a † may not offer that feature at every location.)

Additions
Abbaye
Adriatica
Alison/Blue Bell
Bamboo Club
Bella
Blue Pacific
Bourbon Blue
Cafe M/NJ
Caffe Casta Diva
Carmella's
Chops
Citron Bistro
Denim Lounge
Elements Café/NJ
Esca
Eulogy Belgian
Fatou & Fama
Jones
Lacroix/Rittenhse.
La Lupe
Little Tuna/NJ
Loie
Marg. Kuo's
Max's/NJ
Mixto
Mokas
Moro/DE
Moshulu
Penne
Plate
Radicchio
Ravenna
Roux 3
Salt
Sprigs
Tartine
Tavern
Teikoku
Tir Na Nog
Twenty21
Vesuvio
Vientiane Café
Vivo Enoteca
White Elephant
World Fusion
Yardley Inn

Breakfast
(See also Hotel Dining)
Ardmore Station
Blue in Green†
Carman's Country
Down Home Din.
Famous 4th St.
Hank's Place
Hymie's Merion
Little Pete's†
Main-ly Café
Mayfair Diner
Melrose Diner
Miller's Smorg./LB
Mixto
Morning Glory
Murray's Deli
Nifty Fifty's
Pink Rose Pastry
Ponzio's/NJ
Rat's/NJ
Reading Terminal
Sage Diner/NJ
Shank's & Evelyn's
Silk City
Spotted Hog
Spring Mill Café
Tenth St. Pour Hse.
Tierra Colombiana
Tony Luke Jr.'s
Windmill/LB
Zinn's Diner/LB

Brunch
Alberto's
Andreotti's/NJ
Ardmore Station
Astral Plane
Avalon
Azalea
Back Burner/DE
Barrymore Rm.
Bay Pony Inn
Beau Monde
Bitar's†
Black Bass Hotel
Blue in Green
Braddock's Tav./NJ

Special Feature Index

Buckley's Tav./DE
Café Gallery/NJ
Cafette
California Cafe
Caribou Cafe
Carman's Country
Carr's/LB
Carversville Inn
Chadds Ford Inn
Chart House
Cock 'n Bull
Columbus Inn/DE
Continental
Cresheim Cottage
Crier/Country
Cuttalossa Inn
Davio's
Epicurean
Famous 4th St.
Fayette St. Grille
Fork
Founders
Fountain Rest.
Goat Hollow
Golden Pheasant
Green Room/DE
Gullifty's
Gypsy Rose
Hadley's Bistro
Harry's Savoy Grill/DE
Hymie's Merion
Inn Philadelphia
Iron Hill Brewery
Jack's Firehse.
Jake's
John Harvard's†
Judy's Cafe
Kimberton Inn
Knave of Hearts
La Campagne/NJ
Lambertville Stat./NJ
La Padella
Las Cazuelas
La Terrasse
Le Bus†
London Grill
Mainland Inn
Marathon Grill
Marathon/Square
Marigold Din. Rm.
Marker
Mayfair Diner
Melrose Diner
Mendenhall Inn
Monk's Cafe
Morning Glory
Mothers'
Murray's Deli
New Orleans Cafe
Odette's
Olde Greenfield/LB
Olive/NJ
Opus 251
Pace One
Palace of Asia
Passerelle
Plough & Stars
Plumsteadville Inn
Rembrandt's
Roller's
Roselena's Coffee
Silk City
Society Hill Hotel
Solaris Grille
Sonoma
Spring Mill Café
Striped Bass
Swann Lounge
Tavern on Green
Tenth St. Pour Hse.
Terrace/Greenhill/DE
Thomas'
333 Belrose
U.S. Hotel B&G
Vietnam Palace
Village Porch
Washington Cross.
Washington Hse.
Washington St. Ale/DE
White Dog Cafe
William Penn Inn
Yellow Springs
ZanzibarBlue†

Buffet Served
(Check availability)
Alberto's
America B&G
Aoi
Azalea
Bay Pony Inn
Bird-in-Hand/LB
Black Bass Hotel
Café Gallery/NJ
Cock 'n Bull
Columbus Inn/DE
Crier/Country
Darbar Grill

vote at zagat.com

Special Feature Index

Drafting Room
Fatou & Fama
Founders
General Lafayette
Green Room/DE
Gypsy Rose
Hadley's Bistro
Hibachi
Hunan
Khajuraho
Kingdom of Veg.
Lambertville Stat./NJ
La Padella
Le Mas
Lucy's Hat Shop
Ludwig's Garten
Marg. Kuo's Mand.
Marker
Mendenhall Inn
Miller's Smorg./LB
Moriarty's
New Delhi
Odette's
Otto's
Passage/India
Plumsteadville Inn
Rat's/NJ
Roselena's Coffee
Samosa
Shivnanda
Sitar India
Swann Lounge
Taj Mahal
Tandoor India
Trolley Car Diner
William Penn Inn
Willow Valley/LB
Yardley Inn

Business Dining

Alberto's
Bamboo Club
Blue Bell Inn
Brandywine Rm./DE
Brasserie Perrier
Capital Grille
Catelli/NJ
Chops
Columbus Inn/DE
Deux Cheminées
Dilworthtown Inn
Fountain Rest.
Green Room/DE
Grill
Il Portico
Jolly's
Joseph Poon
Kansas City Prime
La Veranda
La Vigna
Le Bec-Fin
Le Bus†
Le Castagne
Le Mas
Maggiano's†
Mallorca
Marg. Kuo's
Marker
Max's/NJ
McCorm./Schmick's
Melrose Diner
Morton's/Chicago†
Palm
Prime Rib
Rest. Taquet
Rist. Panorama
Roy's
Ruth's Chris
Saloon
Sansom St. Oyster
Savona
Shula's Steak
Smith & Wollensky
Striped Bass
Sullivan's Steak.
Susanna Foo
Tangerine
Twenty21
Villa Strafford
Washington Hse.

BYO

Abacus
Aden
Alisa Cafe
Alison/Blue Bell
Amara Cafe
Arpeggio
Athena
Audrey Claire
Azafran
Barnacle Ben's/NJ
Barone Tratt./NJ
Beijing
Bella Luna
Birchrunville Store
Bistro La Baia
Bistro La Viola

Special Feature Index

Blue Sage Veg.
Bunha Faun
Butcher's Cafe
Cafe M/NJ
Cafe Preeya
Caffe Casta Diva
Carambola
Carman's Country
Carmine's Cafe
Chef Charin
Chez Elena Wu/NJ
Chlöe
Django
Dmitri's†
East of Amara
Effie's
Elements Café/NJ
El Sombrero
Emerald Fish/NJ
Fayette St. Grille
Fellini Café†
Figs
Fountain Side
Franco & Luigi's
Fuji/NJ
FuziOn
Garnian Wa
Gilmore's
Gnocchi
Horizons Cafe
Hosteria Da Elio
Hunan
Il Cantuccio
Inn at Phillips Mill
Isaac's Rest.†
Jamaican Jerk
Kabul
Khajuraho
Kimono Sushi
Kingdom of Veg.
Kisso Sushi
Korea Garden
La Boheme
La Campagne/NJ
La Locanda
L'Angolo
Langostino
Las Cazuelas
Lauletta's Grille
Le Petit Café
Little Fish
Little Marakesh
Little Tuna/NJ
Lombardi's
Lourdas Greek
Mamma Maria
Marg. Kuo's Mand.
Marigold Din. Rm.
Max's/NJ
Mirna's Cafe
Mr. Martino's
Nais Cuisine
Nan
Noodle Heaven
Norma's/NJ
Olga's Diner/NJ
Ooka Jap.
Overtures
Paganini Pizza
Pepper's Cafe
Pif
Porcini
Radicchio
Ravenna
Rest. La Encina
Ritz Seafood/NJ
Roma
Rx
Sabrina's Cafe
Sagami/NJ
Siam Cuisine†
Silk Cuisine
Singapore Kosher
Sitar India
Spezia
Spring Mill Café
State St. Grill
Stefano's
Summer Kit.
Sweet Bay Cafe/LB
Taj Mahal
Tamarindo's
Tandoor India
Taq. Moroleon
Tartine
Teresa's Café
Thai Orchid†
Thai Pepper†
Tony Wang's/LB
Tre Scalini
Umbria
Vientiane Café
Viggiano's
Village Porch
White Elephant

Catering
Abbaye
Abyssinia

vote at zagat.com

Special Feature Index

Adobe Cafe
Alyan's
America B&G
Ardmore Station
August Moon
Azafran
Bamboo Club
Beijing
Ben & Irv
Big George's
Bistro St. Tropez
Bitar's†
Black Swan/NJ
Blüe Ox
Blue Pacific
Blue Sage Veg.
Buca di Beppo†
Butcher's Cafe
Cafe Arielle
Cafette
Caffe Aldo Lam./NJ
Campo's Deli
Caribou Cafe
Carmine's Cafe
Cedars
Celebre's Pizz.
Chez Elena Wu/NJ
Cibucán
Citron Bistro
City Tavern
Continental
Country Club
Coyote Crossing
Cuba Libre
Cuisines
Dahlak†
Day by Day
Deep Blue/DE
Down Home Din.
East of Amara
Effie's
El Azteca†
Emerald Fish/NJ
Famous 4th St.
Fatou & Fama
Fayette St. Grille
Fez Moroccan
FuziOn
Girasole Rist.
Giumarello's/NJ
Gypsy Rose
Hank's Place
Hibachi†
Hunan

Il Sol D'Italia
Indonesia
Isaac's Rest.
Italian Bistro/DE†
Izzy & Zoe's
Jack's Firehse.
Jamaican Jerk
Jim's Steaks†
Joe's Peking
Joseph Poon
Joy Tsin Lau
Kabul
Kansas City Prime
Khajuraho
Kisso Sushi
La Boheme
La Campagne/NJ
Lamberti's/DE†
La Pergola†
Las Cazuelas
La Terrasse
Lauletta's Grille
Lee How Fook
Le Mê Toujours/NJ
Liberties
Little Café/NJ
Little Marakesh
Little Tuna/NJ
Log Cabin/LB
Lombardi's
L'Osteria Cuc. Ital./DE
Lourdas Greek
Ludwig's Garten
Mallorca
Mamma Maria
Manila Bay B&G
Marathon Grill
Marathon/Square
Marg. Kuo's Mand.
Mikado
Minar Palace
Mirna's Cafe
Mixto
Mokas
Moonstruck
Moriarty's
Mrs. Robino's/DE
New Delhi
New Orleans Cafe
Norma's/NJ
Odette's
Old Guard Hse.
Ooka Jap.
Ortlieb's

176   subscribe to zagat.com

Special Feature Index

Otto's
Pace One
Pantheon
Passage/India
Pat's King/Steaks
Peking
Penang
Pepper's Cafe
Persian Grill
Philadelphia Fish
Pho Xe Lua
Pizzicato
Prime Rib
Rest. 821/DE
Rest. La Encina
Rist. Positano
Rist. San Carlo
Ritz Seafood/NJ
Roller's
Roma
Roselena's Coffee
Sabrina's Cafe
Sang Kee†
Seafood Unlimited
Shiroi Hana
Shivnanda
Siam Cuisine†
Silk Cuisine
Sitar India
State St. Grill
Taj Mahal
Tamarindo's
Tandoor India
Taq. Moroleon
Teikoku
Tex Mex Conn.
Thai Orchid/NJ†
Thai Singha
Tierra Colombiana
Tira Misu Rist.
Tir Na Nog
Tony Luke Jr.'s†
Toscana Cuc. Rust.
2 Goodfellas
Upstares/Varalli
Victor Café
Villa di Roma
Village Porch
Washington Cross.
White Elephant
Yardley Inn
Yellow Springs
Ye Olde Concordville

Child-Friendly
(Besides the normal fast-food places; *children's menu available)
Abilene*
Adobe Cafe*
Alison/Blue Bell*
Bamboo Club
Barnacle Ben's/NJ*
Barone Tratt./NJ†
Basil Bistro*
Bay Pony Inn
Bella Trattoria*
Bird-in-Hand/LB*
Blue in Green*
Bookbinders*
Braddock's Tav./NJ*
Brandywine Brew./DE*
Bravo Bistro*
Brew HaHa!†
Bridget Foy's*
Buca di Beppo†
Buckley's Tav./DE*
Cafette*
California Cafe*
California Piz. Kit.*
Carmella's
Carr's/LB*
Chadds Ford Inn*
Charcoal Pit/DE†
Chart House*
Cheesecake Fact.*
Chestnut Grill*
China Royal/DE
City Tavern*
Cock 'n Bull*
Columbus Inn/DE*
Cuisines
Dalessandro's
Dave & Buster's*
Day by Day*
Devon Seafood
D'Ignazio's*
DiNardo's*
East Side Mario's*
El Azteca
El Sombrero*
Engine 46*
Epicurean*
Eulogy Belgian*
Feby's Fishery/DE*
Filomena Cuc. Ital./NJ†
Filomena Cuc. Rust./NJ*
Founders

vote at zagat.com 177

Special Feature Index

Fountain Rest.*
Four Dogs Tav.*
General Lafayette*
Goat Hollow*
Good 'N Plenty/LB
Green Room/DE*
Groff's Farm/LB*
Gullifty's*
Gypsy Rose*
Hadley's Bistro*
Hank's Place
Hard Rock Cafe*
Harry's Savoy Grill/DE*
Havana*
Haydn Zug's/LB*
Hibachi†
Historic Revere/LB*
Hoss's Family/LB†
Hymie's Merion*
Il Sol D'Italia*
Iron Hill Brewery*
Isaac's Rest./LB†
Italian Bistro†
Izzy & Zoe's*
Jenny's Bistro*
Jim's Steaks*
John Harvard's†
Joseph Poon
Joy Tsin Lau
Kegel's Seafood/LB*
Kobe*
Koch's Deli
Lamberti's†
Lambertville Stat./NJ*
Landing*
La Padella*
La Tolteca/DE†
Le Bus†
Little Pete's†
London Grill
Mama Palma's
Ma Ma Yolanda's
Mamma Maria
Marabella's
Marathon Grill
Marg. Kuo's
Marrakesh*
Mayfair Diner*
Melrose Diner
Melting Pot
Mendenhall Inn*
Mexican Food/NJ*
Miller's Smorg./LB
Mixto*

Moriarty's*
Mrs. Robino's/DE*
Murray's Deli
New Orleans Cafe*
Nifty Fifty's
Norma's/NJ
Olga's Diner/NJ*
Olive/NJ*
Otto's*
Outback Steak.†
Philly Crab
Pietro's
Pizzicato*
Plain & Fancy/LB
Plate*
Plumsteadville Inn*
Ponzio's/NJ*
Pub/NJ*
Reading Terminal
Red Caboose/LB*
Roselena's Coffee
Ruby's*
Saffron House*
Sage Diner/NJ*
Seven Stars Inn*
Silk City*
Snockey's Oyster*
Solaris Grille*
South St. Souvlaki
Spaghetti Warehse.*
Spotted Hog*
Sprigs*
Stoltzfus Farm/LB*
Stoudt's/LB*
Tacconelli's Pizz.
Tavern*
Teresa's Café*
Terrace/Greenhill/DE*
Tex Mex Conn.*
Tony Luke Jr.'s
Trolley Car Diner*
Village Porch*
Washington Cross.*
Washington Hse.*
White Dog Cafe*
William Penn Inn
Willow Valley/LB
Windmill/LB*
Yardley Inn*
Zesty's*
Zinn's Diner/LB*

Cigars Welcome
Abilene
Alberto's

Special Feature Index

Basil Bistro
Blue Bell Inn
Blue in Green†
Blüe Ox
bluezette
Capital Grille
Catelli/NJ
Chickie's & Pete's
circa
Copabanana
Cuisines
D'Angelo's Rist.
Davio's
Devon Seafood
Drafting Room†
East Side Mario's/NJ†
Engine 46
Fadó Irish Pub
Fergie's Pub
Finnigan's Wake
Four Dogs Tav.
Frederick's
General Lafayette
Happy Rooster
Havana
Il Portico
Il Sol D'Italia
Independence Brew
Iron Hill Brewery
John Harvard's†
Jolly's
Kansas City Prime
Keating's
La Veranda
Le Bar Lyonnais
Liberties
Manayunk Brew.
McFadden's
McGillin's
Monte Carlo
Morton's/Chicago†
Olive/NJ
Ortlieb's
Outback Steak./NJ†
Pace One
Palm
Paradigm
Passerelle
Peacock/Parkway
Prime Rib
Rist. Positano
Rock Bottom
Rose Tree Inn
Ruth's Chris
Sansom St. Oyster
Seven Stars Inn
Shula's Steak
Smith & Wollensky
Spaghetti Warehse.
Stoudt's/LB
Sullivan's Steak.†
Tavern on Green
Tex Mex Conn.
Tira Misu Rist.
Tony Luke Jr.'s†
Totaro's
Villa Strafford
Warmdaddy's
Washington Cross.
Wooden Iron
Yellow Springs
ZanzibarBlue†

Critic-Proof
(Get lots of business despite so-so food)
Abilene
Adobe Cafe
Al Dar Bistro
Bookbinders
Cosi†
Country Club
Dave & Buster's
East Side Mario's
Elephant & Castle†
Engine 46
Gullifty's
Hard Rock Cafe
John Harvard's†
Little Pete's†
Mad 4 Mex
Manayunk Brew.
McGillin's
Moriarty's
Noodle Heaven
Olga's Diner/NJ
Ortlieb's
Potcheen
Ruby's
Society Hill Hotel
Spaghetti Warehse.
Spotted Hog
Valley Forge Brew.
Zinn's Diner/LB

Dancing
Andreotti's/NJ
Azalea

vote at zagat.com

Special Feature Index

Blue Bell Inn
Brasil's
Brick Hotel
Café Habana
Casablanca
circa
Cuttalossa Inn
D'Angelo's Rist.
Finnigan's Wake
Founders
Fountain Rest.
Frederick's
General Lafayette
Hadley's Bistro
Il Sol D'Italia
Independence Brew
Kennedy-Supplee
La Collina
Lambertville Stat./NJ
Latest Dish
Loie
McFadden's
Monte Carlo
Ravenna
Silk City
Stoudt's/LB
Tierra Colombiana
Washington Cross.

Delivery/Takeout

(D=delivery, T=takeout)
Abilene (D,T)
Abyssinia (T)
Adobe Cafe (T)
Al Dar Bistro (T)
America B&G (T)
Ardmore Station (T)
Ariana (T)
Astral Plane (T)
Athena (T)
Audrey Claire (T)
Avalon (T)
Azafran (T)
Bamboo Club (T)
Bards (T)
Barnacle Ben's/NJ (T)
Barone Tratt./NJ (T)
Basil Bistro (T)
Beau Monde (T)
Bella Luna (T)
Big George's (T)
Bistro La Baia (T)
Bistro Romano (D,T)
Bistro St. Tropez (T)
Bleu (T)
Blüe Ox (T)
Blue Pacific (T)
Blue Sage Veg. (T)
bluezette (T)
Bookbinders (T)
Bourbon Blue (T)
Bravo Bistro (T)
Brick Hotel (D,T)
Bridget Foy's (T)
Bridgid's (T)
Buca di Beppo†
Buckley's Tav./DE (T)
Butcher's Cafe (T)
Cafe M/NJ (T)
Cafe Preeya (T)
Cafe San Pietro (T)
Cafe Spice (D,T)
Cafette (T)
Caffe Aldo Lam./NJ (T)
Caffe Casta Diva (T)
Carambola (T)
Caribou Cafe (T)
Carmella's (T)
Carmine's Cafe (T)
Carr's/LB (T)
Carversville Inn (T)
Century House (T)
Chadds Ford Inn (T)
Charles Plaza (D,T)
Chestnut Grill (T)
Chlöe (T)
Cibucán (T)
circa (T)
Columbus Inn/DE (T)
Continental (T)
Cresheim Cottage (T)
Crier/Country (T)
Cuba Libre (T)
Cuisines (T)
Culinaria/DE (T)
Dahlak†
Damon's Grill/LB (T)
Darbar Grill (D,T)
Davio's (D,T)
Deep Blue/DE (T)
Devon Seafood (T)
DiPalma (T)
Dmitri's (T)
Drafting Room (T)
Eclipse/DE (T)
Elements Café/NJ (T)
Emerald Fish/NJ (T)
Engine 46 (T)

Special Feature Index

Epicurean (T)
Eulogy Belgian (T)
Fadó Irish Pub (T)
Fatou & Fama (T)
Fayette St. Grille (T)
Fellini Café†
Fergie's Pub (T)
Food for Thought/NJ (T)
Fountain Side (T)
Friday Sat. Sun. (T)
FuziOn (T)
Gnocchi (T)
Goose Creek Grill (T)
Green Hills Inn/LB (T)
Gullifty's (T)
Gypsy Rose (T)
Hank's Place (T)
Harry's Savoy Grill/DE (T)
Havana (T)
Hibachi†
Historic Revere/LB (T)
Horizons Cafe (T)
Illuminare (T)
Il Portico (T)
Il Sol D'Italia (T)
Il Tartufo (T)
Indonesia (T)
Inn on Blue. Hill (T)
Jack's Firehse. (T)
Jake's (T)
Jasmine Thai (D,T)
John Harvard's†
Jolly's (T)
Kabul (T)
Kansas City Prime (T)
Keating's (T)
King George II (T)
Knave of Hearts (T)
Knight House (T)
La Boheme (T)
La Campagne/NJ (D,T)
La Lupe (D,T)
Landing (D,T)
L'Angolo (T)
Langostino (T)
La Pergola (T)
Las Cazuelas (T)
La Tolteca/DE†
Lauletta's Grille (T)
Le Castagne (T)
Liberties (T)
Little Café/NJ (D,T)
Little Fish (T)
Little Marakesh (T)

Little Tuna/NJ (T)
Log Cabin/LB (T)
Lombardi's (D,T)
London Grill (T)
Lourdas Greek (T)
L2 (T)
Ludwig's Garten (T)
Maccabeam (D,T)
Mallorca (T)
Manila Bay B&G (T)
Marco Polo (T)
Marg. Kuo's (T)
Max's/NJ (T)
Mélange Café/NJ (T)
Mirna's Cafe (T)
Mixto (T)
Mokas (T)
Mona Lisa/DE (T)
Monk's Cafe (T)
Moody Monkey (T)
Moonstruck (T)
Moriarty's (T)
Morimoto (T)
Moshulu (T)
Mothers' (T)
New Orleans Cafe (T)
New Wave (T)
Novelty (T)
N. 3rd (T)
Olde Greenfield/LB (T)
Ooka Jap. (T)
Ortlieb's (T)
Otto's (T)
Pace One (T)
Palm (T)
Paradigm (T)
¡Pasión! (T)
Peacock/Parkway (T)
Pelican Fish Co./NJ (T)
Penne (T)
Pepper's Cafe (T)
Pigalle (T)
Plate (T)
Portofino (T)
Prime Rib (T)
Pub/NJ (T)
Radicchio (T)
Ravenna (T)
Red Caboose/LB (T)
Rist. Positano (T)
Rist. Primavera (T)
Rist. San Carlo (T)
Ritz Seafood/NJ (T)
Roller's (T)

vote at zagat.com 181

Special Feature Index

Rose Tattoo Cafe (T)
Ruth's Chris†
Rx (D,T)
Sabrina's Cafe (T)
Sansom St. Oyster (T)
Sassafras (T)
Savannah (T)
Seafood Unlimited (D,T)
Serrano (T)
Seven Stars Inn (T)
Society Hill Hotel (T)
Solaris Grille (T)
Sonoma (T)
Sotto Varalli (T)
Spasso (T)
Spence Cafe (T)
Spezia (T)
Spotted Hog (T)
Sprigs (T)
Spring Mill Café (T)
Stefano's (T)
Stoney's/DE (T)
Stoudt's/LB (T)
Summer Kit. (T)
Swanky Bubbles (T)
Sweet Bay Cafe/LB (T)
Syrenka (T)
Tangerine (T)
Taq. Moroleon (T)
Tavern on Green (T)
Teikoku (T)
Terrace/Greenhill/DE (T)
Thai Orchid/NJ†
Thomas' (T)
Tierra Colombiana (D,T)
Tira Misu Rist. (T)
Tir Na Nog (T)
Toscana Cuc. Rust. (T)
Toscana Kitchen/DE (T)
Toto (T)
Tratt. Alberto (T)
Upstares/Varalli (T)
Valanni (T)
Valley Forge Brew. (T)
Vientiane Café (T)
Viggiano's (T)
Villa di Roma (T)
Village Porch (T)
Walter's Steak./DE (T)
Warmdaddy's (T)
Warsaw Cafe (T)
Washington Cross. (T)
Washington Hse. (T)
White Dog Cafe (T)
White Elephant (T)
William Penn Inn (T)
Willistown Grille (T)
Wooden Iron (D,T)
Yardley Inn (T)
Ye Olde Concordville (T)
ZanzibarBlue/DE†

Dining Alone
(Other than hotels and places with counter service)
Aoi
Ardmore Station
Beau Monde
Ben & Irv
Big George's
Bitar's†
Black Sheep Pub
Brew HaHa!†
Cafette
Caribou Cafe
Copabanana
Cosi
Dalessandro's
Devon Seafood
Down Home Din.
Effie's
Famous 4th St.
Horizons Cafe
Izzy & Zoe's
Jim's Steaks
Judy's Cafe
Koch's Deli
La Pergola
Maccabeam
Marathon Grill
Mayfair Diner
Mexican Post
Monk's Cafe
Morning Glory
Nifty Fifty's
Pat's King/Steaks
Reading Terminal
Sage Diner/NJ
Sang Kee
Seafood Unlimited
Shank's & Evelyn's
Tango
Tony Luke Jr.'s
Trolley Car Diner

Entertainment
(Call for days and times of performances)
Abbaye (DJs)
Abilene (blues/rock)

Special Feature Index

Alberto's (piano)
Andreotti's/NJ (vocals)
Azalea (jazz)
Bay Pony Inn (guitar/vocals)
Beau Monde (cabaret/DJ)
Bistro Romano (piano)
Black Bass Hotel (piano)
Blue Bell Inn (varies)
Blüe Ox (accordion)
Bourbon Blue (blues/funk)
Brandywine Brew./DE (jazz)
Brasil's (Brazilian/Latin)
Brew HaHa!†
Brick Hotel (acoustic/modern)
Café Habana (DJ/jazz/Latin)
Cafe San Pietro (piano)
Cafe Spice (DJ)
Casablanca†
Catelli/NJ (piano)
Chadds Ford Inn (bands)
Chickie's & Pete's†
Christopher's (karaoke)
City Tavern (harpsichord)
Cock 'n Bull (mystery dinners)
Columbus Inn/DE (varies)
Creed's Seafood (jazz/piano)
Crier/Country (varies)
Cuba Libre (DJ)
Cuttalossa Inn (acoustic/piano)
Dahlak†
D'Angelo's Rist. (DJ)
Deep Blue/DE (jazz/rock)
Delmonico's (piano)
Denim Lounge (DJs)
D'Ignazio's (piano)
Dilworthtown Inn (jazz)
Doc Holliday's/LB (bands/DJ)
Drafting Room†
Elephant & Castle†
Epicurean (acoustic)
Fadó Irish Pub (Irish)
Fergie's Pub (blues/rock)
Fez Moroccan (belly dancer)
Filomena Cuc. Ital./NJ†
Filomena Cuc. Rust./NJ (DJ)
Finnigan's Wake (bands)
Founders (jazz/piano)
Fountain Rest. (bands)
Four Dogs Tav. (acoustic)
Franco & Luigi's (mandolin/piano)
Frederick's (band/piano/vocals)
Gables/Chadds Ford (jazz)
General Lafayette (folk)
Goat Hollow (varies)
Gracie's/LB (varies)
Green Room/DE (harp/piano)
Grill Rest. (piano)
Groff's Farm/LB (acoustic rock)
Gullifty's (karaoke)
Hadley's Bistro (piano)
Half Moon (blues/jazz/R&B)
Harry's Savoy Grill/DE (piano)
Havana (bands)
Hibachi†
Il Portico (guitar)
Il Sol D'Italia (jazz/rock)
Independ. Brew (bands/DJ)
Inn at Phillips Mill (vocals)
Inn Philadelphia (piano)
Iron Hill Brewery†
Jack's (bluegrass/country)
Jamaican Jerk (varies)
Jenny's Bistro (piano)
John Harvard's†
Johnny Mañana's (varies)
Jones (DJ)
Joseph Ambler (jazz)
Joy Tsin Lau (karaoke)
Kabul (varies)
Kansas City Prime (piano)
Kennedy-Supplee (piano)
Kimberton Inn (harp/piano)
King George II (piano)
La Collina (varies)
Lambertville Stat./NJ (varies)
La Padella (piano)
La Terrasse (piano)
La Tolteca/DE†
Liberties (jazz)
Little Marakesh (belly dancer)
Log Cabin/LB (piano)
Loie (DJ)
London Grill (bands)
L2 (jazz)
Manayunk Brew. (blues/jazz)
Marathon Grill†
Marker (piano)
McFadden's (DJ)
McGillin's (bands)
Mendenhall Inn (harp/piano)
Mixto (varies)
Mokas (piano)
Monte Carlo (piano)
New Orleans Cafe (varies)
Nodding Head (jazz)
Norma's/NJ (belly dancer)
N. 3rd (varies)
Odette's (cabaret/piano)

vote at zagat.com

Special Feature Index

Olde Greenfield/LB (piano)
Olive/NJ (jazz)
Ortlieb's (jazz)
Pace One (jazz)
Paradigm (bands)
Passage/India (piano)
Plate (bands/DJ)
Plough & Stars (Irish)
Plumsteadville Inn (piano)
Primavera Pizza†
Prime Rib (piano)
Rat's/NJ (piano)
Rembrandt's (varies)
Rest. at Doneckers/LB (piano)
Rist. Mediterraneo (piano)
Rock Bottom (karaoke)
Rose Tree Inn (piano)
Roux 3 (varies)
Saffron House (jazz)
Serrano (acoustic)
Silk City (DJ)
Singapore Kosher†
Society Hill Hotel (jazz/piano)
Solaris Grille (jazz)
Spagh. Warehse. (theme dinner)
Spence Cafe (jazz/rock)
Stella Notte (blues/jazz)
Stoudt's/LB (bands)
Sukhothai (DJ)
Sullivan's Steak. (jazz)
Susanna Foo (harp)
Swann Lounge (jazz)
Tai Lake (karaoke)
Tavern on Green (jazz/rock)
Tex Mex Conn. (bands/karaoke)
Tierra Colom. (merengue/salsa)
Tira Misu Rist. (piano)
Tir Na Nog (DJ/Irish)
Toscana Kitchen/DE (jazz)
Upstares/Varalli (piano)
U.S. Hotel B&G (jazz)
Valanni (cabaret/DJ/open mike)
Vickers Tavern (jazz/piano)
Victor Café (opera)
Viggiano's (Italian)
Villa Strafford (jazz)
Vincent's (blues/jazz/piano)
Warmdaddy's (blues)
Washington Cross. (piano)
White Dog Cafe (piano)
William Penn Inn (jazz)
Yangming (piano)
Ye Olde Concordville (piano)
ZanzibarBlue†
Zesty's (guitar)

Fireplaces
Alberto's
Avalon
Bay Pony Inn
Beau Monde
Beau Rivage/NJ
Black Bass Hotel
Black Sheep Pub
Blüe Ox
Braddock's Tav./NJ
Brandywine Brew./DE
Brick Hotel
Bridgid's
Buckley's Tav./DE
Carversville Inn
Centre Bridge Inn
Chadds Ford Inn
Cock 'n Bull
Columbus Inn/DE
Coyote Crossing
Creed's Seafood
Cresheim Cottage
Crier/Country
Cuttalossa Inn
Dante & Luigi's
Davio's
Delmonico's
Deux Cheminées
D'Ignazio's
Dilworthtown Inn
Drafting Room†
Duling-Kurtz Hse.
Effie's
Elephant & Castle
Epicurean
Esca
Fadó Irish Pub
Filomena Cuc. Ital./NJ†
Filomena Cuc. Rust./NJ
Finnigan's Wake
Four Dogs Tav.
General Lafayette
Gilmore's
Giumarello's/NJ
Golden Pheasant
Gracie's/LB
Green Hills Inn/LB
Groff's Farm/LB
Harry's Savoy Grill/DE
Havana
Historic Revere/LB
Hotel Du Village
Inn at Phillips Mill
Inn Philadelphia

Special Feature Index

Joseph Ambler
Kennedy-Supplee
Kimberton Inn
King George II
Krazy Kat's/DE
La Bonne Aub.
La Campagne/NJ
Lamberti's/NJ†
Landing
Le Mas
Log Cabin/LB
Lucy's Hat Shop
Marker
Max's/NJ
Michael's
Mokas
Moriarty's
Odette's
Olde Greenfield/LB
Old Guard Hse.
Olive/NJ
Otto's
Pantheon
Passerelle
Plough & Stars
Plumsteadville Inn
Rat's/NJ
Ravenna
Rest. at Doneckers/LB
Rose Tree Inn
Saloon
Sassafras
Serrano
Stella Notte
Swann Lounge
Vickers Tavern
Villa Strafford
Vincent's
Washington Cross.
Washington St. Ale/DE
William Penn Inn
Willistown Grille
Yardley Inn
Yellow Springs

Game in Season
Abilene
Alisa Cafe
America B&G
Azalea
Back Burner/DE
Bay Pony Inn
Beau Rivage/NJ
Birchrunville Store
Bistro St. Tropez
Black Bass Hotel
Blüe Ox
Brasserie Perrier
Brick Hotel
Bridget Foy's
Cafe Unicorn/LB
Carversville Inn
Centre Bridge Inn
Chadds Ford Inn
circa
Citron Bistro
City Tavern
Creole Café/NJ
Crier/Country
Davio's
Deux Cheminées
Dilworthtown Inn
DiPalma
Eclipse/DE
Founders
Fountain Rest.
General Warren
Gilmore's
Golden Pheasant
Gracie's/LB
Grasshopper
Green Hills Inn/LB
Half Moon
Harry's Savoy Grill/DE
Hotel Du Village
Il Portico
Inn at Phillips Mill
Inn on Blue. Hill
Inn Philadelphia
Iron Hill Brewery†
Jack's Firehse.
Joseph Ambler
Joseph Poon
Kennedy-Supplee
King George II
Krazy Kat's/DE
La Campagne/NJ
Lacroix/Rittenhse.
La Locanda
Lambertville Stat./NJ
La Tolteca/DE†
Le Petit Café
Loie
London Grill
L2
Luigi Vitrone's/DE
Mainland Inn
Monte Carlo

vote at zagat.com

Special Feature Index

Moshulu
Nais Cuisine
New Orleans Cafe
New Wave
Odette's
Old Guard Hse.
Opus 251
Passerelle
Plough & Stars
Rat's/NJ
Rembrandt's
Rest. Taquet
Rose Tree Inn
Roux 3
Salt
State St. Grill
Swann Lounge
Tango
Tartine
333 Belrose
Totaro's
Trinacria
Umbria
Vickers Tavern
Victor Café
Villa Strafford
Vincent's
Washington Hse.
White Dog Cafe
Yellow Springs

Historic Places

(Year opened; * building)
1681 King George II*
1683 Blüe Ox
early 1700s Bistro Romano*
1700 Ye Olde Concordville*
1714 William Penn Inn*
1722 Yellow Springs*
1725 Gypsy Rose*
1736 Chadds Ford Inn*
1736 Joseph Ambler*
1736 Seven Stars Inn*
1740 Crier/Country*
1740 Historic Revere/LB*
1740 Pace One*
1740s Black Bass Hotel*
1742 Washington Hse.
1743/1945 Blue Bell Inn
1745 General Warren
1748 Cresheim Cottage*
1751 Plumsteadville Inn*
1754 Dilworthtown Inn*
1755 Havana*
1756 Groff's Farm/LB*
1756 Inn at Phillips Mill*
1764 Brick Hotel*
1772 La Bonne Aub.*
1773 (replica) City Tavern
1780 Columbus Inn/DE
1780 Olde Greenfield/LB*
1790 Old Guard Hse.*
1792 Birchrunville Store*
1794 Odette's*
1796 Kimberton Inn*
1800 Cuttalossa Inn*
1800 Inn on Blue. Hill*
1805 Green Hills Inn/LB*
1813 Carversville Inn*
1817 Washington Cross.*
1823 Braddock's Tav./NJ*
1824 Inn Philadelphia*
1830 Bay Pony Inn*
1830 Duling-Kurtz Hse.*
1848 Saffron House*
1852 Kennedy-Supplee*
1856 Haydn Zug's/LB*
1857 Golden Pheasant*
1860 McGillin's
1880 Spring Mill Café
1893 Reading Terminal*
1899 Dante & Luigi's
1900 Ralph's
circa 1900 Hotel Du Village*

Hotel Dining

Adam's Mark Philadelphia
  Marker
Bay Pony Inn
  Bay Pony Inn
Best Western Concordville
  Ye Olde Concordville
Best Western Inn
  Palace of Asia
Best Western Revere Inn
  Historic Revere/LB
Black Bass Hotel
  Black Bass Hotel
Brick Hotel
  Brick Hotel
Centre Bridge Inn
  Centre Bridge Inn
Chadds Ford Inn
  Chadds Ford Inn
Chestnut Hill Hotel
  Chestnut Grill
  Stella Notte
Clarion Hotel
  Elephant & Castle

Special Feature Index

Crier in the Country
   Crier/Country
Crowne Plaza Philadelphia
   Elephant & Castle
Duling-Kurtz House
   Duling-Kurtz Hse.
EverMay On The Delaware
   EverMay/Delaware
Four Seasons Philadelphia
   Fountain Rest.
   Swann Lounge
General Lafayette Inn
   General Lafayette
General Warren Inne
   General Warren
Golden Pheasant Inn
   Golden Pheasant
Hilton Philadelphia
   Delmonico's
Hilton Valley Forge
   Kobe
Hotel du Pont
   Brandywine Rm./DE
   Brew HaHa!/DE
   Green Room/DE
Hotel Du Village
   Hotel Du Village
Hyatt Regency
   Keating's
Inn at Montchanin Village
   Krazy Kat's/DE
Inn at Penn
   Penne
   Pod
Inn at Phillips Mill
   Inn at Phillips Mill
Joseph Ambler Inn
   Joseph Ambler
Latham Hotel
   Jolly's
Mendenhall Hotel
   Mendenhall Inn
Omni Hotel
   Azalea
Pace One Country Inn
   Pace One
Park Hyatt at the Bellevue
   Barrymore Rm.
   Founders
   Palm
Penn's View Hotel
   Rist. Panorama
Plumsteadville Inn
   Plumsteadville Inn
Radisson Plaza Warwick
   Capriccio's
   Prime Rib
Rittenhouse Hotel
   Cassatt Lounge
   Lacroix/Rittenhse.
   Smith & Wollensky
Ritz-Carlton Philadelphia
   Grill
   Pantheon
Sheraton Rittenhouse Sq.
   Bleu
   Potcheen
Sheraton Society Hill
   Hadley's Bistro
Society Hill Hotel
   Society Hill Hotel
Sofitel Philadelphia
   Chez Colette
Wayne Hotel
   Rest. Taquet
Westin Philadelphia
   Grill Rest.
William Penn Inn
   William Penn Inn
Willow Valley Resort
   Willow Valley/LB
Wyndham Philadelphia
   Shula's Steak

"In" Places

Adriatica
Alison/Blue Bell
Alma de Cuba
Audrey Claire
Bleu
bluezette
Buddakan
Cafe Spice
Capital Grille
Chickie's & Pete's†
Chops
Cibucán
circa
Continental
Cuba Libre
Denim Lounge
Django
Dmitri's†
Eulogy Belgian
Fadó Irish Pub
Judy's Cafe
Kisso Sushi
Krazy Kat's/DE

Special Feature Index

Latest Dish
Le Mas
Loie
London Grill
Los Catrines/Teq.
L2
Maggiano's†
Marmont
Max's/NJ
Mixto
Morimoto
North by NW
Novelty
Paradigm
¡Pasión!
Pod
Rest. at Doneckers/LB
Ritz Seafood/NJ
Rouge
Savannah
Spezia
Swanky Bubbles
Tangerine
Tir Na Nog
Twenty Manning
Valanni
Vetri
Vivo Enoteca
Wooden Iron
Yangming
ZanzibarBlue/DE†

Jacket Required

Beau Rivage/NJ
Dilworthtown Inn
EverMay/Delaware
Fountain Rest.
Green Room/DE
Il Portico
Joseph Ambler
La Bonne Aub.
Lacroix/Rittenhse.
La Famiglia
Le Bec-Fin
Monte Carlo
Moshulu
Prime Rib
Ritz Seafood/NJ
Savona

Late Dining

(Weekday closing hour)
Abbaye (1 AM)
Billy Wong's (2 AM)
Brandywine Brew./DE (1 AM)

Christopher's (1 AM)
Copabanana (1 AM)
Copa Too (1 AM)
Jim's Steaks†
Jones (12 AM)
La Lupe (12 AM)
Loie (1 AM)
Mad 4 Mex (2:45 AM)
Marmont (1 AM)
McGillin's (1 AM)
Monk's Cafe (1 AM)
Moriarty's (1 AM)
North Sea (3 AM)
N. 3rd (2 AM)
Olga's Diner/NJ (2 AM)
Penang (1 AM)
Plough & Stars (1:30 AM)
Ponzio's/NJ (1 AM)
Rib Crib (1 AM)
Rouge (1 AM)
Sage Diner/NJ (1 AM)
Savannah (1 AM)
Standard Tap (1 AM)
Stoney's/DE (1 AM)
Sugar Mom's (2 AM)
Swanky Bubbles (1 AM)
Swann Lounge (1 AM)
Tai Lake (3 AM)
Washington St. Ale/DE (1 AM)

Meet for a Drink

Abbaye
Adriatica
Alberto's
Al Dar Bistro
Alma de Cuba
Bamboo Club
Bards
Bella
Billy Wong's
Black Sheep Pub
bluezette
Brasil's
Brasserie Perrier
Capital Grille
Caribou Cafe
Chops
Cibucán
circa
Citron Bistro
Continental
Copa Too
Coyote Crossing
Cuba Libre
Dark Horse Pub

Special Feature Index

Davio's
Delmonico's
Denim Lounge
Engine 46
Esca
Eulogy Belgian
Fadó Irish Pub
Fergie's Pub
Filomena Cuc. Ital./NJ†
Finnigan's Wake
Happy Rooster
Independence Brew
Iron Hill Brewery
Jones
Le Mas
Loie
London Grill
Los Catrines/Teq.
L2
Manayunk Brew.
Marker
McCorm./Schmick's
McFadden's
Mixto
Monk's Cafe
Moriarty's
New Wave
Oasis
Odette's
Penne
Plough & Stars
Prime Rib
Rist. Panorama
Savannah
Society Hill Hotel
Sonoma
Standard Tap
Swann Lounge
Tango
Tir Na Nog
Twenty Manning
Twenty21
Valanni
Vivo Enoteca
Wooden Iron
World Fusion
ZanzibarBlue/DE†

Microbreweries
Brandywine Brew./DE
Independence Brew
Iron Hill Brewery
John Harvard's†
Manayunk Brew.
Valley Forge Brew.
Victory Brew.

Offbeat
Astral Plane
Bamboo Club
Bitar's†
Buca di Beppo†
Butcher's Cafe
Carman's Country
Gracie's/LB
Jones
Judy's Cafe
Knave of Hearts
La Lupe
Little Pete's†
Maggiano's†
Manila Bay B&G
Melrose Diner
Morimoto
Morning Glory
Moshulu
Penang
Pod
Shank's & Evelyn's
Silk City
Simon Pearce
Syrenka
Tacconelli's Pizz.
Trolley Car Diner
Vientiane Café
Zinn's Diner/LB

Outdoor Dining
(G=garden; P=patio;
S=sidewalk; T=terrace)
Aden (G,S)
Adobe Cafe (P)
America B&G (P)
Astral Plane (S)
Athena (P)
Azafran (P)
Bamboo Club (P)
Barnacle Ben's/NJ (G)
Barone Tratt./NJ (P)
Bella Trattoria (S)
Birchrunville Store (T)
Bistro La Baia (S)
Bitar's†
Black Bass Hotel (T)
Bleu (S)
Blüe Ox (G)
bluezette (S)
Braddock's Tav./NJ (G)

vote at zagat.com 189

Special Feature Index

Bravo Bistro (P)
Brick Hotel (G)
Bridget Foy's (S)
Buca di Beppo†
Café Gallery/NJ (T)
Cafe M/NJ (S)
Cafette (G)
Caribou Cafe (T)
Carmella's (T)
Centre Bridge Inn (T)
Chart House (T)
Chestnut Grill (P,S)
City Tavern (G)
Columbus Inn/DE (T)
Continental (S)
Coyote Crossing (P)
Creed's Seafood (P)
Cresheim Cottage (P)
Crier/Country (G)
Cuba Libre (S)
Cuttalossa Inn (G,P,T)
Devon Seafood (P)
D'Ignazio's (T)
Dilworthtown Inn (G)
Effie's (G)
Elements Café/NJ (S)
Esca (P)
Eulogy Belgian (S)
Filomena Cuc. Rust./NJ (P)
Four Dogs Tav. (P)
General Warren (T)
Geno's Steaks (S)
Golden Pheasant (G)
Goose Creek Grill (T)
Gracie's/LB (G,P)
Groff's Farm/LB (P)
Gypsy Rose (T)
Harry's Savoy Grill/DE (P,T)
Havana (P)
Hotel Du Village (G)
Il Sol D'Italia (P)
Inn at Phillips Mill (G)
Inn Philadelphia (G)
Iron Hill Brewery†
Isaac's Rest.†
Jamaican Jerk (G)
Jenny's Bistro (P)
John Harvard's/DE†
Joseph Ambler (P)
Kansas City Prime (S)
Keating's (P)
Knave of Hearts (S)
Knight House (P)
Krazy Kat's/DE (P)

La Campagne/NJ (T)
La Lupe (S)
Landing (G,T)
La Terrasse (T)
La Tolteca/DE†
La Veranda (T)
La Vigna (P)
Le Mas (G)
Lemon Grass/LB†
Little Café/NJ (S)
Little Fish (S)
Little Pete's†
Loie (S)
Mad 4 Mex (P)
Maggiano's†
Main-ly Café (S)
Manayunk Brew. (T)
Marmont (S)
Mélange Café/NJ (P,T)
Mexican Food/NJ (P)
Mirna's Cafe†
Mokas (P)
Morning Glory (P)
Moshulu (T)
Mothers' (P)
New Orleans Cafe (P)
New Wave (S)
North by NW (P)
Odette's (G)
Olde Greenfield/LB (G,P)
Olive/NJ (T)
Opus 251 (G)
Otto's (G)
Pace One (G)
Pat's King/Steaks (S)
Pattaya Grill (P,S)
Peacock/Parkway (P)
Penne (P)
Pepper's Cafe (P)
Philadelphia Fish (P)
Pif (S)
Places! Bistro (G)
Plate (P)
Primavera Pizza†
Rat's/NJ (P)
Ravenna (P)
Red Caboose/LB (S)
Rembrandt's (S)
Rest. La Encina (P)
Rest. Taquet (P)
Roller's (S)
Roma (S)
Rouge (P)
Roux 3 (P)

Special Feature Index

Salt (S)
Savannah (S)
Savona (T)
Shivnanda (S)
Siam Cuisine†
Society Hill Hotel (S)
Solaris Grille (G,P)
Sonoma (G,P,S)
Sprigs (S)
Spring Mill Café (T)
Summer Kit. (P)
Swann Lounge (T)
Tango (P)
Tartine (G)
Tavern (P)
Tavern on Green (S)
Terrace/Greenhill/DE (T)
Thomas' (S)
Three Little Pigs (P)
333 Belrose (P)
Tir Na Nog (P)
Tony Luke Jr.'s†
Toscana Cuc. Rust. (T)
Toscana Kitchen/DE (P)
Tratt. Alberto (G,S)
Twenty Manning (P)
Twenty21 (G)
2 Goodfellas (P)
Vickers Tavern (P)
Viggiano's (P)
Vincent's (P)
Washington Cross. (G,P)
Washington St. Ale/DE (P)
White Dog Cafe (P)
Winberie's (P)
World Fusion (S)
Yardley Inn (P)
Zesty's (S)
Zocalo (P)

Parking

(V=valet, *=validated)
Adriatica (V)
Alberto's (V)
Alma de Cuba (V)
Ariana*
Azalea (V)
Barrymore Rm. (V)*
Beau Rivage/NJ (V)
Black Bass Hotel (V)
bluezette (V)
Bookbinders*
Bourbon Blue (V)
Brandywine Rm./DE (V)
Brasserie Perrier (V)
Bravo Bistro (V)
Buca di Beppo†
Buddakan (V)
Caffe Aldo Lam./NJ (V)
Cassatt Lounge (V)
Cedars*
Centre Bridge Inn (V)
Chart House (V)
Cherry St. Veg.*
Chez Colette (V)
Chops (V)
circa (V)
Columbus Inn/DE (V)
Creed's Seafood (V)
Cuba Libre (V)
D'Angelo's Rist.*
Dave & Buster's*
Davio's (V)
Delmonico's (V)
DiNardo's*
Felicia's (V)
Finnigan's Wake (V)
Founders (V)*
Fountain Rest. (V)
Frederick's (V)
Genji*
Giumarello's/NJ (V)
Grasshopper (V)
Green Room/DE (V)
Grill (V)
Grill Rest. (V)
Hadley's Bistro*
Hibachi†
H.K. Gold. Phoenix*
Il Portico (V)
Imperial Inn*
Iron Hill Brewery†
Jake's (V)
Joe's Peking*
Jolly's (V)
Jones (V)
Joseph Poon*
Joy Tsin Lau*
Kabul*
Kansas City Prime (V)
Keating's (V)
King George II (V)
Kristian's Rist. (V)
La Collina (V)
Lacroix/Rittenhse. (V)
La Famiglia (V)
La Veranda (V)
Le Bar Lyonnais (V)

vote at zagat.com

Special Feature Index

Le Bec-Fin (V)
Le Mas (V)
Los Catrines/Teq. (V)
Maggiano's*
Mallorca (V)
Manayunk Brew. (V)
Marabella's (V)
Marker (V)*
Marmont (V)
McCorm./Schmick's (V)
Mendenhall Inn (V)
Michael's (V)
Monte Carlo (V)
Moriarty's*
Morimoto (V)
Morton's/Chicago†
New Orleans Cafe (V)
Noodle Heaven*
Odette's (V)
Palm (V)*
Pantheon (V)
¡Pasión!*
Penne (V)
Pho Xe Lua*
Plough & Stars*
Pod (V)
Porcini*
Portofino*
Potcheen (V)
Prime Rib (V)
Rat's/NJ (V)
Rest. 821/DE (V)
Rist. La Buca*
Rist. Panorama (V)*
Rist. Primavera†
Roy's (V)
Ruth's Chris†
Saffron House (V)
Saloon (V)
Sansom St. Oyster*
Savona (V)
Seafood Unlimited (V)
Shivnanda*
Shula's Steak*
Smith & Wollensky (V)
Solaris Grille*
Sonoma (V)*
Striped Bass (V)*
Susanna Foo (V)*
Swanky Bubbles (V)
Swann Lounge (V)
Tai Lake*
Tangerine (V)
Tir Na Nog (V)
Tratt. Alberto (V)
Twenty21*
U.S. Hotel B&G*
Victor Café (V)
Villa Strafford (V)*
Warmdaddy's (V)*
William Penn Inn (V)
World Fusion (V)
ZanzibarBlue†
Zesty's (V)

People-Watching

Adriatica
Alma de Cuba
America B&G
Audrey Claire
Bamboo Club
Bleu
Blue Pacific
bluezette
Bourbon Blue
Brasserie Perrier
Bridget Foy's
Buddakan
Cafe M/NJ
Capital Grille
Carmella's
Catelli/NJ
Chickie's & Pete's
Chops
Cibucán
circa
Citron Bistro
Continental
Copabanana
Creed's Seafood
Cuba Libre
Denim Lounge
Devon Seafood
Dmitri's†
Eulogy Belgian
Fadó Irish Pub
Famous 4th St.
Fork
Geno's Steaks
Grill
Hymie's Merion
Jake's
Jolly's
Jones
Judy's Cafe
Kansas City Prime
Koch's Deli
Krazy Kat's/DE

subscribe to zagat.com

Special Feature Index

Lacroix/Rittenhse.
Latest Dish
Le Castagne
Le Mas
Loie
London Grill
Los Catrines/Teq.
L2
Maggiano's†
Max's/NJ
McCorm./Schmick's
Melrose Diner
Mirna's Cafe
Mixto
Morimoto
Moro/DE
Moshulu
N. 3rd
Oasis
Outback Steak.†
Palm
Pantheon
¡Pasión!
Pat's King/Steaks
Pif
Plate
Pod
Prime Rib
Pub/NJ
Radicchio
Rat's/NJ
Rist. Panorama
Rouge
Roux 3
Roy's
Savannah
Smith & Wollensky
Sonoma
Striped Bass
Sullivan's Steak.
Tangerine
Tango
Tavern
Teikoku
Tir Na Nog
Tony Luke Jr.'s
Toscana Cuc. Rust.
Twenty Manning
Upstares/Varalli
Valanni
Vesuvio
Vinny T's
Vivo Enoteca
Warmdaddy's
ZanzibarBlue†

Power Scenes
Alma de Cuba
bluezette
Brasserie Perrier
Buddakan
Capital Grille
Catelli/NJ
Chops
Fountain Rest.
Green Room/DE
Grill Rest.
Jones
Kansas City Prime
Lacroix/Rittenhse.
La Veranda
Le Bec-Fin
Le Castagne
Le Mas
Max's/NJ
McCorm./Schmick's
Morimoto
Morton's/Chicago†
Palm
Prime Rib
Rouge
Roy's
Ruth's Chris
Saloon
Shula's Steak
Smith & Wollensky
Striped Bass
Sullivan's Steak.
Susanna Foo
Wooden Iron

Pre-Theater Menus
(Call for prices and times)
Abacus
Adobe Cafe
Andreotti's/NJ
Barnacle Ben's/NJ
Bay Pony Inn
Blue Bell Inn
Blüe Ox
Bookbinders
Brandywine Rm./DE
Caffè Bellissimo/DE†
Deep Blue/DE
D'Ignazio's
DiNardo's
Hank's Place
Harry's Savoy Grill/DE
Hymie's Merion
Lambertville Stat./NJ

vote at zagat.com 193

Special Feature Index

La Pergola†
Little Café/NJ
London Grill
Marker
Moonstruck
Olga's Diner/NJ
Otto's
Pattaya Grill
Plumsteadville Inn
Ron's Schoolhouse
Sonoma
Tavern on Green
Washington Hse.
William Penn Inn
Ye Olde Concordville

Private Rooms
(Restaurants charge less at off times; call for capacity)

Adobe Cafe
Adriatica
Alberto's
Al Dar Bistro
Alma de Cuba
America B&G
Andreotti's/NJ
August Moon
Azalea
Back Burner/DE
Barnacle Ben's/NJ
Barone Tratt./NJ
Bay Pony Inn
Beau Rivage/NJ
Bella Luna
Bird-in-Hand/LB
Bistro St. Tropez
Black Bass Hotel
Black Sheep Pub
Black Swan/NJ
Blue Bell Inn
Blüe Ox
Blue Pacific
bluezette
Bourbon Blue
Braddock's Tav./NJ
Brandywine Brew./DE
Brandywine Rm./DE
Brasserie Perrier
Brick Hotel
Bridget Foy's
Bridgid's
Buca di Beppo†
Buddakan
Bunha Faun

Café Gallery/NJ
Cafe San Pietro
Cafe Unicorn/LB
Caffe Aldo Lam./NJ
Caffè Bellissimo
California Cafe
Capital Grille
Carmine's Cafe
Carr's/LB
Casablanca†
Catelli/NJ
Centre Bridge Inn
Chestnut Grill
Chez Elena Wu/NJ
Chops
CinCin
circa
Citron Bistro
City Tavern
Cock 'n Bull
Columbus Inn/DE
Continental
Copabanana
Creed's Seafood
Cresheim Cottage
Crier/Country
Cuba Libre
Cuisines
Cuttalossa Inn
Dahlak†
D'Angelo's Rist.
Dante & Luigi's
Dark Horse Pub
Dave & Buster's
Davio's
Deep Blue/DE
Denim Lounge
D'Ignazio's
Dilworthtown Inn
DiPalma
Drafting Room†
Duling-Kurtz Hse.
Effie's
El Azteca†
Epicurean
Eulogy Belgian
EverMay/Delaware
Fergie's Pub
Filomena Cuc. Ital./NJ†
Filomena Cuc. Rust./NJ
Finnigan's Wake
Food for Thought/NJ
Founders
Fountain Rest.

subscribe to zagat.com

Special Feature Index

Four Dogs Tav.
Gables/Chadds Ford
General Lafayette
General Warren
Genji
Gilmore's
Giumarello's/NJ
Goat Hollow
Golden Pheasant
Gracie's/LB
Green Hills Inn/LB
Green Room/DE
Groff's Farm/LB
Gypsy Rose
Hadley's Bistro
Hard Rock Cafe
Harmony Veg.
Harry's Savoy Grill/DE
Haydn Zug's/LB
Hibachi†
Historic Revere/LB
H.K. Gold. Phoenix
Hotel Du Village
Hunan
Il Portico
Inn on Blue. Hill
Inn Philadelphia
Io E Tu Rist.
Iron Hill Brewery†
Isaac's Rest./LB†
Italian Bistro†
Jack's Firehse.
Jasmine Thai
John Harvard's†
Jolly's
Joseph Ambler
Kansas City Prime
Kawabata
Keating's
Kegel's Seafood/LB
Kennedy-Supplee
Kimberton Inn
King George II
Knight House
Korea Garden
Krazy Kat's/DE
La Bonne Aub.
La Campagne/NJ
La Collina
Lacroix/Rittenhse.
La Famiglia
Lai Lai Garden
Lamberti's†
Lambertville Stat./NJ

La Terrasse
La Veranda
La Vigna
Lee How Fook
Le Mas
Le Mê Toujours/NJ
Liberties
Lily's on Main/LB
Log Cabin/LB
London Grill
Los Catrines/Teq.
L2
Lucy's Hat Shop
Ludwig's Garten
Maggiano's
Mainland Inn
Mallorca
Ma Ma Yolanda's
Mamma Maria
Marabella's
Marathon Grill†
Marg. Kuo's
Marg. Kuo's Mand.
Marrakesh
Marra's
McCorm./Schmick's
Melting Pot
Mendenhall Inn
Mexican Food/NJ
Michael's
Mixto
Mokas
Monte Carlo
Moody Monkey
Moonstruck
Moriarty's
Morton's/Chicago
Moshulu
Mrs. Robino's/DE
Mustard Greens
Nais Cuisine
New Orleans Cafe
Odette's
Olde Greenfield/LB
Old Guard Hse.
Opus 251
Pace One
Palm
Pantheon
Passage/India
Passerelle
Pattaya Grill
Peking
Pho Xe Lua

vote at zagat.com

Special Feature Index

Plain & Fancy/LB
Plate
Plumsteadville Inn
Pod
Ponzio's/NJ
Portofino
Prime Rib
Pub/NJ
Ralph's
Ravenna
Red Caboose/LB
Rest. at Doneckers/LB
Rest. 821/DE
Rest. Taquet
Rist. La Buca
Rist. Panorama
Rist. Positano
Rist. Primavera†
Rock Bottom
Rose Tattoo Cafe
Rose Tree Inn
Roux 3
Ruth's Chris
Saffron House
Saloon
Sang Kee†
Savona
Sawan's Med.
Serrano
Seven Stars Inn
Shivnanda
Siam Cuisine†
Silk Cuisine
Simon Pearce
Singapore Kosher†
Siri's Thai French/NJ
Smith & Wollensky
Solaris Grille
Sonoma
Sotto Varalli
Spaghetti Warehse.
Spotted Hog
Spring Mill Café
Stella Notte
Stoudt's/LB
Sullivan's Steak./DE†
Susanna Foo
Sweet Bay Cafe/LB
Tai Lake
Tangerine
Tango
Tavern
Terrace/Greenhill/DE
Thomas'
333 Belrose
Tierra Colombiana
Tira Misu Rist.
Tir Na Nog
Toscana Cuc. Rust.
Totaro's
Toto
Tratt. Alberto
Trinacria
Twenty21
211 York
Vickers Tavern
Viggiano's
Village Porch
Villa Strafford
Vincente's/DE
Vincent's
Walter's Steak./DE
Washington Cross.
Washington Hse.
White Dog Cafe
White Elephant
William Penn Inn
Yangming
Yellow Springs
Zocalo

Prix Fixe Menus
(Call for prices and times)

Alberto's
America B&G
Andreotti's/NJ
Azalea
Back Burner/DE
Bay Pony Inn
Bistro St. Tropez
Black Bass Hotel
Bookbinders
Braddock's Tav./NJ
Brasserie Perrier
Buca di Beppo
Café Gallery/NJ
Casablanca
Cassatt Lounge
Cedars
Century House
CinCin
City Tavern
Cock 'n Bull
Crier/Country
Darbar Grill
Denim Lounge
Deux Cheminées
DiNardo's

subscribe to zagat.com

Special Feature Index

DiPalma
Drafting Room
EverMay/Delaware
Fayette St. Grille
Fez Moroccan
Figs
Founders
Fountain Rest.
Fuji/NJ
General Lafayette
Giumarello's/NJ
Golden Pheasant
Green Hills Inn/LB
Groff's Farm/LB
Gypsy Rose
Inn Philadelphia
Kimberton Inn
Kingdom of Veg.
La Campagne/NJ
Lacroix/Rittenhse.
Lambertville Stat./NJ
La Padella
Le Bec-Fin
Le Mas
Lemon Grass†
Ludwig's Garten
Mainland Inn
Mamma Maria
Mandarin Garden
Marrakesh
Max's/NJ
Michael's
Monte Carlo
Moriarty's
Moshulu
My Thai
New Delhi
Overtures
Pantheon
Passerelle
Peacock/Parkway
Rat's/NJ
Rest. 821/DE
Rest. Taquet
Rist. La Buca
Sansom St. Oyster
Singapore Kosher/NJ†
Summer Kit.
Susanna Foo
Swann Lounge
Taj Mahal
Tango
Toto
Vivo Enoteca
Washington Hse.
Yangming
ZanzibarBlue†

Quiet Conversation

Barrymore Rm.
Bella
Birchrunville Store
Caffe Casta Diva
Deux Cheminées
Dilworthtown Inn
Founders
Fountain Rest.
Gilmore's
Inn at Phillips Mill
Inn Philadelphia
Kennedy-Supplee
Knave of Hearts
La Bonne Aub.
Lacroix/Rittenhse.
La Famiglia
Le Mê Toujours/NJ
Overtures
Rat's/NJ
Roselena's Coffee
Sagami/NJ
Salt
Simon Pearce
Singapore Kosher†
Susanna Foo
Swann Lounge
Tartine
Umbria
Yardley Inn

Raw Bars

Bamboo Club
Bookbinders
Carr's/LB
Creed's Seafood
Feby's Fishery/DE
Filomena Cuc. Rust./NJ
Lamberti's/DE†
Le Mas
Mikimotos/DE
Oasis
Olive/NJ
Pace One
Philadelphia Fish
Sansom St. Oyster
Seafood Unlimited
Snockey's Oyster
Sotto Varalli
Stoudt's/LB
Striped Bass

vote at zagat.com 197

Special Feature Index

Swanky Bubbles
U.S. Hotel B&G
Walter's Steak./DE

Reserve Ahead
Athena
Avalon
Back Burner/DE
Barone Tratt./NJ
Birchrunville Store
Bistro La Viola
Black Bass Hotel
Black Swan/NJ
Blue Bell Inn
Buca di Beppo†
Buckley's Tav./DE
Buddakan
Café Gallery/NJ
Cafe San Pietro
Cafe Unicorn/LB
Caffe Aldo Lam./NJ
Carversville Inn
Centre Bridge Inn
Century House
Citron Bistro
Creole Café/NJ
Deep Blue/DE
Dilworthtown Inn
Eclipse/DE
Elements Café/NJ
Emerald Fish/NJ
Esca
EverMay/Delaware
Fatou & Fama
Feby's Fishery/DE
Filomena Cuc. Rust./NJ
Food for Thought/NJ
Founders
Fountain Rest.
Fuji/NJ
Giumarello's/NJ
Gracie's/LB
Green Room/DE
Grill Rest.
Harry's Savoy Grill/DE
Il Portico
Inn at Phillips Mill
Inn Philadelphia
John Harvard's/DE†
Joseph Ambler
Kabul
Kennedy-Supplee
Kobe
Krazy Kat's/DE
Kristian's Rist.

La Bonne Aub.
La Campagne/NJ
Lacroix/Rittenhse.
La Famiglia
Lambertville Stat./NJ
L'Angolo
La Terrasse
Lauletta's Grille
La Veranda
La Vigna
Le Bec-Fin
Le Castagne
Le Mas
Le Mê Toujours/NJ
Le Petit Café
Lily's on Main/LB
Little Café/NJ
Little Fish
Little Marakesh
L'Osteria Cuc. Ital./DE
Lourdas Greek
Luigi Vitrone's/DE
Mainland Inn
Marg. Kuo's
Marigold Din. Rm.
Marrakesh
Max's/NJ
McCorm./Schmick's
Mélange Café/NJ
Mendenhall Inn
Mezza Luna
Mikado
Mikimotos/DE
Miller's Smorg./LB
Mirna's Cafe†
Mona Lisa/DE
Morimoto
Morton's/Chicago†
Mrs. Robino's/DE
Nais Cuisine
Nan
New Orleans Cafe
Norma's/NJ
Ortlieb's
Overtures
Paloma
¡Pasión!
Pattaya Grill
Pelican Fish Co./NJ
Penne
Pif
Pigalle
Portofino
Rat's/NJ

Special Feature Index

Ravenna
Rest. 821/DE
Rest. Taquet
Rist. Panorama
Rist. Positano
Rist. San Carlo
Ritz Seafood/NJ
Roller's
Roselena's Coffee
Rose Tattoo Cafe
Ruth's Chris
Salt
Savona
Sawan's Med.
Spasso
Spence Cafe
Spezia
Stella Notte
Stoudt's/LB
Sullivan's Steak./DE†
Sweet Bay Cafe/LB
Tangerine
Terrace/Greenhill/DE
Tex Mex Conn.
Thomas'
333 Belrose
Tierra Colombiana
Tira Misu Rist.
Toscana Cuc. Rust.
Totaro's
Tratt. Alberto
Tre Scalini
Trinacria
Twenty Manning
211 York
Umbria
Valanni
Vetri
Victor Café
Viggiano's
Villa Strafford
Vincente's/DE
Warmdaddy's
Warsaw Cafe
Washington Cross.
William Penn Inn
Willistown Grille
Yangming
Yellow Springs
Ye Olde Concordville
ZanzibarBlue†
Zocalo

Romantic Places
Astral Plane
Beau Monde
Beau Rivage/NJ
Bella
Bistro Romano
Brew HaHa!/DE†
Caffe Casta Diva
Carversville Inn
Chlöe
Deux Cheminées
Dilworthtown Inn
Duling-Kurtz Hse.
EverMay/Delaware
Fountain Rest.
Gilmore's
Golden Pheasant
Hotel Du Village
Inn at Phillips Mill
Inn on Blue. Hill
Inn Philadelphia
Kennedy-Supplee
Knave of Hearts
La Bonne Aub.
Le Bar Lyonnais
Le Bec-Fin
Log Cabin/LB
Mendenhall Inn
Monte Carlo
Mr. Martino's
Opus 251
Overtures
¡Pasión!
Passerelle
Rat's/NJ
Roselena's Coffee
Rose Tattoo Cafe
Rouge
Simon Pearce
Spring Mill Café
Summer Kit.
Tangerine
Tartine
Twenty Manning
Umbria
Valanni
Vetri
Vickers Tavern
Washington Hse.
Yardley Inn
Yellow Springs
ZanzibarBlue/DE†

Senior Appeal
Abacus
Bay Pony Inn
Ben & Irv

vote at zagat.com

Special Feature Index

Bird-in-Hand/LB
Blüe Ox
Cafe Preeya
Caffe Casta Diva
Catelli/NJ
D'Ignazio's
Emerald Fish/NJ
Ernesto's 1521
Frederick's
General Lafayette
Good 'N Plenty/LB
Hank's Place
Hoss's Family/LB†
Inn on Blue. Hill
Isaac's Rest./LB†
Italian Bistro†
Jenny's Bistro
Kegel's Seafood/LB
Koch's Deli
Lamberti's†
Lambertville Stat./NJ
La Pergola
Little Pete's†
Little Tuna/NJ
Marg. Kuo's
Max's/NJ
Mayfair Diner
Melrose Diner
Miller's Smorg./LB
Moonstruck
Murray's Deli
Norma's/NJ
Old Guard Hse.
Olga's Diner/NJ
Otto's
Plain & Fancy/LB
Plate
Pub/NJ
Radicchio
Rat's/NJ
Salt
Simon Pearce
Time Out Falafel
Vesuvio
Viggiano's
Villa Strafford
Vinny T's
Washington Hse.
White Elephant
William Penn Inn
Willow Valley/LB
Windmill/LB
Yardley Inn
Ye Olde Concordville
Zinn's Diner/LB

Singles Scenes
Abilene
Alma de Cuba
Bards
Billy Wong's
Black Sheep Pub
Bourbon Blue
Brandywine Brew./DE
Café Habana
Cibucán
circa
Coyote Crossing
Cuba Libre
Denim Lounge
Eulogy Belgian
Fadó Irish Pub
Fergie's Pub
Independence Brew
Jones
Judy's Cafe
Kisso Sushi
Latest Dish
Loie
Los Catrines/Teq.
L2
Manayunk Brew.
Marathon/Square
McFadden's
Mixto
North by NW
N. 3rd
Ortlieb's
Plough & Stars
Pod
Sonoma
Standard Tap
Sugar Mom's
Swanky Bubbles
Tir Na Nog
Twenty Manning
Valanni
Valley Forge Brew.

Sleepers
(Good to excellent food, but little known)
China Royal/DE
Culinaria/DE

200   subscribe to zagat.com

Special Feature Index

Feby's Fishery/DE
Gracie's/LB
Green Hills Inn/LB
Groff's Farm/LB
Log Cabin/LB
L'Osteria Cuc. Ital./DE
Luigi Vitrone's/DE
Mikimotos/DE
Olde Greenfield/LB
Stoudt's/LB
Vincente's/DE
Walter's Steak./DE

Tasting Menus

America B&G
Birchrunville Store
Food for Thought/NJ
Fountain Rest.
Inn Philadelphia
La Campagne/NJ
Little Marakesh
Max's/NJ
Morimoto
Moro/DE
Rat's/NJ
Rest. 821/DE
Rest. Taquet
Savona
Seafood Unlimited
Solaris Grille
Striped Bass
Susanna Foo
Vetri

Views

Ardmore Station
Barrymore Rm.
Bistro St. Tropez
Black Bass Hotel
Bleu
Bravo Bistro
Café Gallery/NJ
Carmella's
Chart House
Cuttalossa Inn
EverMay/Delaware
Gypsy Rose
King George II
Lacroix/Rittenhse.
La Veranda
Moshulu
Odette's

Passerelle
Radicchio
Rat's/NJ
Simon Pearce
Society Hill Hotel
Upstares/Varalli

Visitors on Expense Account

Brasserie Perrier
Capital Grille
Catelli/NJ
Chops
Deux Cheminées
Dilworthtown Inn
Founders
Fountain Rest.
Grill
Il Portico
Kansas City Prime
Le Bec-Fin
Le Mas
Mallorca
McCorm./Schmick's
Monte Carlo
Morimoto
Morton's/Chicago†
Pantheon
Prime Rib
Roy's
Ruth's Chris†
Shula's Steak
Smith & Wollensky
Striped Bass
Sullivan's Steak.
Susanna Foo
Tangerine

Waterside

Black Bass Hotel
Bravo Bistro
Café Gallery/NJ
Carmella's
Centre Bridge Inn
Chart House
Cuttalossa Inn
Golden Pheasant
Gypsy Rose
Keating's
King George II
Lambertville Stat./NJ
Landing

Special Feature Index

La Veranda
Manayunk Brew.
Moshulu
Odette's

Winning Wine Lists
Back Burner/DE
Bamboo Club
Beau Rivage/NJ
Blue Bell Inn
Brandywine Rm./DE
Capital Grille
Caribou Cafe
Catelli/NJ
Chops
circa
Deux Cheminées
Dilworthtown Inn
Fountain Rest.
Green Hills Inn/LB
Grill
Harry's Savoy Grill/DE
Haydn Zug's/LB
Inn on Blue. Hill
Jake's
Kansas City Prime
La Bonne Aub.
Lacroix/Rittenhse.
La Famiglia
Le Bar Lyonnais
Le Bec-Fin
Le Castagne
Le Mas
Mainland Inn
Monte Carlo
Morton's/Chicago†
Opus 251
Pantheon
Penne
Prime Rib
Rat's/NJ
Rest. 821/DE
Rest. Taquet
Rist. Panorama
Rist. Positano
Roux 3
Saloon
Salt
Savona
Shula's Steak
Striped Bass
Sullivan's Steak.
Toscana Cuc. Rust.
Trinacria
Twenty21
Vetri
Yardley Inn

Worth a Trip
PENNSYLVANIA
Birchrunville
  Birchrunville Store
Blue Bell
  Alison/Blue Bell
Carversville
  Carversville Inn
Doylestown
  Inn on Blue. Hill
Dresher
  Carambola
Ephrata
  Rest. at Doneckers/LB
Exton
  Duling-Kurtz Hse.
Havertown
  Carmine's Cafe
Kennett Square
  Taq. Moroleon
Kimberton
  Kimberton Inn
Lancaster
  Log Cabin/LB
Lansdale
  Ravenna
Mainland
  Mainland Inn
Mendenhall
  Mendenhall Inn
New Hope
  Hotel Du Village
  Inn at Phillips Mill
  La Bonne Aub.
  Odette's
Pine Forge
  Gracie's/LB
Reading
  Green Hills Inn/LB
Southampton
  Blue Sage Veg.
Upper Darby
  Alisa Cafe
West Chester
  Gilmore's
  Simon Pearce
Yardley
  Yardley Inn

Special Feature Index

NEW JERSEY
Cherry Hill
  La Campagne
  Mélange Café
Cinnaminson
  Fuji
  Max's
Collingswood
  Sagami
Hamilton
  Rat's

Medford
  Braddock's Tav.
DELAWARE
Hockessin
  Back Burner
Wilmington
  Moro
  Toscana Kitchen
  ZanzibarBlue

Wine Vintage Chart

This chart is designed to help you select wine to go with your meal. It is based on the same 0 to 30 scale used throughout this *Survey*. The ratings (prepared by our friend **Howard Stravitz**, a professor at the University of South Carolina) reflect both the quality of the vintage and the wine's readiness for present consumption. Thus, if a wine is not fully mature or is over the hill, its rating has been reduced. We do not include 1987, 1991–1993 vintages because they are not especially recommended for most areas.

	'85	'86	'88	'89	'90	'94	'95	'96	'97	'98	'99	'00	'01
WHITES													
French:													
Alsace	24	18	22	28	28	26	25	23	23	25	23	25	26
Burgundy	26	25	17	25	24	15	29	28	25	24	25	22	20
Loire Valley	–	–	–	–	25	23	24	26	24	23	24	25	23
Champagne	28	25	24	26	29	–	26	27	24	24	25	25	–
Sauternes	21	28	29	25	27	–	20	23	27	22	22	22	28
California (Napa, Sonoma, Mendocino):													
Chardonnay	–	–	–	–	–	–	22	27	23	27	25	25	23	26
Sauvignon Blanc/Semillon	–	–	–	–	–	–	–	–	–	24	24	25	22	26
REDS													
French:													
Bordeaux	25	26	24	27	29	22	26	25	23	24	23	25	23
Burgundy	23	–	21	25	28	–	26	27	25	22	27	22	20
Rhône	25	19	27	29	29	24	25	23	25	28	26	27	24
Beaujolais	–	–	–	–	–	–	–	–	23	22	25	25	18
California (Napa, Sonoma, Mendocino):													
Cab./Merlot	26	26	–	21	28	29	27	25	28	23	26	23	26
Pinot Noir	–	–	–	–	–	27	24	24	26	25	26	25	27
Zinfandel	–	–	–	–	–	25	22	23	21	22	24	19	24
Italian:													
Tuscany	26	–	24	–	26	22	25	20	28	24	27	26	25
Piedmont	26	–	26	28	29	–	23	26	28	26	25	24	22

Is that a Zagat in your pocket?

NTRODUCING
ZAGAT TO GO℠
2003 Restaurant and Nightlife Guide
FOR POCKET PC & PALM OS® DEVICES

Extensive Coverage: Includes over 20,000 establishments in 45+ cities

Search: Find the perfect spot by locale, price, cuisine and more

Free Updates: Stay current with new content downloads throughout the year

One-Touch Scheduling: Add your plans directly to your Date Book or Calendar

Available wherever books and software are sold

or for download at www.zagat.com/software